THE YOGA SUTRAS
OF PATANJALI

Other Theosophy Trust Books

Meditation and Self-Study
by Raghavan Iyer
compiled by The Editorial Board of Theosophy Trust

The Origins of Self-Consciousness
in The Secret Doctrine
by H.P. Blavatsky
compiled by The Editorial Board of Theosophy Trust

Wisdom in Action
Essays on the Spiritual Life
by Raghavan Iyer

The Dawning of Wisdom
Essays on Walking the Path
by Raghavan Iyer

Teachers of the Eternal Doctrine
From Tsong-Ka-Pa to Nostradamus
by Elton Hall

Symbols of the Eternal Doctrine
From Shamballa to Paradise
by Helen Valborg

The Key to Theosophy
An Exposition of the
Ethics, Science, and Philosophy
by H. P. Blavatsky

Evolution and Intelligent Design
in The Secret Doctrine
by H.P. Blavatsky
compiled by The Editorial Board of Theosophy Trust

The Yoga Sutras
of Patanjali

BY

Raghavan Iyer

Compiled by
The Editorial Board of Theosophy Trust

Theosophy Trust Books
Washington, D.C.

The Yoga Sutras
of Patanjali

Theosophy Trust books may be ordered through Amazon.com, Barnes & Noble, Books-A-Million, and other booksellers, or by visiting:

http://www.theosophytrust.org/online_books.php

ISBN 978-0-9832220-7-1
ISBN 098322207X

Library of Congress Control Number: 2011943515

Printed in the United States of America

Dedicated To

All Those Who Have Tried

to Learn Meditation and the

Practice of Self-Study, and Even More,

Those Who Have Tried and Failed

May This Work Help Them Succeed

KRISHNA

"He who has attained to meditation should constantly strive to stay at rest in the Supreme, remaining in solitude and seclusion, having his body and his thoughts under control, without possessions and free from hope. He should in an undefiled spot place his seat, firm, neither too high nor too low, and made of kusa grass which is covered with a skin and a cloth. There, for the self's purification he should practice meditation with his mind fixed on one point, the modifications of the thinking principle controlled and the action of the senses and organs restrained. Keeping his body, head, and neck firm and erect, with mind determined, and gaze directed to the tip of his nose without looking in any direction, with heart at peace and free from fear, the Yogee should remain, settled in the vow of a Brahmacharya, his thoughts controlled, and heart fixed on me. The devotee of controlled mind who thus always bringeth his heart to rest in the Supreme reacheth that tranquility, the supreme assimilation with me."

The Bhagavad-Gita, Ch. VI

CONTENTS

INTRODUCTION

When Professor Iyer spoke to theosophical students of either meditation or self-study, he invariably employed the phrases "deep, daily meditation" and "thorough self-examination" to emphasize the importance of these practices to the successful endeavours of spiritual aspirants. In his private discourses, meetings and conversations, and in his public lectures and writings, Prof. Iyer pointed to Patanjali's *Yoga Sutras* as the model upon which a real discipline of spiritual meditation should be based, and took great pains to separate that ancient system of meditation from all of the forms of self-hypnosis that currently pass as "meditation". In Patanjali's system, which is that of the *Raja Yoga* school, meditation is a distinct quotidian practice that has well-charted points of entry, a cycle or rhythm of activity, and points of exit; it is also the dominant undertone to one's life, that upon which the heart is set, the "line of life's meditation". Whether meditation is considered as a constant undercurrent carried on while engaged in the necessary duties of life, or as a distinct and daily practice undertaken at specific time, both aspects of real meditation must be nourished, strengthened, and sustained.

Likewise Prof. Iyer consistently pointed to the practice of self-study enjoined upon the brotherhood of Pythagoras and expressed in his *Golden Verses*: "Do not let sleep close your tired eyes until you have three times gone over the events of the day. 'What did I do wrong? What did I accomplish? What did I fail to do that I should have done?' Starting from the beginning, go through to the end. Then, reproach yourself for the things you did wrong, and take pleasure in the good things you did."

In his article, *Pythagoras and His School*, Prof. Iyer notes "what is said in the *Golden Verses* about proper self-examination, which is an activity very different from offering a confessional before a priest, or going to a psychiatrist and having oneself analysed, or engaging in one or another form of tedious, furtive and repressive discussion of the shadow. In the Pythagorean teaching, the shadow cannot understand itself. The shadow is void of the very possibility of self-knowledge. Real understanding can come solely through the light of self-awareness which is inherent in every human being." The heart of the matter is this: we must learn to conduct a patient and thorough examination of the lower, personal self by the light of the Higher Self, accompanied by an affirmation of one's fundamental identity with one's true Self, the Self of All, and a simultaneous negation of any false identification with the personal and transitory self. Such an activity could become a daily discipline that makes the quest for self-definition and authentic self-actualization possible.

The purpose of this book is to bring together in a convenient and coherent form the many HERMES articles written by Prof. Iyer that dealt with this subject. In truth, meditation and self-study represent two sides of one human activity, something analogous to the operation of the systolic and diastolic movements of the human heart. The one is the centrifugal movement of consciousness expanding to Universals beyond the limits of Self; the other is the centripetal movement focusing with laser-like precision upon the particulars within the limits of Self. They represent roughly the sub-principles of *Buddhi* and *Manas* acting within the incarnated Manasic principle; for the spiritual aspirant they should – in time - become as natural as breathing in and breathing out. These two aspects of the inbreathing and outbreathing within the neophyte's consciousness are dealt with in the three treatises of *The Voice of the Silence,* as well as in Prof. Iyer's seminal article, *Meditation and Self-Study*:

> We might begin to wonder whether perhaps there is a golden chord that connects the golden sphere of a man of meditation and the complex intermediary realms in which he must, by pain and anguish and awakening, by knitting together minute golden moments rescued from a great deal of froth and self-deception, come to know himself. If there were not a fundamental connection between meditation and self-study, something of the uniquely precious wisdom in this great text would be lost to us. When we begin to realize this in our lives, we come to appreciate that, while we may not be in a position to make judgments about teachers and schools in a vast and largely unrecorded history or in our own time,

nonetheless we do know that there is something profoundly important in stressing both meditation and self-study, in bringing the two together. We must reconcile what looked like a pair of opposites and get beyond despair to something else which allows an existential and dynamic balance between meditation and self-study.

Alas, most of us find this existential balance to be elusive, as there are many obstacles to such a natural and easy relationship to meditation and self-study, obstacles that have been self-created and reinforced over many lifetimes of misdirected thought and attempts to short-circuit what is unavoidable in the spiritual path: the careful and painstaking unwinding of the coils of self-induced delusions. These obstacles are detailed in the *Yoga Sutras* with surprising brevity and familiarity, suggesting to the perceptive reader that the author had so thoroughly studied and mastered the subject that he is able to reduce the issues to their fewest essential elements. Early in the First Book (*Samadhi Pada*, verses 30-32), Patanjali gives the diagnosis of the hindrances and the prescription for their removal:

> 30. The hindrances which cause mental distractions are disease, dullness, doubt, heedlessness, indolence, addiction to sense-objects, distorted perception, failure to find a footing and instability in any state.
>
> 31. These distractions are accompanied by sorrow, depression, bodily restlessness and spasmodic breathing.
>
> 32. To check these, there should be constant practice of one truth or principle (*eka-tattva*).

Patanjali also notes the antidote to self-induced mental pollution, that one's mind "becomes purified through the practice of friendliness, compassion, gladness and indifference respectively towards happiness, sorrow, virtue and vice." (V. 33) It may be at this point that the practitioner gains his/her first intimation that in this Path, "to whatever place one would go, that place one's own self becomes". (*Dhyanesvari*, quoted in *The Voice of the Silence*.)

The obstacles noted above are not to be taken lightly or ignored, as they are the product of spiritual negligence in this and previous lifetimes, and, by law, must produce the same result in future lives. They are not easily overcome. These obstacles produce the condition – familiar to everyone who has honestly attempted meditation and self-study – of the interior consciousness appearing to oneself like a void, a dark and lightless place, where the interior space seems to be utterly empty of light, life and hope. But as we discover by perseverance and consulting the experiences of those who have gone before, in this endeavor, we must create our own light. In *The Gayatri Invocation*, Prof. Iyer points to the root cause of the major obstacles to this endeavor: ignorance combined with inertia (*tamas*), which, when conjoined together, produce a "stony and indifferent heart" and a "repeated persistence in a restricted view of the world". It may seem strange, but some individuals contract to the point where they actually enjoy "the dingy, the cloudy, the chaotic and the claustrophobic." This self-torture produces a condition in which the tormented soul cannot attach meaning to the common language of the most simple acts of decency and kindness, and because of their pollution, cannot believe they are capable of resonating to a sense of the sacred. They may be able to use sacred language in stringing together sentences that produce the illusion of intimate knowledge, but such acts only result in an empty analytical familiarity and routinized repetitions. Their heart light is nearly extinguished, and the electric fire of wisdom finds no tinder in the ashes in their hearts. Such is the sad result of lives of misuse of the sacred Teachings.

Persistence in dullness, heedlessness, and distorted perception will also cause additional obstacles for the future, as Prof. Iyer notes in his article, *The Six Dharshanas*.

> "A thorough training in logic is required not only in all philosophical reasoning, exposition and disputation, but it is also needed by those who seek to stress mastery of *praxis* over a lifetime and thereby become spiritual exemplars. This at once conveys the enormous strength of an immemorial tradition as well as the pitiable deficiencies of most professors and pundits, let alone the self-styled so-called exoteric *gurus* of the contemporary East. Neither thaumaturgic wonders nor mass hypnosis can compensate for mental muddles and shallow thinking; indeed, they become insuperable obstacles

to even a good measure of *gnosis* and noetic theurgy, let alone authentic enlightenment and self-mastery."

However, the most common obstacles to the moderating influence of the *yamas* and *niyamas* – the restraints and observances - of the *Yoga* discipline outlined by Patanjali are the negative and self-destructive thoughts that swarm round humankind like unwelcome flies: thoughts of impure acts; the desire to do harm to others because of a perceived wrong or injustice; self-indulgence, self-deception and self-assertion. Providing a home to such thoughts creates an atmosphere that can only result in the defeat of one's spiritual resolves and commitments. Rather than give in to these energies, the wise aspirant should treat with great respect the advice offered in the article *Sadhana Pada*:

> Instead of suppressing such scattered thoughts or wallowing in hideous self-pity, one must firmly and deliberately insert into the mind their potent opposites – love for hate, tenderness for temerity, sweetness for spite, virile confidence for the devilry of self-doubt, authentic self-conquest for compulsive self-indulgence. Thus what begins as a shrewd defence against deleterious thoughts becomes a deft substitution of one kind of thought for another and results in sublimation, the skilful transformation of the tonality and texture of consciousness. Strict and consistent measures are needed to deal with subversive thoughts, not in order to repress them or to hide guilt for having them, but only because they induce depression and self-loathing, with predictable and pathetic consequences. Facing unworthy thoughts firmly, and thereby exorcising them, is to free oneself from their nefarious spell.

In much the same way that the delights of the *sattva guna* can become a distraction or obstacle in the way of the yogin, Prof. Iyer shows, in the article *Vibhuti Pada*, how shifts in the activity of the *gunas* in one's perceptions can produce an entirely different sort of obstacle, one that is difficult to identify as such because it is so welcome and attractive:

> "Since any significant refocussing of the mind produces dazzling insights and diverse phenomena, Patanjali conveyed their range and scope. For *yoga* they are not important in themselves because the goal is *kaivalya*, liberation, but they are vitally important as aids or obstacles on the way to achieving

the goal. Patanjali could not dismiss or overlook them, since they are real enough and inescapable, and so he delineated them clearly, knowing fully that all such arcane information can be abused. One who willingly uses such knowledge to stray off the arduous path to emancipation brings misery upon himself. One who would use this knowledge wisely needs to understand the many ways one can be misled into wasting the abundant resources accessible to the *yogin*. Profound alterations in states of consciousness through *sanyama* can bring about awakened powers called *siddhis*, attainments, many of which may seem to be supernatural and supernormal to the average person. They are, however, neither miraculous nor supernatural, since they suspend, circumvent or violate no laws. Rather, they merely indicate the immense powers of controlled consciousness within the perspective of great Nature, powers that are largely latent, untapped and dormant in most human beings. They are suggestive parameters of the operation of the vast scope and potency of consciousness in diverse arenas of *prakriti*."

Finally, any viable conception of perfectibility requires a continuous and attentive care for the imperfections in the lunar vestures and what we so mistakenly call ' I '. These imperfections may be transmuted if a vigilant individual generates fresh patterns of thought or feeling, which can then do their magical work. Prof. Iyer was noted for oft expressing his unshakable faith that for every incarnate human being, it is always possible to change the polarity and quality of the life-atoms in the lower vestures by attracting new sets of elementals with greater degrees of porosity than those we have attracted by our negative and ultimately self-destructive patterns of thought. This is a creative and courageous task, and it can be carried out only if one faces the facts about oneself. In the path of self-purification, we must always be willing to face up to and settle our karmic accounts. We must always be willing to look honestly where we stand in relation to the ideal of the perfected human being and to the moment of death. We must learn to see through and beyond entire realms of appearances and so take a moral stand based on well thought out and rational ethical principles. Their deeper meanings and deft applications must be located within the sacred sphere of one's duty.

The goal of meditative purification is to strengthen the spiritual will and garner continuous inspiration in the daily performance of duty such that one's commitment to the discipline becomes irrevocable and indefatigable. After a point, as Prof. Iyer notes in "*The Descent of Manas*", rather than see encounters with the spiritual as an unwelcome intrusion upon one's precious "personal time", the aspirant will come to look forward to them, and one's mind will naturally turn to sacred themes. The benefit of this mental discipline is a simplicity of stance that takes nothing for granted, but rather finds joy in the profound privilege of contemplating and reaffirming the fundamental principles of the spiritual life. No longer prone to the errors of futile speculation, and having forsaken attempts to reconcile the irreconcilable by adapting the spiritual sciences to material conceptions, the joyous aspirant will honour the basic rules of their self-chosen discipline by sharpening their Buddhic discernment through practice, staying within the forward current, and gaining true self-respect. They will come to see that the mere thought of falling away from the discipline through attaching blame upon the external world rapidly destroys that which they hold most sacred, the foundation of discipleship.

Metaphysically, there is no other more fundamental reason to engage in self-purification than the "duty one owes oneself as a trustee of Nature and a servant of mankind. If one grasps the idea of monadic evolution metaphysically, and not merely statistically or speculatively, it is evident that there are myriad daily opportunities for engaging in sacrificial acts of service to others." It is the exalted privilege of a *Manasa* - a self-conscious human being - to be able to serve all life-atoms through the concentrated power of compassionate thought. To a true spiritual seeker, a *sadhaka*, who thinks in this archetypal mode, the sole reason for skillfully performing any act in life is to render gentle and gracious service to others, to human beings as well as to all the life-atoms that one encounters and interacts with in every circumstance of life.

Prof. Iyer frequently made the observation that every authentic spiritual tradition insisted upon the purification and cleansing of the heart as a precondition and constant companion of real spiritual meditation.

Before the mind can be mastered, he insisted, the heart must be cleansed of its impurities - those distorted, complex and awkward elements in one's feeling nature, the hideous deformities of one's feeling nature - which can only be perceived as such because of the soul's awareness of its intrinsic beauty and purity. "Like a craftsman with the highest standard of excellence, the soul surveys its self-evolved vestures with an objective and critical eye."

Self-purification must encompass purification of one's motive and steadfastness in relation to our deepest integrity, honesty, and fidelity of commitment. Eventually, this arduous task produces *Bodhichitta,* the seed of Enlightenment, where we can "rejoice in the inner purification that has taken place. Even one's perspective changes in regard to what is truly helpful to the immortal soul and what is harmful. Once one touches the current of this supreme detachment and begins to enter the light of the void through efforts at *dhyana,* one may begin to make one's own honest and yet heroic, courageous and cheerful way towards gaining greater continuity, control and proficiency in meditation. Blending the mind and heart, one may enter the way that leads to the *dhyana* haven."

> The *Dhyana* gate is like an alabaster vase, white and transparent; within there burns a steady golden fire, the flame of *Prajna* that radiates from *Atma.*
>
> Thou art that vase.
>
> *The Voice of the Silence*

Editor, Theosophy Trust
November 17, 2011

(The articles in this book and many others by Prof. Iyer can also be found separately in the Lead Articles section of Theosophytrust.org at http://www.theosophytrust.org/rni_articles.php)

PATANJALI AND THE YOGA SUTRAS

Almost nothing is known about the sage who wrote the *Yoga Sutras*. The dating of his life has varied widely between the fourth century B.C.E. and the sixth century C.E., but the fourth century B.C.E. is the period noted for the appearance of aphoristic literature. Traditional Indian literature, especially the *Padma Purana*, includes brief references to Patanjali, indicating that he was born in *Illavrita Varsha*. *Bharata Varsha* is the ancient designation of Greater India as an integral part of *Jambudvipa*, the world as conceived in classical topography, but *Illavrita Varsha* is not one of its subdivisions. It is an exalted realm inhabited by the gods and enlightened beings who have transcended even the rarefied celestial regions encompassed by the sevenfold *Jambudvipa*. Patanjali is said to be the son of Angira and Sati, to have married Lolupa, whom he discovered in the hollow of a tree on the northern slope of Mount Sumeru, and to have reduced the degenerate denizens of Bhotabhandra to ashes with fire from his mouth. Such legendary details conceal more than they reveal and suggest that Patanjali was a great *Rishi* who descended to earth in order to share the fruits of his wisdom with those who were ready to receive it.

Some commentators identify the author of the *Yoga Sutras* with the Patanjali who wrote the *Mahabhashya* or *Great Commentary* on Panini's famous treatise on Sanskrit grammar sometime between the third and first centuries B.C.E. Although several scholars have contended that internal evidence contradicts such an identification, others have not found this reasoning conclusive. King Bhoja, who wrote a well-known commentary in the tenth century, was inclined to ascribe both works to a single author, perhaps partly as a reaction to others who placed Patanjali several centuries C.E. owing to his alleged implicit criticisms of late Buddhist doctrines. A more venerable tradition, however, rejects this identification altogether and holds that the author of the *Yoga Sutras* lived long before the commentator on Panini. In this view, oblique references to Buddhist doctrines are actually allusions to modes of thought found in some *Upanishads*.

In addition to our lack of definite knowledge about Patanjali's life, confusion arises from contrasting appraisals of the *Yoga Sutras* itself. There is a strong consensus that the *Yoga Sutras* represents a masterly compendium of various *Yoga* practices which can be traced back through the *Upanishads* to the *Vedas*. Many forms of *Yoga* existed by the time this treatise was written, and Patanjali came at the end of a long and ancient line of *yogins*. In accord with the free-thinking tradition of *shramanas*, forest recluses and wandering mendicants, the ultimate vindication of the *Yoga* system is to be found in the lifelong experiences of its ardent votaries and exemplars. The *Yoga Sutras* constitutes a practitioner's manual, and has long been cherished as the pristine expression of *Raja Yoga*. The basic texts of *Raja Yoga* are Patanjali's *Yoga Sutras*, the *Yogabhashya* of Vyasa and the *Tattvavaisharadi* of Vachaspati Mishra. *Hatha Yoga* was formulated by Gorakshanatha, who lived around 1200 C.E. The main texts of this school are the *Goraksha Sutaka*, the *Natha Yoga Pradipika* of Yogindra of the fifteenth century, and the later *Shivasamhita*. Whereas *Hatha Yoga* stresses breath regulation and bodily discipline, *Raja Yoga* is essentially concerned with mind control, meditation and self-study.

The *Yoga Sutras* of Patanjali is universal in the manner of the *Bhagavad Gita*, including a diversity of standpoints whilst fusing *Sankhya* metaphysics with *bhakti* or self-surrender. There is room for differences of emphasis, but every diligent user of Patanjali's aphorisms is enabled to refine aspirations, clarify thoughts, strengthen efforts, and sharpen focus on essentials in spiritual self-discipline. Accommodating a variety of exercises – mind control, visualization, breath, posture, moral training – Patanjali brings together the best in differing approaches, providing an integrated discipline marked by moderation, flexibility and balance, as well as degrees of depth in meditative absorption. The text eludes any simple classification within the vast resources of Indian sacred literature and *a fortiori* among the manifold scriptures of the world. Although it does not resist philosophical analysis in the way many mystical treatises do, it is primarily a practical aid to the quest for spiritual freedom, which transcends the concerns of theoretical clarification. Yet like any arcane science which necessarily pushes beyond the shifting boundaries of sensory experience, beyond conventional concepts of inductive reasoning and mundane reality, it reaffirms at every point its vital connection with the universal search for meaning and deliverance from bondage to shared illusions. It is a summons to systematic self-mastery which can aspire to the summits of *gnosis*.

The actual text as it has come down to the present may not be exactly what Patanjali penned. Perhaps he reformulated in terse aphoristic language crucial insights found in time-honoured but long-forgotten texts. Perhaps he borrowed terms and phrases from diverse schools of thought and training. References to breath control, *pranayama*, can be found in the oldest *Upanishads*, and the lineaments of systems of *Yoga* may be discerned in the *Maitrayana, Shvetashvatara* and *Katha Upanishads*, and veiled instructions are given in the 'Yoga' *Upanishads* – *Yogatattva, Dhyanabindu, Hamsa, Amritanada, Shandilya, Varaha, Mandala Brahmana, Nadabindu* and *Yogakundali* – though a leaning towards *Sankhya* metaphysics occurs only in the *Maitrayana*. The *Mahabharata* mentions the *Sankhya* and the *Yoga* as ancient systems of thought. *Hiranyagarbha* is traditionally regarded as the propounder of *Yoga*, just as Kapila is known as the original expounder of *Sankhya*. The *Ahirbudhnya* states that *Hiranyagarbha* disclosed the entire science of *Yoga* in two texts – the *Nirodha Samhita* and the *Karma Samhita*. The former treatise has been called the *Yoganushasanam*, and Patanjali also begins his work with the same term. He also stresses *nirodha* in the first section of his work.

In general, the affinities of the *Yoga Sutras* with the texts of *Hiranyagarbha* suggest that Patanjali was an adherent of the *Hiranyagarbha* school of *Yoga*, and yet his own manner of treatment of the subject is distinctive. His reliance upon the fundamental principles of *Sankhya* entitle him to be considered as also belonging to the *Sankhya Yoga* school. On the other hand, the significant variations of the later *Sankhya* of Ishvarakrishna from older traditions of proto-*Sankhya* point to the advantage of not subsuming the *Yoga Sutras* under broader systems. The author of *Yuktidipika* stresses that for Patanjali there are twelve capacities, unlike Ishvarakrishna's thirteen, that egoity is not a separate principle for Patanjali but is bound up with intellect and volition. Furthermore, Patanjali held that the subtle body is created anew with each embodiment and lasts only as long as a particular embodiment, and also that the capacities can only function from within. Altogether, Patanjali's work provides a unique synthesis of standpoints and is backed by the testimony of the accumulated wisdom derived from the experiences of many practitioners and earlier lineages of teachers.

Some scholars and commentators have speculated that Patanjali wrote only the first three *padas* of the *Yoga Sutras*, whilst the exceptionally short fourth *pada* was added later. Indeed, as early as the writings of King Bhoja, one verse in the fourth *pada* (IV. 16) was recognized as a line interpolated from Vyasa's seventh commentary in which he dissented from *Vijnanavadin* Buddhists. Other interpolations may have occurred even in the first three *padas*, such as III. 22, which some classical commentators questioned. The fact that the third *pada* ends with the word *iti* ('thus', 'so', usually indicating the end of a text), as it does at the end of the fourth *pada*, might suggest that the original contained only three books. However, the philosophical significance of the fourth *pada* is such that the coherence of the entire text need not be questioned on the basis of inconclusive speculations.

Al-Biruni translated into Arabic a book he called *Kitab Patanjal* (*The Book of Patanjali*), which he said was famous throughout India. Although his text has an aim similar to the *Yoga Sutras* and uses many of the same concepts, it is more theistic in its content and even has a slightly Sufi tone. It is not the text now known as the *Yoga Sutras*, but it may be a kind of paraphrase popular at the time, rather like the *Dnyaneshwari*, which stands both as an independent work and a helpful restatement of the *Bhagavad Gita*. The *Kitab* translated by al-Biruni illustrates the pervasive influence of Patanjali's work throughout the Indian subcontinent.

For the practical aspirant to inner tranquillity and spiritual realization, the recurring speculations of scholars and commentators, stimulated by the lack of exact historical information about the author and the text, are of secondary value. Whatever the precise details regarding the composition of the treatise as it has come down through the centuries, it is clearly an integrated whole, every verse of which is helpful not only for theoretical understanding but also for sustained practice. The *Yoga*

Sutras constitutes a complete text on meditation and is invaluable in that every *sutra* demands deep reflection and repeated application. Patanjali advocated less a doctrinaire method than a generous framework with which one can make experiments with truth, grow in comprehension and initiate progressive awakenings to the supernal reality of the *Logos* in the cosmos.

The word *Yoga* is derived from the Sanskrit verbal root *yuj*, 'to yoke' or 'to join', related to the Latin *jungere*, 'to join', 'to unite'. In its broadest usages it can mean addition in arithmetic; in astronomy it refers to the conjunction of stars and planets; in grammar it is the joining of letters and words. In *Mimamsa* philosophy it indicates the force of a sentence made up of united words, whilst in *Nyaya* logic it signifies the power of the parts taken together. In medicine it denotes the compounding of herbs and other substances. In general, *Yoga* and *viyoga* pertain to the processes of synthesis and analysis in both theoretical and applied sciences. Panini distinguishes between the root *yuj* in the sense of concentration (*Samadhi*) and *yujir* in the sense of joining or connecting. Buddhists have used the term *Yoga* to designate the withdrawal of the mind from all mental and sensory objects. *Vaishesika* philosophy means by *Yoga* the concentrated attention to a single subject through mental abstraction from all contexts. Whereas the followers of Ramanuja use the term to depict the fervent aspiration to join one's *ishtadeva* or chosen deity, *Vedanta* chiefly uses the term to characterize the complete union of the human soul with the divine spirit, a connotation compatible with its use in *Yoga* philosophy. In addition, Patanjali uses the term *Yoga* to refer to the deliberate cessation of all mental modifications.

Every method of self-mastery, the systematic removal of ignorance and the progressive realization of Truth, can be called *Yoga*, but in its deepest sense it signifies the union of one's apparent and fugitive self with one's essential nature and true being, or the conscious union of the embodied self with the Supreme Spirit. The *Maitrayana Upanishad* states:

> Carried along by the waves of the qualities darkened in his
> imagination, unstable, fickle, crippled, full of desires, vacillating, he

enters into belief, believing I am he, this is mine, and he binds his self by his self as a bird with a net. Therefore a man, being possessed of will, imagination and belief, is a slave, but he who is the opposite is free. For this reason let a man stand free from will, imagination and belief. This is the sign of liberty, this is the path that leads to *brahman*, this is the opening of the door, and through it he will go to the other shore of darkness.

Thus, *Yoga* refers to the removal of bondage and the consequent attainment of true spiritual freedom. Whenever *Yoga* goes beyond this and actually implies the fusion of an individual with his ideal, whether viewed as his real nature, his true self or the universal spirit, it is gnostic self-realization and universal self-consciousness, a self-sustaining state of serene enlightenment. Patanjali's metaphysical and epistemological debt to *Sankhya* is crucial to a proper comprehension of the *Yoga Sutras*, but his distinct stress on *praxis* rather than *theoria* shows a deep insight of his own into the phases and problems that are encountered by earnest practitioners of *Yoga*. His chief concern was to show how and by what means the spirit, trammelled in the world of matter, can withdraw completely from it and attain total emancipation by transforming matter into its original state and thus realize its own pristine nature. This applies at all levels of self-awakening, from the initial cessation of mental modifications, through degrees of meditative absorption, to the climactic experience of spiritual freedom.

Patanjali organized the *Yoga Sutras* into four *padas* or books which suggest his architectonic intent. *Samadhi Pada*, the first book, deals with concentration of mind (*Samadhi*), without which no serious practice of *Yoga* is possible. Since *Samadhi* is necessarily experiential, this *pada* explores the hindrances to and the practical steps needed to achieve alert quietude. Both restraint of the senses and of the discursive intellect are essential for *Samadhi*. Having set forth what must be done to attain and maintain meditative absorption, the second book, *Sadhana Pada*, provides the method or means required to establish full concentration. Any effort to subdue the tendency of the mind to become diffuse, fragmented or agitated demands a resolute, consistent and continuous practice of self-imposed, steadfast restraint, *tapas*, which cannot become stable without a commensurate disinterest in all phenomena. This relaxed disinterestedness, *vairagya*, has nothing to do with passive indifference, positive disgust, inert apathy or feeble-minded *ennui* as often experienced in the midst of desperation and tension in daily affairs. Those are really the self-protective responses of one who is captive to the pleasure-pain principle and is deeply vulnerable to the flux of events and the vicissitudes of fortune. *Vairagya* implies a conscious transcendence of the pleasure-pain principle through a radical reappraisal of expectations, memories and habits. The pleasure-pain principle, dependent upon passivity, ignorance and servility for its operation, is replaced by a reality principle rooted in an active, noetic apprehension of psycho-spiritual causation. Only when this impersonal perspective is gained can the *yogin* safely begin to alter significantly his psycho-physical nature through breath control, *pranayama*, and other exercises.

The third book, *Vibhuti Pada*, considers complete meditative absorption, *sanyama*, its characteristics and consequences. Once calm, continuous attention is mastered, one can discover an even more transcendent mode of meditation which has no object of cognition whatsoever. Since levels of consciousness correspond to planes of being, to step behind the uttermost veil of consciousness is also to rise above all manifestations of matter. From that wholly transcendent standpoint beyond the ever-changing contrast between spirit and matter, one may choose any conceivable state of consciousness and, by implication, any possible material condition. Now the *yogin* becomes capable of tapping all the *siddhis* or theurgic powers. These prodigious mental and moral feats are indeed magical, although there is nothing miraculous or even supernatural about them. They represent the refined capacities and exalted abilities of the perfected human being. Just as any person who has achieved proficiency in some specialized skill or knowledge should be careful to use it wisely and precisely, so too the *yogin* whose spiritual and mental powers may seem practically unlimited must not waste his energy or misuse his hard-won gifts. If he were to do so, he would risk getting entangled in worldly concerns in the myriad ways from which he had sought to free himself. Instead, the mind must be merged into the inmost spirit, the result of which is *kaivalya*, steadfast isolation or eventual emancipation from the bonds of illusion and the meretricious glamour of terrestrial existence.

In *Kaivalya Pada*, the fourth book which crowns the *Yoga Sutras*, Patanjali conveys the true nature of isolation or supreme spiritual freedom insofar as it is possible to do so in words. Since *kaivalya* is the term used for the sublime state of consciousness in which the enlightened soul has gone beyond the differentiating sense of 'I am', it cannot be characterized in the conceptual languages that are dependent on the subject-object distinction. Isolation is not nothingness, nor is it a static condition. Patanjali throws light on this state of *gnosis* by providing a metaphysical and metapsychological explanation of cosmic and human intellection, the operation of karma and the deep-seated persistence of the tendency of self-limitation. By showing how the suppression of modifications of consciousness can enable it to realize its true nature as pure potential and master the lessons of manifested Nature, he intimates the immense potency of the highest meditations and the inscrutable purpose of cosmic selfhood.

The metapsychology of the *Yoga Sutras* bridges complex metaphysics and compelling ethics, creative transcendence and critical immanence, in an original, inspiring and penetrating style, whilst its aphoristic method leaves much unsaid, throwing aspirants back upon themselves with a powerful stimulus to self-testing and self-discovery. Despite his sophisticated use of *Sankhya* concepts and presuppositions, Patanjali's text has a universal appeal for all ardent aspirants to Raja *Yoga*. He conveys the vast spectrum of consciousness, diagnoses the common predicament of human bondage to mental ailments, and offers practical guidance on the arduous pathway of lifelong contemplation that could lead to the summit of self-mastery and spiritual freedom.

Hermes, January 1989

THE SIX DHARSHANAS

*To contemplate these things is the privilege of the gods and to
do so is also the aspiration of the immortal soul of men generally
– though only in a few cases is such aspiration realized.*

Plato

I – THEORIA AND PRAXIS

Throughout its long and largely unrecorded history, Indian thought preserved its central concern with ontology and epistemology, with noetic psychology as the indispensable bridge between metaphysics and ethics, employing introspection and self-testing as well as logical tools, continually confronting the instruments of cognition with the fruits of contemplation. Through its immemorial oral teachings and a vast variety of written texts, the fusion of *theoria* and *praxis*, theory and practice, was never sacrificed to the demands of academic specialization or the compartmentalization of human endeavour. Diverse schools of thought shared the conviction that true understanding must flow from the repeated application of received truths. Coming to know is a dynamic, dialectical process in which thought stimulates contemplation and regulates conduct, and in turn is refined by them. Although an individual who would be healthy and whole thinks, feels and acts, *gnosis* necessarily involves the fusion of thought, will and feeling, resulting in *metanoia*, a radically altered state of being. The Pythagorean conception of a philosopher as a lover of wisdom is close to the standpoint of an earnest seeker of truth in the Indian tradition.

Indian thought did not suffer the traumatic cognitive disruption caused by the emergence of ecclesiastical Christianity in the Mediterranean world, where an excessive concern with specification of rigid belief, sanctioned and safeguarded by an institutional conception of religious authority and censorship, sundered thought and action to such an extent that it became common to think one way and act in another with seeming impunity. The chasms which opened up between thought, will and feeling provided fertile soil for every kind of psychopathology, in part because such a fragmentation of the human being engenders inversions, obsessions and even perversities, and also in part because for a thousand years it has been virtually impossible to hold up a credible paradigm of the whole and healthy human being. The philosophical quest became obscured in the modern West by the linear succession of schools, each resulting from a violent reaction to its predecessors, each claiming to possess the Truth more or less exclusively, and often insisting upon the sole validity of its method of proceeding. The slavish concern with academic respectability and the fear of anathemization resulted in the increasing alienation of thought from being, of cognition from conduct, and philosophical disputation from the problems of daily life.

Indian thought did not spurn the accumulated wisdom of its ancients in favour of current fashions and did not experience a violent disruption of its traditional hospitality to multiple standpoints. The so-called *astika* or orthodox schools found no difficulty in combining their veneration of the Vedic hymns with a wide and diverse range of views, and even the *nastika* or heterodox schools, which repudiated the canonical 'authority' of the *Vedas*, retained much of Vedic and Upanishadic metaphysics and almost the whole of their psychology and ethics. Indian philosophical schools could not see themselves as exclusive bearers of the total Truth. They emerged together from a long-standing and continuous effort to enhance our common understanding of God, Man and Nature, and they came to be considered as *darshanas* or paradigmatic standpoints shedding light from different angles on noumenal and phenomenal realities. They refrained from claiming that any illumination which can be rendered in words – or even in thoughts – can be either final or complete.

II – THE SIX SCHOOLS

It may be pointed out here that a system of philosophy however lofty and true it may be should not be expected to give us an absolutely correct picture of the transcendent truths as they really exist. Because philosophy works through the medium of the intellect and the intellect has its inherent limitations, it cannot understand or formulate truths which are beyond its scope.... We have to accept these limitations when we use the intellect as an instrument for understanding and discovering these truths in the initial stages. It is no use throwing away this instrument, poor and imperfect though it is, because it gives us at least some help in organizing our effort to know the truth in the only way it can be known – by Self-realization.

I. K. Taimni

The ageless and dateless *Vedas*, especially the exalted hymns of the *Rig Veda*, have long been esteemed as the direct expression of what gods and divine seers, *rishis* or immortal sages, saw when they peered into the imperishable centre of Being which is also the origin of the entire cosmos. The *Upanishads* (from *upa, ni* and *sad*, meaning 'to sit down near' a sage or *guru*), included in the *Vedas*, constitute the highest transmission of the fruits of illumination attained by these *rishis*. Often cast in the form of memorable dialogues between spiritual teachers and disciples, they represent rich glimpses of truth, not pieced together from disparate intellectual insights, but as they are at once revealed to the divine eye, *divya chakshu*, which looks into the core of Reality, freely intimated in idioms, metaphors and *mantras* suited to the awakening consciousness and spiritual potentials of diverse disciples. However divergent their modes of expression, they are all addressed to those who are ready to learn, willing to meditate deeply, and seek greater self-knowledge through intensive self-questioning. The *Upanishads* do not purport to provide discursive knowledge, conceptual clarification or speculative dogmas, but rather focus on the fundamental themes which concern the soul as a calm spectator of the temporal succession of states of mind from birth to death, seeking for what is essential amidst the ephemeral, the enduring within the transient, the abiding universals behind the flux of fleeting appearances.

From this standpoint, they are truly therapeutic in that they heal the sickness of the soul caused by passivity, ignorance and delusion. This ignorance is not that of the malformed or malfunctioning personality, maimed by childhood traumas or habitual vices. It is the more fundamental ignorance (*avidya*) of the adroit and well-adapted person who has learnt to cope with the demands of living and fulfil his duties in the world at a certain level without however, coming to terms with the causes of his longings and limitations, his dreams and discontinuities, his entrenched expectations and his hidden potentials. The sages spoke to those who had a measure of integrity and honesty and were willing to examine their presuppositions, but lacked the fuller vision and deeper wisdom that require a sustained search and systematic meditation. For such an undertaking, mental clarity, moral sensitivity, relaxed self-control and spiritual courage are needed, as well as a willingness to withdraw for a period from worldly concerns. The therapeutics of self-transcendence is rooted in a recondite psychology which accommodates the vast spectrum of self-consciousness, different levels of cognition and degrees of development, reaching up to the highest conceivable self-enlightenment.

Upanishadic thought presupposed the concrete and not merely conceptual continuity of God, Nature and Man. Furthermore, Man is the self-conscious microcosm of the macrocosm, where the part is not only inseparably one with the whole but also reflects and resonates with it. Man could neither be contemplated properly nor fully comprehended in any context less than the entirety of visible and invisible Nature, and so too, ethics, logic and psychology could not be sundered from metaphysics. 'Is', the way things are, is vitally linked to 'must', the ways things must be, as well as to 'ought', the way human beings should think and act, through 'can', the active exploration of human potentialities and possibilities, which are not different, save in scope and degree, from cosmic potencies. A truly noetic psychology bridges metaphysics and ethics through a conscious mirroring of *Rta*, ordered cosmic harmony, in *dharma*, righteous human conduct that freely acknowledges what is due to each and every aspect of Nature, including all humanity, past, present and future.

The ancient sages resolved the One-many problem at the mystical, psychological, ethical and social levels by affirming the radical metaphysical and spiritual unity of all life, whilst fully recognizing (and refusing to diminish through any form of reductionism) the immense diversity of human types and the progressive awakenings of human consciousness at different stages of material evolution and spiritual involution. The immemorial pilgrimage of humanity can be both universally celebrated and act as a constant stimulus to individual growth. Truth, like the sun shining over the summits of a Himalayan range, is one, and the pathways to it are as many and varied as there are people to tread them.

As if emulating the sculptor's six perspectives to render accurately any specific form in space, ancient Indian thinkers stressed six *darshanas*, which are sometimes called the six schools of philosophy. These are *astika* or orthodox in that they all find inspiration in different ways in the *Vedas*. And like the sculptor's triple set of perspectives – front-back, left side-right side, top-bottom – the six *darshanas* have been seen as three complementarities, polarized directions that together mark the trajectory of laser light through the unfathomable reaches of ineffable wisdom. Each standpoint has its integrity and coherence in that it demands nothing less than the deliberate and radical reconstitution of consciousness from its unregenerate and unthinking modes of passive acceptance of the world. Yet none can claim absoluteness, finality or infallibility, for such asseverations would imply that limited conceptions and discursive thought can capture ultimate Reality. Rather, each *darshana* points with unerring accuracy towards that cognition which can be gained only by complete assimilation, practical self-transformation and absorption into it. At the least, every *darshana* corresponds with a familiar state of mind of the seeker, a legitimate and verifiable mode of cognition which makes sense of the world and the self at some level.

All genuine seekers are free to adopt any one or more of the *darshanas* at any time and even to defend their chosen standpoint against the others but they must concede the possibility of synthesizing and transcending the six standpoints in a seventh mode which culminates in *taraka*, transcendental, self-luminous *gnosis*, the goal of complete enlightenment often associated with the secret, incommunicable way of *buddhiyoga* intimated in the fourth, seventh and eighteenth chapters of the *Bhagavad Gita*.

Although scholars have speculated on the sequential emergence of the *darshanas*, and though patterns of interplay can be discerned in their full flowering, their roots lie in the ancient texts and they arise together as distinctive standpoints. It has also been held that the six schools grew out of sixty-two systems of thought lost in the mists of antiquity. At any rate, it is generally agreed that each of the later six schools was inspired by a sage and teacher who struck the keynote which has reverberated throughout its growth, refinement and elaboration. As the six schools are complementary to each other, they are traditionally viewed as the six branches of a single tree. All six provide a theoretical explanation of ultimate Reality and a practical means of emancipation. The oldest are *Yoga* and *Sankhya*, the next being *Vaishesika* and *Nyaya*, and the last pair are *Purva Mimamsa* and *Vedanta* (sometimes called *Uttara Mimamsa*). The founders of these schools are considered to be Patanjali of *Yoga*, Kapila of *Sankhya*, Kanada of *Vaishesika*, Gautama of *Nyaya*, Jaimini of *Purva Mimamsa* and Vyasa of *Vedanta*, though the last is also assigned to *Badarayana*. All of them propounded the tenets of their philosophical systems or schools in the form of short *sutras*, whose elucidation required and stimulated elaborate commentaries. Since about 200 C.E., a vast crop of secondary works has emerged which has generated some significant discussions as well as a welter of scholastic disputation and didactic controversies, moving far away from *praxis* into the forests of *theoria*, or reducing *praxis* to rigid codes and *theoria* to sterile formulas. At the same time, there has remained a remarkable vitality to most of these schools, owing to their transmission by long lineages which have included many extraordinary teachers and exemplars. This cannot be recovered merely through the study of texts, however systematic and rigorous, in a philosophical tradition which is essentially oral, even though exceptional powers of accurate recall have been displayed in regard to the texts.

Nyaya and *Vaishesika* are schools primarily concerned with analytic approaches to the objects of knowledge, using carefully tested principles of logic. The word *Nyaya* suggests that by which the mind reaches a conclusion, and since the word also means 'right' or 'just', *Nyaya* is the science of correct thinking. The founder of this school, Gautama, lived about 150 B.C.E., and its source-book is the *Nyaya Sutra*. Whilst knowledge requires an object, a knowing subject and a state of knowing, the validity of cognition depends upon *pramana*, the means of cognition. There are four acceptable *pramanas*, of which *pratyaksha* – direct perception or intuition – is most important. Perception requires the mind, *manas*, to mediate between the self and the senses, and perception may be determinate or indeterminate. Determinate perception reveals the class to which an object of knowledge belongs, its specific qualities and the union of the two. Indeterminate perception is simple apprehension without regard to genus or qualities. In the *Nyaya* school, indeterminate perception is not knowledge but rather its prerequisite and starting-point.

Anumana or inference is the second *pramana* or means of cognition. It involves a five-fold syllogism which includes a universal statement, an illustrative example and an application to the instance at hand. *Upamana* is the apt use of analogy, in which the similarities which make the analogy come alive are essential and not superficial. *Shabda*, sound or verbal expression, is the credible testimony of authority, which requires not uncritical acceptance but the thoughtful consideration of words, meanings and the modes of reference. As the analytic structure of *Nyaya* logic suggests, its basic approach to reality is atomistic, and so the test of claims of truth is often effectiveness in application, especially in the realm of action. Typically, logical discussion of a proposition takes the form of a syllogism with five parts: the proposition (*pratijna*) the cause (*hetu*), the exemplification (*drishtanta*), the recapitulation (*upanaya*) and the conclusion (*nigamana*).

However divergent their views on metaphysics and ethics, all schools accept and use *Nyaya* canons of sound reasoning. A thorough training in logic is required not only in all philosophical reasoning, exposition and disputation, but it is also needed by those who seek to stress mastery of *praxis* over a lifetime and thereby become spiritual exemplars. This at once conveys the enormous strength of an immemorial tradition as well as the pitiable deficiencies of most professors and pundits, let alone the self-styled so-called exoteric *gurus* of the contemporary East. Neither thaumaturgic wonders nor mass hypnosis can compensate for mental muddles and shallow thinking; indeed, they become insuperable obstacles to even a good measure of *gnosis* and noetic theurgy, let alone authentic enlightenment and self-mastery.

The *Vaishesika* school complements *Nyaya* in its distinct pluralism. Its founder, Kanada, also known as Kanabhaksha, lived around 200 C.E., and its chief work is the *Vaishesika Sutra.* Its emphasis on particulars is reflected in its name, since *vishesha* means 'particularity', and it is concerned with properly delineating the categories of objects of experience. These objects of experience, *padarthas*, are six: substance (*dravya*), quality (*guna*), and *karma* or movement and activity (forming the triplicity of objective existence), and generality (*samanya*), particularity (*vishesha*) and *samavayi* or inherence (forming a triad of modes of intellectual discernment which require valid logical inference). A seventh object of experience, non-existence (*shunya*), was eventually added to the six as a strictly logical necessity. The *Vaishesika* point of view recognizes nine irreducible substances: earth, water, air, fire, aether (*Akasha*), time, space, self and mind, all of which are distinct from the qualities which inhere in them. The self is necessarily a substance – a substrate of qualities – because consciousness cannot be a property of the physical body, the sense-organs or the brain-mind. Although the self as a substance must be everywhere pervasive, its everyday capacity for feeling, willing and knowing is focussed in the bodily organism.

Since the self experiences the consequences of its own deeds, there is, according to *Vaishesika*, a plurality of souls, each of which has its *vishesha*, individuality or particularity. What we experience is made up of parts, and is non-eternal, but the ultimate components – atoms – are eternal. Individuality is formed by imperceptible souls and certain atoms, which engender the organ of thought. At certain times, during immense cosmogonic cycles, nothing is visible, as both souls and atoms are asleep, but when a new cycle of creation begins, these souls reunite with certain atoms. Gautama asserted that even during incarnated existence, emancipation may be attained through ascetic detachment and the highest stages of contemplative absorption or *Samadhi*. Though the *Vaishesika* school wedded an atomistic standpoint to a strict atheism, over time thinkers accepted a rationalistic concept of Deity as a prime mover in the universe, a philosophical requisite acceptable to *Nyaya*. The two schools or systems were combined by Kusumanjali of *Udayana* about 900 C.E. in his proof of the existence of God. Since then, both schools have been theistic. The Jains claim early parentage for the *Vaishesika* system, and this merely illustrates what is very common in the Indian tradition, that innovators like Gautama and Kanada were reformulating an already ancient school rather than starting *de novo*.

The *Purva Mimamsa* of Jaimini took as its point of departure neither knowledge nor the objects of experience, but *dharma*, duty, as enjoined in the *Vedas* and *Upanishads*. As the accredited sources of *dharma*, these sacred texts are not the promulgations of some deity who condescended to step into time and set down principles of correct conduct. Rather, the wisdom in such texts is eternal and uncreate, and true *rishis* have always been able to see them and to translate that clear vision into mantramic sounds and memorable utterances. Hence *Mimamsa* consecrates the mind to penetrating the words which constitute this sacred transmission. Central to the *Mimamsa* school is the theory of self-evidence – *svata pramana:* truth is its own guarantee and the consecrated practice of faith provides its own validation. Repeated testings will yield correct results by exposing discrepancies and validating real cognitions. There is a recognizable consensus amidst the independent visions of great seers, and each individual must recognize or rediscover this consensus by proper use and concentrated enactment of *mantras* and hymns. Every sound in the fifty-two letters of Sanskrit has a cosmogonic significance and a theurgic effect. Inspired *mantras* are exact mathematical combinations of sounds which emanate potent vibrations that can transform the magnetic sphere around the individual as well as the magnetosphere of the earth. Self-testing without self-deception can become a sacred activity, which is *sui generis.*

From the *Mimamsa* perspective, every act is necessarily connected to perceptible results. One might say that the effects are inherent in the act, just as the fruit of the tree is in the seed which grew and blossomed. There is no ontological difference between act and result, for the apparent gap between them is merely the consequence of the operation of time. Since the fruit of a deed may not follow immediately upon the act, or even manifest in the same lifetime, the necessary connection between act and result takes the form of *apurva*, an unseen force which is the unbreakable link between them. This testable postulate gives significance to the concept of *dharma* in all its meanings – 'duty', 'path', 'teaching', 'religion', 'natural law', 'righteousness', 'accordance with cosmic harmony' – but it cannot by itself secure complete liberation from conditioned existence. Social duties are important, but spiritual duties are even more crucial, and the saying "To thine own self be true" has an array of meanings reaching up to the highest demands of soul-tendance. In the continual effort to work off past karma and generate good karma, there is unavoidable tension between different duties, social and spiritual. The best actions, paradigmatically illustrated in Vedic invocations and rituals, lead to exalted conditions, even to some heavenly condition or blissful state. Nonetheless, as the various *darshanas* interacted and exchanged insights, *Mimamsa* came to consider the highest action as resulting in a cessation of advances and retreats on the field of merit, whereby *dharma* and *adharma* were swallowed up in a sublime and transcendental state of unbroken awareness of the divine.

In striving to penetrate the deepest arcane meaning of the sacred texts, *Mimamsa* thinkers accepted the four *pramanas* or modes of knowledge set forth in *Nyaya*, and added two others: *arthapatti* or postulation, and *abhava* or negation and non-existence. They did this in part because, given their view of the unqualified eternality of the *Vedas*, they held that all cognition is valid at some level and to some degree. There can be no false knowledge; whatever is known is necessarily true. As a consequence, they saw no reason to prove the truth of any cognition. Rather, they sought to demonstrate its falsity, for if disproof were successful, it would show that there had been no cognition at all. The promise of *gnosis* rests upon the sovereign method of falsifiability rather than a vain attempt to seek total verification in a public sense. Shifting the onus of proof in this way can accommodate the uncreate *Vedas*, which are indubitably true and which constitute the gold standard against which all other claims to truth are measured. *Mimamsa* rests upon the presupposition of the supremacy of Divine Wisdom, the sovereignty of the Revealed Word and the possibility of its repeated realization. Even among those who cannot accept the liturgical or revelatory validity and adequacy of the *Vedas*, the logic of disproof can find powerful and even rigorous application. As a method, it became important to the philosophers of *Vedanta*.

Vedanta, meaning 'the end or goal of the *Vedas*', sometimes also called *Uttara Mimamsa*, addresses the spiritual and philosophical themes of the *Upanishads*, which are considered to complete and form the essence of the *Vedas*. Badarayana's magisterial *Brahma Sutras* ordered the Upanishadic Teachings in a logically coherent sequence which considers the nature of the supreme *brahman*, the ultimate Reality, and the question of the embodiment of the unconditioned Self. Each of the five hundred and fifty-five *sutras* (literally, 'threads') are extremely short and aphoristic, requiring a copious commentary to be understood. In explaining their meaning, various commentators presented Vedantic doctrines in different ways. Shankaracharya, the chief of the commentators and perhaps the greatest philosopher in the Indian tradition, espoused the *advaita*, non-dual, form of *Vedanta*, the purest form of monism, which has never been excelled. He asked whether in human experience there is anything which is impervious to doubt. Noting that every object of cognition – whether dependent on the senses, the memory or pure conceptualization – can be doubted, he recognized in the doubter that which is beyond doubt of any kind. Even if one reduces all claims to mere avowals – bare assertions about what one seems to experience – there nonetheless remains that which avows. It is proof of itself, because nothing can disprove it. In this, it is also different from everything else, and this difference is indicated by the distinction between subject and object. The experiencing Self is subject; what it experiences is an object. Unlike objects, nothing can affect it: it is immutable and immortal.

For Shankara, this Self (*atman*) is *sat-chit-ananda*, being or existence, consciousness or cognition, and unqualified bliss. If there were no world, there would be no objects of experience, and so although the world as it is experienced is not ultimately real, it is neither *abhava*, non-existent, nor *shunya*, void. Ignorance is the result of confusing *atman*, the unconditioned subject, with *anatman*, the external world. From the standpoint of the cosmos, the world is subject to space, time and causality, but since these categories arise from nascent experience, they are inherently inadequate save to point beyond themselves to the absolute, immutable, self-identical *brahman*, which is absolute Being (*sat*). *Atman* is *brahman*, for the immutable singularity of the absolute subject, the Self, is not merely isomorphic, but radically identical with the transcendent singularity of the ultimate Reality. Individuals who have yet to realize this fundamental truth, which is in fact the whole Truth, impose out of ignorance various attitudes and conceptions on the world, like the man who mistakes an old piece of rope discarded on the trail for a poisonous serpent. He reacts to the serpent, but his responses are inappropriate and cause him to suffer unnecessarily, because there is no serpent on the trail to threaten him. Nonetheless, the rope *is* there. For Shankara, the noumenal world is real, and when a person realizes its true nature, gaining wisdom thereby his responses will be appropriate and cease to cause suffering. He will realize that he *is* the *atman* and that the *atman* is *brahman.*

Although *brahman* is ultimately *nirguna*, without qualities, the aspirant to supreme knowledge begins by recognizing that the highest expression of *brahman* to the finite mind is *Ishvara*, which is *saguna brahman*, Supreme Reality conceived through the modes of pure logic. Taking *Ishvara*, which points beyond itself to That (*Tat*), as his goal and paradigm, the individual assimilates himself to *Ishvara* through the triple path of ethics, knowledge and devotion – the *karma, jnana* and *bhakti yogas* of the *Bhagavad Gita* – until *moksha*, emancipation and self-realization, is attained. For Shankara, *moksha* is not the disappearance of the world but the dissolution of *avidya*, ignorance.

Ramanuja, who lived much later than Shankara, adopted a qualified non-dualism, *Vishishtadvaita Vedanta*, by holding that the supreme *brahman* manifests as selves and matter. For him, both are dependent on *brahman*, and so selves, not being identical with the Ultimate, always retain their separate identity. As a consequence, they are dependent on *brahman*, and that dependency expresses itself self-consciously as *bhakti* or devotion. In this context, however, the dependence which is manifest as *bhakti* is absurd unless *brahman* is thought to be personal in some degree, and so *brahman* cannot be undifferentiated. Emancipation or freedom is not union with the divine, but rather the irreversible and unwavering intuition of Deity. The Self is not identical with *brahman*, but its true nature is this intuition, which is freedom. Faith that *brahman* exists is sufficient and individual souls are parts of *brahman*, who is the creator of universes. Yet *brahman* does not create anything new; what so appears is merely a modification of the subtle and the invisible to the gross which we can see and sense. Because we can commune with this God by prayer, devotion and faith, there is the possibility of human redemption from ignorance and delusion. The individual is not effaced when he is redeemed; he maintains his self-identity and enjoys the fruits of his faith.

About a century and a half after Ramanuja, Madhava promulgated a dualistic (*dvaita*) *Vedanta*, in which he taught that *brahman*, selves and the world are separate and eternal, even though the latter two depend forever upon the first. From this standpoint, *brahman* directs the world, since all else is dependent, and is therefore both transcendent and immanent. As that which can free the self, *brahman* is identified with Vishnu. Whereas the ultimate Reality or *brahman* is neither independent (*svatantra*) nor dependent (*paratantra*), God or Vishnu is independent, whereas souls and matter are dependent. God did not cause the cosmos but is part of it, and by his presence keeps it in motion. Individual souls are dependent on *brahman* but are also active agents with responsibilities which require the recognition of the omnipresence and omnipotence of God. For the individual self, there exists either the bondage which results from ignorance and the karma produced through acting ignorantly, or release effected through the adoration, worship and service of Deity. The self is free when its devotion is pure and perpetual. Although the later forms of *Vedanta* lower the sights of human potentiality from the lofty goal of universal self-consciousness and conscious immortality taught by Shankaracharya, they all recognize the essential difference between bondage and freedom. The one is productive of suffering and the other offers emancipation from it. But whereas for Shankara the means of emancipation is wisdom (*jnana*) as the basis of devotion (*bhakti*) and *nishkama karma* or disinterested action, the separation between *atman* and *brahman* is crucial for Ramanuja and necessitates total *bhakti*, whilst for Madhava there are five distinctions within his dualism – between God and soul, God and matter, soul and matter, one form of matter and another, and especially between one soul and another – thus requiring from all souls total obeisance to the omnipresent and omnipotent God.

Suffering is the starting point of the *Sankhya darshana* which provides the general conceptual framework of *Yoga* philosophy. Patanjali set out the *Taraka Raja Yoga* system, linking transcendental and self-luminous wisdom (*taraka*) with the alchemy of mental transformation, and like the exponents of other schools, he borrowed those concepts and insights which could best delineate his perspective. Since he found *Sankhya* metaphysics useful to understanding, like a sturdy boat used to cross a stream and then left behind when the opposite bank has been reached, many thinkers have traditionally presented *Sankhya* as the theory for which *Yoga* is the practice. This approach can aid understanding, providing one recognizes from the first and at all times that *yoga* is the path to metaconsciousness, for which no system of concepts and discursive reasoning, however erudite, rigorous and philosophical, is adequate. More than any other school or system, *Yoga* is essentially experiential, in the broadest, fullest and deepest meaning of that term.

Hermes, June 1988

THE SANKHYA DARSHANA

The term 'Sankhya' is ultimately derived from the Sanskrit root khya, meaning 'to know', and the prefix san, 'exact'. Exact knowing is most adequately represented by Sankhya, 'number', and since the precision of numbers requires meticulous discernment, Sankhya is that darshana which involves a thorough discernment of reality and is expressed through the enumeration of diverse categories of existence. Philosophically, Sankhya is dualistic in its discernment of the Self (Purusha) from the non-self (prakriti). In distinguishing sharply between Purusha, Self or Spirit, on the one hand, and prakriti, non-self or matter, on the other, the Sankhya standpoint requires a rigorous redefinition of numerous terms used by various schools. Even though later Sankhya freely drew from the Vedic-Upanishadic storehouse of wisdom which intimates a rich variety of philosophical views, its earliest concern does not appear to have been philosophical in the sense of delineating a comprehensive conceptual scheme which describes and explains reality. Early Sankhya asked, "What is real?" and only later on added the question, "How does it all fit together?"

Enumerations of the categories of reality varied with individual thinkers and historical periods, but the standard classification of twenty-five tattvas or fundamental principles of reality is useful for a general understanding of the darshana. Simply stated, Sankhya holds that two radically distinct realities exist: Purusha, which can be translated 'Spirit', 'Self' or 'pure consciousness', and mulaprakriti, or 'pre-cosmic matter', 'non-self' or 'materiality'. Nothing can be predicated of Purusha except as a corrective negation; no positive attribute, process or intention can be affirmed of it, though it is behind all the activity of the world. It might be called the Perceiver or the Witness, but, strictly speaking, no intentionality can be implied by these words, and so Purusha cannot be conceived primarily as a knower. Mulaprakriti, however, can be understood as pure potential because it undergoes ceaseless transformation at several levels. Thus, of the twenty-five traditional *tattvas*, only these two are distinct. The remaining twenty-three are transformations or modifications of *mulaprakriti*. *Purusha* and *mulaprakriti* stand outside conceptual cognition, which arises within the flux of the other *tattvas*. They abide outside space and time, are simple, independent and inherently unchanging, and they have no relation to one another apart from their universal, simultaneous and mutual presence.

Mulaprakriti is characterized by three qualities or *gunas: sattva* or intelligent and noetic activity, *rajas* or passionate and compulsive activity, and *tamas* or ignorant and impotent lethargy, represented in the *Upanishads* by the colours white, red and black. If *mulaprakriti* were the only ultimate reality, its qualities would have forever remained in a homogeneous balance, without undergoing change, evolution or transformation. Since *Purusha* is co-present with *mulaprakriti*, the symmetrical homogeneity of *mulaprakriti* was disturbed, and this broken symmetry resulted in a progressive differentiation which became the world of ordinary experience. True knowledge or pure cognition demands a return to that primordial stillness which marks the utter disentanglement of Self from non-self. The process which moved the *gunas* out of their perfect mutual balance cannot be described or even alluded to through analogies, in part because the process occurred outside space and time (and gave rise to them), and in part because no description of what initiated this universal transformation can be given in the language of logically subsequent and therefore necessarily less universal change. In other words, all transformation known to the intellect occurs in some context – minimally that of the intellect itself – whilst the primordial process of transformation occurred out of all context, save for the mere co-presence of *Purusha* and *mulaprakriti*.

This imbalance gave rise, first of all, logically speaking, to *mahat* or *Buddhi*. These terms refer to universal consciousness, primordial consciousness or intellect in the classical and neo-Platonic sense of the word. *Mahat* in turn gave rise to *ahankara*, the sense of 'I' or egoity. (*Ahankara* literally means 'I-making'.) Egoity as a principle or *tattva* generated a host of offspring or evolutes, the first of which was *manas* or mind, which is both the capacity for sensation and the mental ability to act, or intellectual volition. It also produced the five *buddhindriyas* or capacities for sensation: *shrota* (hearing), *tvac* (touching), *chaksus* (seeing), *rasana* (tasting) and *ghrana* (smelling). In addition to sensation, *ahankara* gave rise to their dynamic and material correlates, the five *karmendriyas* or capacities for action, and the five *tanmatras* or subtle elements. The five *karmendriyas* are *Vach* (speaking), *pani* (grasping), *pada* (moving), *payu* (eliminating) and *upastha* (procreating), whilst the five *tanmatras* include *shabda* (sound), *sparsha* (touch), *rupa* (form), *rasa* (taste) and *gandha* (smell). The *tanmatras* are called 'subtle' because they produce the *mahabhutas* or gross elements which can be perceived by ordinary human beings. They are *Akasha* (aether or empirical space), *vayu* (air), *tejas* (fire, and by extension, light), *ap* (water) and *prithivi* (earth).

This seemingly elaborate system of the elements of existence (*tattvas*) is a rigorous attempt to reduce the kaleidoscope of reality to its simplest comprehensible components, without either engaging in a reductionism which explains away or denies what does not fit its classification, or falling prey to a facile monism which avoids a serious examination of visible and invisible Nature. Throughout the long history of *Sankhya* thought, enumerations have varied, but this general classification has held firm. Whilst some philosophers have suggested alternative orders of evolution, for instance, making the subtle elements give rise to the capacities for sensation and action, Ishvarakrishna expressed the classical consensus in offering this classification of twenty-five *tattvas*.

Once the fundamental enumeration was understood, *Sankhya* thinkers arranged the *tattvas* by sets to grasp more clearly their relationships to one another. At the most general level, *Purusha* is neither generated nor generating, whilst *mulaprakriti* is ungenerated but generating. *Buddhi, ahankara* and the *tanmatras* are both generated and generating, and *manas*, the *buddhindriyas, karmendriyas* and *mahabhutas* are generated and do not generate anything in turn. In terms of their mutual relationships, one can speak of kinds of *tattvas* and indicate an order of dependence from the standpoint of the material world.

No matter how subtle and elaborate the analysis, however, one has at best described ways in which consciousness functions in *prakriti,* the material world. If one affirms that *Purusha* and *prakriti* are radically and fundamentally separate, one cannot avoid the challenge which vexed Descartes: how can *res cogitans*, thinking substance, be in any way connected with *res extensa*, extended (material) substance? *Sankhya* avoided the most fundamental problem of Cartesian dualism by willingly admitting that there can be no connection, linkage or interaction between *Purusha* and *prakriti*. Since consciousness is a fact, this exceptional claim involved a redefinition of consciousness itself. Consciousness is necessarily transcendent, unconnected with *prakriti*, and therefore it can have neither cognitive nor intuitive awareness, since those are activities which involve some centre or egoity and surrounding field from which it separates itself or with which it identifies. Egoity or perspective requires some mode of action, and all action involves the *gunas*, which belong exclusively to *prakriti*. Consciousness, *Purusha*, is mere presence, *sakshitva*, without action, dynamics or content. Awareness, *chittavritti*, is therefore a function of *prakriti*, even though it would not have come into being – any more than anything would have evolved or the *gunas* would have become unstable – without the universal presence of *Purusha*. Thus it is said that *Purusha* is unique in that it is neither generated nor generating, whereas all other *tattvas* are either generating, generated or both.

In this view, mind is material. Given its capacity for awareness, it can intuit the presence of *Purusha*, but it is not that *Purusha*. All mental functions are part of the complex activity of *prakriti*. Consciousness is bare subjectivity without a shadow of objective content, and it cannot be said to have goals, desires or intentions. *Purusha* can be said to exist (*sat*) – indeed, it necessarily exists – and its essential and sole specifiable nature is *chit*, consciousness. Unlike the Vedantin *atman*, however, it cannot also be said to be *ananda*, bliss, for *Purusha* is the pure witness, *sakshi*, with no causal connection to or participation in *prakriti*. Yet it is necessary, for the *gunas* could not be said to be active save in the presence of some principle of sentience. Without *Purusha* there could be no *prakriti*. This is not the simple idealistic and phenomenological standpoint summarized in Berkeley's famous dictum, *esse est percipi*, "to be is to be perceived". Rather, it is closer to the recognition grounded in Newtonian mechanics that, should the universe achieve a condition of total entropy, it could not be said to exist, for there would be no possibility of differentiation in it. Nor could its existence be denied. The presence of *Purusha*, according to *Sankhya*, is as necessary as is its utter lack of content.

Given the distinction between unqualified, unmodified subjectivity as true or pure consciousness, and awareness, which is the qualified appearance of consciousness in the world, consciousness appears as what it cannot be. It appears to cause and initiate, but cannot do so, since *Purusha* cannot be said to be active in any sense; it appears to entertain ideas and chains of thought, but it can in reality do neither. Rather, the action of the *gunas* appears as the activity of consciousness until the actual nature of consciousness is realized. The extreme break with previous understanding resulting from this realization – that consciousness has no content and that content is not conscious – is emancipation, the freeing of *Purusha* from false bondage to *prakriti*. It is akin to the Vedantin realization of *atman* free of any taint of *maya*, and the Buddhist realization of *shunyata*. Philosophical conceptualization is incapable of describing this realization, for pure consciousness can only appear, even to the subtlest cognitive understanding, as nothing. For *Sankhya*, *Purusha* is not nothing, but it is nothing that partakes of *prakriti* (which all awareness does).

Sankhya's unusual distinction between consciousness and what are ordinarily considered its functions and contents implies an operational view of *Purusha*. Even though no properties can be predicated of *Purusha*, the mind or intellect intuits the necessity of consciousness behind it, as it were. That is, the mind becomes aware that it is not itself pure consciousness. Since this awareness arises in individual minds, *Purusha* is recognized by one or another egoity. Without being able to attribute qualities to *Purusha*, it must therefore be treated philosophically as a plurality. Hence it is said that there are literally innumerable *purushas*, none of which have any distinguishing characteristics. The Leibnizian law of the identity of indiscernibles cannot be applied to *Purusha*, despite the philosophical temptation to do so, precisely because philosophy necessarily stops at the limit of *prakriti*. *Purusha* is outside space and time, and so is also beyond space-time identities. Since the minimum requirements of differentiation involve at least an indirect reference to either space or time, their negation in the concept of indiscernibility also involves such a reference, and cannot be applied to *Purusha*. Even though *Sankhya* affirms a plurality of *purushas*, this stance is less the result of metaphysical certitude than of the limitations imposed by consistency of method. The plurality of *purushas* is the consequence of the limits of understanding.

Within the enormous and diverse history of Indian thought, the six *darshanas* viewed themselves and one another in two ways. Internally, each standpoint sought clarity, completeness and consistency without reference to other *darshanas*. Since, however, the *darshanas* were committed to the proposition that they were six separate and viable perspectives on the same reality, they readily drew upon one another's insights and terminology and forged mutually dependent relationships. They were less concerned with declaring one another true or false than with understanding the value and limitations of each in respect to a complete realization of the ultimate and divine nature of things. Whilst some Western philosophers have pointed to the unprovable Indian presupposition that the heart of existence is divine, the *darshanas* reverse this standpoint by affirming that the core of reality is, almost definitionally, the only basis for thinking of the divine. In other words, reality is the criterion of the divine, and no other standard can make philosophical sense of the sacred, much less give it a practical place in human psychology and ethics. In their later developments, the *darshanas* strengthened their internal conceptual structures and ethical architectonics by taking one another's positions as foils for self-clarification. Earlier developments were absorbed into later understanding and exposition. Historically, *Sankhya* assimilated and redefined much of what had originally belonged to *Nyaya* and *Vaishesika*, and even *Mimamsa*, only to find much of its terminology and psychology incorporated into Vedanta, the most trenchantly philosophical of the *darshanas*. At the same time, later *Sankhya* borrowed freely from Vedantin philosophical concepts to rethink its own philosophical difficulties.

Despite *Sankhya's* unique distinction between consciousness and awareness, which allowed it to preserve its fundamental dualism in the face of monistic arguments – and thereby avoid the metaphysical problems attending monistic views – it could not avoid one fundamental philosophical question: What is it to say that *prakriti* is dynamic *because* of the presence of *Purusha*? To say that *prakriti* reflects the presence of *Purusha*, or that *Purusha* is reflected in *prakriti*, preserves a rigid distinction between the two, for neither an object reflected in a mirror nor the mirror is affected by the other. But *Sankhya* characterizes the ordinary human condition as one of suffering, which is the manifest expression of the condition of *avidya*, ignorance. This condition arises because *Purusha* falsely identifies with *prakriti* and its evolutes. Liberation, *Mukti*, is the result of *viveka*, discrimination, which is the highest knowledge. Even though *viveka* might be equated with pure perception as the *sakshi* or Witness, the process of attaining it suggests either an intention on the part of *Purusha* or a response on the part of *prakriti*, if not both. How then can *Purusha* be said to have no relation, including no passive relation, to *prakriti*? Even Ishvarakrishna's enchanting metaphor of the dancer before the host of spectators does not answer the question, for there is a significant relationship between performer and audience.

Such questions are worthy of notice but are misplaced from the *Sankhya* standpoint. If philosophical understanding is inherently limited to the functions of the mind (which is an evolute of *prakriti*), it can encompass neither total awareness (*Purusha*) nor the fact that both *Purusha* and *prakriti* exist. This is the supreme and unanswerable mystery of *Sankhya* philosophy, the point at which *Sankhya* declares that questions must have an end. It is not, however, an unaskable or meaningless question. If its answer cannot be found in philosophy, that is because it is dissolved in *Mukti*, freedom from ignorance, through perfect *viveka*, discrimination. In *Sankhya* as in *Vedanta*, philosophy ends where realization begins. Philosophy does not resolve the ultimate questions, even though it brings great clarity to cognition. Philosophy prepares, refines and orients the mind towards a significantly different activity, broadly called 'meditation', the rigorous cultivation of clarity of discrimination and concentrated, pellucid insight. The possibility of this is provided for by *Sankhya* metaphysics through its stress on the asymmetry between *Purusha* and *prakriti*, despite their co-presence. *Prakriti* depends on *Purusha*, but *Purusha* is independent of everything; *Purusha* is pure consciousness, whilst *prakriti* is unself-conscious. *Prakriti* continues to evolve because individual selves in it do not realize that they are really *Purusha* and, therefore, can separate themselves from *prakriti*, whilst there can never be complete annihilation of everything or of primordial matter.

Whereas *Yoga* accepted the postulates of *Sankhya* and also utilized its categories and classifications, all these being in accord with the experiences of developed *yogins*, there are significant divergences between *Yoga* and *Sankhya*. The oldest *Yoga* could have been agnostic in the sense implicit in the *Rig Veda* Hymn to Creation, but Patanjali's *Yoga* is distinctly theistic, diverging in this way from atheistic *Sankhya*. Whilst *Sankhya* is a speculative system, or at least a conceptual framework, *Yoga* is explicitly experiential and therefore linked to an established as well as evolving consensus among advanced *yogins*. This is both illustrated and reinforced by the fact that whereas *Sankhya* maps out the inner world of disciplined ideation in terms of thirteen evolutes – *Buddhi, ahankara, manas* and the ten *indriyas* – Patanjali's *Yoga* subsumes all these under *chitta* or consciousness, which is resilient, elastic and dynamic, including the known, the conceivable, the cosmic as well as the unknown. Whereas *Sankhya* is one of the most self-sufficient or closed systems, *Yoga* retains, as a term and in its philosophy, a conspicuously open texture which characterizes all Indian thought at its best. From the Vedic hymns to even contemporary discourse, it is always open-ended in reference to cosmic and human evolution, degrees of adeptship and levels of initiatory illumination. It is ever seeing, reaching and aspiring, beyond the boundaries of the highest thought, volition and feeling; beyond worlds and rationalist systems and doctrinaire theologies; beyond the limits of inspired utterance as well as all languages and all possible modes of creative expression. Philosophy and mathematics, poetry and myth, idea and icon, are all invaluable aids to the image-making faculty, but they all must point beyond themselves, whilst they coalesce and collapse in the unfathomable depths of the Ineffable, before which the best minds and hearts must whisper *neti neti*, "not this, not that". There is only the Soundless Sound, the ceaseless *AUM* in Boundless Space and Eternal Duration.

Hermes, July 1988

THE YOGA SUTRA

This is the royal knowledge, the royal mystery, the most excellent purifier, clearly comprehensible, not opposed to sacred law, easy to perform, and inexhaustible.

Sri Krishna

A careful study of Patanjali's priceless aphorisms on *Raja Yoga* is immensely valuable to all who wish to learn the discipline of true meditation while at the same time discerning the sharp contrast between the psycho-spiritual and the psycho-physical systems of yogic training. Metaphysics and ethics are linked through psychology. A therapeutic program of self-study, undertaken with discrimination and detachment, is integral to the progressive realization of knowledge of spiritual law and a calm reliance upon the moral order. The subtle externalizations implicit in the separative and pseudo-autonomous portraits of human nature, found in all psycho-physical systems of self-development, are incompatible with gnostic metaphysics of the highest spiritual sort and subvert the ethical ideal of compassionate direction of all one's emanations. 'The divine discipline' involves a grasp of correspondences between the universal and the particular, the macrocosm and the microcosm in man, and requires a noetic fusion of the psychological and spiritual. Patanjali could assist us in this art of self-study and in the science of mind control, but to make full use of his teaching, we must not lose sight of the dual metaphysical and ethical basis of his aphorisms.

Spiritual growth may be regarded as a gradual deepening of perception and strengthening of will. As personal beings, bound by desire to the material limitations of the phenomenal world of sense-objects, our perceptions are crude and our volition is perverted. It is the limited perception of life, the inability to sense conscious or even individual existence outside of form or beyond the material plane, that constitutes real death. "Real life is in the spiritual consciousness of that life, in a conscious existence in Spirit, not Matter." Meditation is needed to free ourselves from the limitations imposed by our fleeting sensory perceptions and by our false sense of identity and personal volition. The point of departure of Patanjali's text is the diffusive, fragmented, ephemeral, limiting nature of our everyday consciousness, i.e., our mental awareness of objects and subjects and of our own natures. Spiritual consciousness is, by contrast, concentrated, deliberate, unifying, liberating and permanent. This is not merely an initial contrast but one that persists even as we ascend through higher levels of awareness, planes of perception and states of will-activity. The aphorisms have meanings and implications that recur with a heightened significance as we proceed with meditation and self-study.

Perception and will are bound up with two forces – noetic (from *nous*) and psychic (from *psyche*), derived from *Buddhi* and *Prana* (moral perception and vital energy) – and the possibility of the former using the latter. We can attach a minimal, everyday sense to the notion of moral power, acting on the will of man. This moral power and energy in man can be consciously cultivated by individuals and by groups and applied courageously to the quest. We must always distinguish between what is salutary and what is pleasant, between *sreyas* and *preyas*, to achieve a harmony between thought, word and deed, so that life becomes a fulfilled oath, a constant vow or *vrita*, a perpetual pilgrimage, a continual sacrifice. The votary of truth is not a muddled idealist but a man who meditates before getting into action. He does not take refuge in theoretical speculation but remains steadfast in contemplation while constantly trying to endow his whole life of conscious activity with a pervading sanctity of *pavitra*. It is only by personal steadfastness, by holding on to his vow that a man may be useful to others to an exceptional degree. It is impossible to live as a *sadhaka* in the midst of society if one's entire life is not a fulfilled oath.

The metaphysical basis of Patanjali's text is laid down in a few aphorisms in each of the four parts of the *sutra*. Book I, the *Samadhi pada*, points to a fundamental truth which must be grasped even before we embark on meditation and self-study:

> The state of abstract meditation may be attained by profound devotedness toward the Supreme Spirit considered in its comprehensible manifestation as *Ishwara*.
>
> *Ishwara* is a spirit, untouched by troubles, works, fruits of works, or desires.
>
> In *Ishwara* becomes infinite that omniscience which in man exists but as a germ.
>
> *Ishwara* is the preceptor of all, even of the earliest of created beings, for He is not limited by time.
>
> Book I: 23-26

Beyond the phenomenal universe lies pure spirit, known in its comprehensive manifestation as *Ishwara*, unmodified by material form or phenomenal change, untouched by sorrow-producing sensations or by particular precipitations, by causal connections and external conditions, or the stimuli of impulses and desires. The germ of omniscience – the knowledge of this unmodified reality – exists in man and becomes infinite in *Ishwara*. Man can move from the atomic to the infinite through mental awareness and change of consciousness if he grasps and applies the truth of the distinction between his ever-modified mind and his status as a soul, a spectator without a spectacle.

> At the time of concentration the soul abides in the state of a spectator without a spectacle.
>
> The student whose mind is thus steadied obtains a mastery which extends from the Atomic to the Infinite.
>
> That meditation which has a subtle object in view ends with the indissoluble element called primordial matter.
>
> Book I: 3, 40, 45

These aphorisms point to the metaphysical realization possible to every monadic consciousness, and also indicate a relationship to primordial matter, the indissoluble element that exists in the very constitution of the manifested universe. Lest a false impression of these states should arise and contribute to moral indifference, Patanjali declares:

> Although the Universe in its objective state has ceased to be, in respect to that man who has attained to the perfection of spiritual cultivation, it has not ceased in respect to all others, because it is common to others besides him.
>
> Book II: 22

Book II of the aphorisms, the *Sadhana pada*, is concerned with the practical means of establishing concentration. Ignorance or *avidya* is identified as the cause of the variety of mental afflictions and is defined in its metaphysical sense:

> Ignorance is the notion that the non-eternal, the impure, the evil, and that which is not soul are, severally, eternal, pure, good and soul.
>
> Book II: 5

The culmination of ignorance, inhibiting self-awareness, is the natural tendency to material manifestation and the self-reproductive power of externalization:

> The tenacious wish for existence upon earth is inherent in all sentient beings, and continues through all incarnations, because it has self-reproductive power. It is felt as well by the wise as the unwise.
>
> Book II: 9

We must see this power for what it is, but our valuations alter if we recognize, as in aphorism 28, that the entire universe, visible and invisible, compounded of the purity of the unmodified *Ishwara* (reflected in primordial matter), the activity and the withdrawal involved in manifestation, the material elements and organs of action, that all exist for the soul's experience and emancipation.

Aphorism 20 of Book II defines the soul as the Perceiver, vision pure and simple, unmodified, which looks directly upon ideas. Hence the possibility of omniscience set forth in Book III:

> By concentrating his mind upon the true nature of the soul as being entirely distinct from any experiences, and disconnected from all material things, and dissociated from the understanding, a knowledge of the true nature of the soul itself arises in the ascetic.
>
> From the particular kind of concentration last described, there arises in the ascetic, and remains with him at all times, a knowledge concerning all things, whether they be those apprehended through the organs of the body or otherwise presented to his contemplation.
>
> In the ascetic who has acquired the accurate discriminative knowledge of the truth and of the nature of the soul, there arises a knowledge of all existences in their essential natures and a mastery over them.
>
> Book III: 36, 37, 50

Aphorisms 23 to 26 of Book II show why man is bound and why he can free himself, why he is actually ignorant and potentially omniscient – the soul is conjoined with the organ of thought and thus with nature. The conjuncture is caused by ignorance, but the quitting of bondage to matter is possible through perfect discriminative knowledge.

Aphorism 9 of Book III, the *Vibhuti pada* concerning yogic attainments, shows that while the modifications of mind produce a train of self-reproductive thought, so too another train of self-reproductive thought arises when the mind is engrossed solely with the truth.

> There are two trains of self-reproductive thought, the first of which results from the mind being modified and shifted by the object or subject contemplated; the second, when it is passing from that modification and is becoming engaged only with the truth itself; at the moment when the first is subdued and the mind is just becoming intent, it is concerned in both of those two trains of self-reproductive thought, and this state is technically called *Nirodha*.
>
> Book III: 9

The cycle of cosmic involvement is ideation, manifestation and retention of transcendence. For the individual the cycle is reversed –

impure involvement or false ideation, disengagement and self-subsisting universal self-awareness. Once attained, this could be followed by a new cycle in which the individual creates in the manner of spirit – by ideation, constructive manifestation (through the power of projection) and retention of transcendence. This divine and human prerogative is enshrined in the doctrine of *Jnana Yagna*, the practice of *Buddhi Yoga*, and the spiritual powers of *Kriyashakti* and *Icchashakti*.

These involve a grasp of Karma (Book III, 23), *sattwa* or the property of luminousness (Book III, 21), *udana* or vital energy (Book III, 40), and the five classes of properties in the manifested universe (Book III, 45). Thus we can gain the knowledge that saves us from involuntary rebirth (Book III, 55) and the condition of emancipation or Isolation of the Soul (Book III, 56). Book IV says more about the perfections (Book IV, 1), the transformation of nature (Book IV, 2), the mental deposits left by Karma (Book IV, 8), the three qualities of objects (Book IV, 13), our awareness of time (Book IV, 32), and the re-absorption of the qualities (Book IV, 33).

All this is abstruse, a statement of principles and possibilities. How are we to make this knowledge accessible? By drawing the ethical corollaries of the metaphysical truths given. The mind cannot be withdrawn from its repeated modifications to the unmodified state of the soul without constant practice – *abhyasa*. To do this we require a firm position, growth in dispassion to displace the power of *tanha* and the desire for externalization through attachment and repulsion, and a knowledge of the soul as distinct from all else.

> This exercise is a firm position observed out of regard for the end in view, and perseveringly adhered to for a long time without intermission.
>
> Dispassion is the having overcome one's desires.
>
> Dispassion, carried to the utmost, is indifference regarding all else than soul, and this indifference arises from a knowledge of soul as distinguished from all else.
>
> Book I: 14-16

The obstacles to concentration are set out in Book I, 30 – sickness, languor, doubt, carelessness, laziness, addiction to sense-objects, erroneous perception, failure to attain to abstraction, instability in any state when attained. To prevent these, according to aphorisms 32 and 39 of Book I, any one truth which one appreciates should be dwelt upon until the mind is steadied. Further, the mind must be purified through the practice of benevolence, tenderness, complacency, disregard for objects of happiness, grief, virtue and vice. Hence the enormous importance of detachment and resignation and forbearance, the essential and universal duties, and special religious observances or ascetic rules.

> Forbearance consists in not killing, veracity, not stealing, continence, and not coveting.
>
> These, without respect to rank, place, time, or compact, are the universal great duties.
>
> Religious Observances are purification of both mind and body, contentment, austerity, inaudible mutterings, and persevering devotion to the Supreme Soul.
>
> Book II: 30-32

These 'Religious Observances' or *niyamas* are especially relevant to all who wish to pursue the path of spiritual growth, but they must be developed on the firm basis of constant practice of the universal great duties, the *mahavritam*. One of the oldest meanings of *vrita*, as found in the *Rig Veda*, is "divine will or command." The order (*Rta*) observable in nature was considered to be the consequence of the *vrita* of the gods, and it could be reflected in human society through the deliberate and vigilant performance of *Dharma*. The instinctual behaviour of the lower kingdoms and the motions of natural objects have a rhythm and a reliability that men must consciously emulate if they are to become conscious embodiments of the divine power that pervades the universe. Any conscious or unconscious infringement of the divine order is to be expiated by imposing on oneself some sort of self-denial. Such a resort to *vrita* was supposed to purify the performer and elevate him spiritually. The observance of vows is even more necessary for the aspirant to a life of complete renunciation or for a seeker after mystical attainment as in the *Yoga Sutra*. Dispassion must accompany the discrimination sought through the special religious observances. Then meditation will become meaningful and fruitful. The task is arduous, but every effort brings strength and joy.

Hermes, August 1976
Raghavan Iyer

YOGA SUTRAS – BOOK I:
SAMADHI PADA

AUM atha yoganushasanam

1. OM. Now begins instruction in yoga. (1)

yogash chitta-vritti-nirodhah

2. Yoga is the restraint of the modifications of the mind. (2)

tada drashtuh svarupe 'vasthanam

3. Then the Seer is established in his own essential nature. (3)

vritti-sarupyam itaratra

4. Otherwise, there is self-identification with the mental modifications. (4)

vrittayah panchatayyah klishtaklishtah

5. The mental modifications are fivefold and are painful or pleasurable. (5)

pramana-viparyaya-vikalpa-nidra-smritayah

6. These are correct cognition, misconception, fantasy, sleep and memory. (6)

pratyakshanumanagamah pramanani

7. Correct cognition is based on direct perception, valid inference and verbal testimony. (7)

viparyayo mithya-jnanam atad-rupa-pratishtham

8. Misconception is illusory knowledge based upon what is other than itself. (8)

shabda-jnananupati-vastu-shunyo vikalpah

9. Fantasy, empty of substance, is engendered by words and concepts. (9)

abhava-pratyayalambana vrittir nidra

10. Sleep is the modification engendered by the abeyance and absence of mental contents. (10)

anubhuta-vishayasanpramosha smritih

11. Memory is the not letting go of an object or image of subjective experience. (11)

abhyasa-vairagyabhyam tan-nirodhah

12. The restraint of these mental modifications comes from assiduous practice (*abhyasa*) and through dispassionate detachment (*vairagya*). (12)

tatra sthitau yatno 'bhyasah

13. Practice (*abhyasa*) is the continuous effort to abide in a steady state. (13)

sa tu dirgha-kala-nairantarya-satkarasevito dridha-bhumih

14. This is indeed firmly grounded when it is persistently exercised for a long time, without interruption, and with earnest, reverential attention and devotion. (14)

drishtanushravika-vishaya-vitrishnasya vashikara-sanjna vairagyam

15. Dispassionate detachment (*vairagya*) is the consciousness of perfect mastery in one who has ceased to crave for objects, seen or unseen. (15)

tat param Purusha-khyater guna-vaitrishnayam

16. That is the supreme dispassion when there is cessation of all craving for the attributes (*gunas*), owing to discernment of the Self (*Purusha*). (16)

vitarka-vicharanandasmitanugamat sanprajnatah

17. Cognitive contemplation is accompanied by reasoning, deliberation, bliss and the awareness of pure being (*asmita*). (17)

virama-pratyayabhyasa-purvah sanskara-shesho 'nyah

18. Another sort of contemplation comes through the previous practice, the cessation of all mental contents, residual potencies alone remaining. (18)

bhava-pratyayo videha-prakritilayanam

19. It is caused by phenomenal existence in the case of the disembodied and of those absorbed into Nature (*prakriti*). (19)

shraddha-virya-smriti-Samadhi-prajnapurvaka itaresham

20. In the case of others, it is preceded by faith (*shraddha*), energy (*virya*), attentiveness (*smriti*), and the intellectual insight (*prajna*) needed for meditative absorption (*Samadhi*). (20)

tivra-sanveganam asannah

21. It is close at hand for those with vehement intensity. (21)

mridu-madhyadhimatratvat tato 'pi visheshah

22. There is also a further differentiation – mild, moderate and intense. (22)

ishvara-pranidhanad va

23. Or by devoted self-surrender to the Lord. (23)

klesha-karma-vipakashayair aparamrishtah purushavishesha ishvarah

24. *Ishvara* is a distinct spirit (*Purusha*), untouched by troubles, actions and their results, and latent impressions. (24)

tatra niratishayam sarvajna-bijam

25. In *Ishvara* the seed of omniscience becomes infinite. (25)

sa purvesham api guruh kalenanavachchedat

26. *Ishvara* is the preceptor even of the Ancients, for He is not fettered by time. (26)

tasya vachakah pranavah

27. His designation is OM. (27)

tajjapas tad-artha-bhavanam

28. Let there be constant chanting of OM and meditation on its meaning. (28)

tatah pratyak-chetanadhigamo 'py antaraya-bhavash cha

29. From that comes the turning inward of consciousness and the removal of hindrances. (29)

vyadhi-styana-sanshaya-pramadalasyavirati-bhranti-darshanalabdhabhumikatvanavasthitatvani chitta-vikshepas te 'ntarayah

30. The hindrances which cause mental distractions are disease, dullness, doubt, heedlessness, indolence, addiction to sense-objects, distorted perception, failure to find a footing and instability in any state. (30)

duhkha-daurmanasyangamejayatva-shvasa-prashrasa vikshepa-sahabhuvah

31. These distractions are accompanied by sorrow, depression, bodily restlessness and spasmodic breathing. (31)

   tat-pratishedhartham eka-tattvabhyasah

32. To check these, there should be constant practice of one truth or principle (*eka-tattva*). (32)

   maitri-karuna-muditopekshanam sukha-duhkha-punyapunya-vishayanam bhavanatash chitta-prasadanam

33. The mind becomes purified through the practice of friendliness, compassion, gladness and indifference respectively towards happiness, sorrow, virtue and vice, (33)

   prachchardana-vidharanabhyam va pranasya

34. Or by expulsion and retention of breath (*prana*). (34)

   vishayavati va pravrittir utpanna manasah sthiti-nibandhani

35. The awakening of subtle sensory vision can hold the mind in a state of steadiness, (35)

   vishoka va jyotishmati

36. Or a state of serene luminosity, (36)

   vita-raga-vishayam va chittam

37. Or the mind is fixed on one free from craving, (37)

   svapna-nidra-jnanalambanam va

38. Or by dwelling on insights gained in dreams and dreamless sleep, (38)

   yathabhimata-dhyanad va

39. Or by meditating on that which is deeply desired. (39)

paramanu-parama-mahattvanto 'sya vashikarah

40. Thus, his mastery extends from the minutest atom to the ultimate infinitude. (40)

kshina-vritter abhijatasyeva maner grahitri-grahana-grahyeshu tatstha-tadanjanata samapattih

41. When the modifications of the mind vanish, it becomes like a transparent crystal, attaining the power of transformation (*samapatti*), taking on the colour of what it rests on, whether it be the cognizer, the cognized or the act of cognition. (41)

tatra shabdartha-jnana-vikalpaih sankirna savitarka

42. Whenever the construction of words and meanings is confused and uncertain, the mind wavers in a polemical and chaotic state (*sankirna savitarka*). (42)

smriti-parishuddhau svarupa-shunyevartha-matra-nirbhasa nirvitarka

43. When the memory is purified, when the mind is void of its own form, it is luminous with true knowledge of its sole object, attaining to an unclouded state (*nirvitarka*). (43)

etayaiva savichara nirvichara cha sukshma-vishaya vyakhyata

44. Also, by this process, the deliberative and non-deliberative states concerning subtle elements (*sukshma-vishaya*) are explained. (44)

sukshma-vishayatvam chalinga-paryavasanam

45. And the subtle elements extend up to the noumenal, primordial and undifferentiated (*alinga*). (45)

ta eva sabijah samadhih

46. They are only the basis of meditation with its seed. (46)

vichara-vaisharadye 'dhyatma-prasadah

47. On attaining the utmost purity of the non-deliberative state, there is the dawning of spiritual light, the gracious peace and luminosity of the supreme Self. (47)

ritambhara tatra prajna

48. Therein is direct cognition (*prajna*), which carries and holds the unalloyed Truth. (48)

shrutanumana-prajnabhyam anya-vishaya vishesharthatvat

49. Direct cognition is essentially different from testimony and inference, owing to its focus upon a specific object, Truth itself. (49)

taj-jah sanskaro 'nya sanskara-pratibandhi

50. The impress engendered therefrom supersedes all other latent impressions. (50)

tasyapi nirodhe sarva-nirodhan nirbijah samadhih

51. On the stoppage of even that, all else being eliminated, there arises meditation without a seed (*nirbijah Samadhi*). (51)

Hermes, May 1987

SAMADHI PADA

*Through yoga let one concentrate on study. By perfection in study
and in yoga, the Supreme Soul shines forth clearly.*

Vyasa

The classic text of Patanjali opens with the simplest statement: *"atha
yoganushasanam"*, "Now begins instruction in *yoga*." The typical reader
today might well expect this terse announcement to be followed by
a full explanation of the term *yoga* and its diverse meanings, perhaps
a polemical digression on different schools of thought and some
methodological guidance concerning the best way to use the text. None
of this occurs. Rather, Patanjali set down his most famous words: *"yogash
chitta-vritti-nirodhah"*: "Yoga is the restraint of the modifications of the
mind." He stated the essential meaning of *yoga* without any argument
or illustration, as if he were providing a basic axiom. He thus showed
at the very start that he was concerned with practical instruction rather
than theoretical exposition. He thereby took for granted that the user
of the text already had some understanding of the task of *yoga* and was
ready to undergo a demanding daily discipline.

Yoga psychology differs radically from more recent, and especially
post-Freudian, schools of thought in its stress on self-emancipation
rather than on self-acceptance in relation to social norms or psychic
tensions. Most modern varieties of psychology, including even the
recent humanistic preoccupation with self-actualization as propounded
by Abraham Maslow and elaborated in different directions by
Carl Rogers and Rollo May, essentially aim at an integration and
harmonizing of otherwise disparate and conflicting elements in a person
in contemporary society. For Patanjali, all these identifiable elements
– thoughts, feelings, intentions, motives and desires (conscious and
unconscious) – are *chittavrittis*, mental modifications which must be seen
as hindrances to contemplative calm. Even if they are deftly balanced

and fully integrated, the individual would at best be a mature person marked by thoughtful and creative responses in a world of suffering and ignorance. Conquering, not coping, transcending, not reconciling, were Patanjali's chief concerns. For him, the latter were by-products of the former, and never the reverse. The psychology of self-emancipation means the deliberate and self-conscious restraint of everything that is productive of mental confusion, weakness and pain.

Patanjali's stipulative definition of *yoga* might seem dogmatic, but this reaction springs from ignorance of his central purpose and unstated presuppositions. Patanjali wrote not from the standpoint of revealed scripture, academic scholarship or of theoretical clarification, but from the standpoint of concrete experience through controlled experiment. If truth is ontologically bound up and intimately fused with self-transcendence, then what from the standpoint of self-emancipation is a stark description is, from the standpoint of the unenlightened, an arbitrary prescription. What would be the naturalistic fallacy on a single plane of manifested Nature becomes a necessary line of thought when multiple planes of unmanifested Nature are taken into account. The ability to alter states of consciousness presupposes the capacity to emulate the architectonics of a higher and less differentiated plane on a lower and more fragmented plane of percepts and concepts. In other words, *yoga* is that science in which the descriptions of reality necessarily function as prescriptions for those who have not experienced it. The analogy would be closer to music or mathematics than to the visual arts or the empirical sciences as normally understood.

Skilful methods are those which provide apt descriptions, giving the instructional guidance needed. Hence, in the hands of a spiritual master, the actual method to be pursued varies with each aspirant, for it is the vital and original link between the adept's transcendent *(taraka)* wisdom and the disciple's mental temperament and devotion *(bhakti)*. There is a reciprocal interaction between the readiness to receive and the mode of giving – of disciple and master. For Patanjali, the true nature of *chitta,* the mind, can be known only when it is not modified by external influences and their internal impresses. For as long as modifications persist without being deliberately chosen for a purpose, the mind unwittingly identifies with them, falling into passivity, habitude, and the pain which results from a state of fragmentation and self-alienation.

Since mental modifications ramify in myriad directions, their root causes need to be grasped clearly if they are to be firmly removed. The essential principle to be understood is central to the second and third of Gautama Buddha's Four Noble Truths. Those persistent misconceptions which, directly or indirectly, produce discontent and suffering have a distinctive set of causes which, if eliminated, inevitably ensure the cessation of their concomitant effects. Patanjali pointed to five *chittavrittis* which are distinct and yet share the common tendency to be pleasurable or painful. Whilst *yoga* psychology fully acknowledges the strength of the pleasure principle – the propensity to be drawn towards pleasurable sensations as if by a magnet and to be repelled by painful ones – it denies its relevance to real individuation as a moral agent, a *Manushya*, whose name comes from *manas*, 'mind', the root of which is *man*, 'to think'. Self- emancipation, the culmination in *yoga* of self-transcendence, requires the complete subordination of the pleasure-pain principle to the reality principle. Reality, in this view, has nothing to do with involuntary change, the inherent propensity of *prakriti*, matter, and not *Purusha*, spirit, whilst pleasure and pain are necessarily bound up with conditioning and change. This is why the most attractive states of mind seem so readily and recurrently to alter into the most repugnant states. In general, mental modifications obscure and obstruct the intrinsically blissful nature of pure consciousness, the serene state of mind of the "spectator without a spectacle."

The five types of mental modifications are: *correct cognition*, based on direct perception, valid inference and verbal testimony; *misconception*, based upon something other than itself, namely the five *kleshas* or sources of sorrow – ignorance, egoism, attachment, hate and the fear of death, according to the *Yogabhashya*; *fantasy*, engendered by words and concepts, when and to the degree that they do not refer to reality; *sleep*, which occurs when other modifications cease and the mind is emptied of mental contents; and *memory*, which is the result of clinging to, or at least not letting go of, objects or images of subjective experiences. The *chittavrittis* can be diagrammatically depicted as follows:

Mental Modifications (*chittavrittis*)				
Correct cognition (*pramana*)	Misconception (*viparyaya*)	Fantasy (*vikalpa*)	Sleep (*nidra*)	Memory (*smriti*)
Direct perception Valid inference Verbal testimony	Illusion (mistaken perception)	Words and concepts	Absence of mental contents	Clinging to objects and images

Although this array of mental modifications is easy to outline, its implications are extensive and radical. When Patanjali included correct cognition amongst the mental modifications, he was adhering to strict theoretical and practical consistency. He was concerned to deny that mundane insight, discursive thought and even scriptural authority can free the mind from bondage to delusion and suffering. Yet without a preliminary apprehension of *yoga* philosophy, how could one adopt its methods and hope to achieve its aims? In part the answer lies in a proper grasp of the pervasiveness of *maya* or illusion. If everything that conceals the changeless Real is *maya,* then the human being who seeks to know the Real by conventional methods is trapped in some sort of metaphysical split or even schizophrenia. Philosophers from the pre-Socratics and Platonists to Descartes and Spinoza recognized that a substance cannot become what it is not. To say that human beings are intrinsically capable of attaining *kaivalya,* self-emancipation or transcendence of *maya,* is to affirm that they are quintessentially what they seek. Their inmost nature is one with the Real. On the other hand, to say that they have to strive in earnest to realize fully what they essentially are implies that they have allowed themselves to become captive to *maya* through persistent self-limitation.

Given this delusive condition, the mere temporary cessation of modifications, such as occurs in sleep, will not help to liberate man's immortal spirit. As *maya* is pervasive illusion, humanity as it knows itself is a part of it. Ignorant or involuntary withdrawal from its action only makes it unconscious, and this is why sleep is classed as one of the *chittavrittis*. Rather, one has to master the rules of *maya* and learn how to extricate oneself gradually from it. Otherwise, one only makes random moves, embedding oneself in deeper ignorance and greater suffering. Patanjali taught that deliverance can only come through *abhyasa*, assiduous practice, and *vairagya*, dispassionate detachment. *Abhyasa is* the active opposite of passive sleep, and *vairagya* frees one from all attachments, including the *kleshas*, which induce misconceptions. Together, these two mirror in the world of change that which is changeless beyond it. In the language of the *Isha Upanishad*, one has to find the transcendent in the immanent, and for Patanjali, *abhyasa* and *vairagya* constitute exactly that mode of awareness.

For Patanjali, however, *abhyasa* is not just striving to *do* something; it is rather the effort to *be* something. "*Abhyasa* is the continuous effort to abide in a steady state." According to the *Yogabhashya*, *abhyasa* is the attempt to preserve *prashantavahita*, continuity of mind or consciousness which is both fully awake and without fluctuations. Like all such spiritual exercises, *abhyasa* becomes richer, more refined and more relaxed with persistence that comes from repeated effort, moral earnestness and joyous devotion. *Abhyasa* is the constant criterion for all effort, and the indispensable tool, whenever and however taken up.

Vairagya cannot be merely passive disinterest in the content of experience any more than sleep can substitute for wakeful serenity. It is true detachment whilst being fully aware of the relative significance of objects, and this element of self-conscious maintenance of calm detachment is exactly what makes it real *vairagya*. Through *vairagya*, one comes to know the world for what it is because one recognizes that every object of sense, whether seen or unseen, is an assemblage of evanescent attributes or qualities (*gunas*) of *prakriti*, whereas the enduring reality, from the standpoint of the seeker for emancipation, is *Purusha*, the Self of all. Shankaracharya stated: "The seer of *Purusha* becomes one who is freed from rejecting or accepting anything.... Detachment is extreme clarity of cognition."

Abhyasa and *vairagya* are fused in the intense yet serene mental absorption known as *Samadhi*. Patanjali characterized *Samadhi* (which means 'concentration', 'contemplation' and 'meditation', depending on the context) in relation to a succession of stages, for if *Samadhi* signifies a specific state, the contemplative seeker would either abide in it or fail to do so. But Patanjali knew that no one can suddenly bridge the gap between fragmented, distracted consciousness and wholly unified meditation. Rather, concentration *(Samadhi)* proceeds by degrees for one who persists in the effort, because one progressively overcomes everything that hinders it. In the arduous ascent from greater degrees of relative *maya* towards greater degrees of reality, the transformation of consciousness requires a calm apprehension of those higher states. The conscious descent from exalted planes of being requires the capacity to bring down a clearer awareness of reality into the grosser regions of *maya*. Continuous self-transformation on the ascent must be converted into confident self-transmutation on the descent.

Patanjali saw in the evolving process of meditation several broad but distinct levels of *Samadhi*. The first is *sanprajnata Samadhi*, cognitive contemplation, in which the meditator is aware of a distinction between himself and the thought he entertains. This form of meditation is also called *sabija Samadhi*, or meditation with a seed *(bija)*, wherein some object or specific theme serves as a focal point on which to settle the mind in a steady state. Since such a point is extrinsic to pure consciousness, the basic distinction between thinker and thought persists. In its least abstracted form, *sanprajnata Samadhi* involves *vitarka* (reasoning), *vichara* (deliberation), *ananda* (bliss) and *asmita* (the sense of ' I '). Meditation is some sort of *bhavana*, or becoming that upon which one ponders, for consciousness identifies with, takes on and virtually becomes what it contemplates. Meditation on a seed passes through stages in which these types of conditioning recede and vanish as the focal point of consciousness passes beyond every kind of deliberation and even bliss itself, until only *asmita* or the pure sense of 'I' remains. Even this, however, is a limiting focus which can be transcended.

Asanprajnata Samadhi arises out of meditation on a seed though it is itself seedless. Here supreme detachment frees one from even the subtlest cognition and one enters *nirbija Samadhi,* meditation without a seed, which is self-sustaining because free of any supporting focalization on an object. From the standpoint of the succession of objects of thought – the type of consciousness all human beings experience in a chaotic or fragmentary way and a few encounter even in meditation on a seed – *nirbija Samadhi* is nonexistence or emptiness, for it is absolutely quiescent consciousness. Nonetheless, it is not the highest consciousness attainable, for it is the retreat of mind to a neutral *(laya)* centre from which it can begin to operate on a wholly different plane of being. This elevated form of pure consciousness is similar to a state experienced in a disembodied condition between death and rebirth, when consciousness is free of the involvement with vestures needed for manifestation in differentiated matter. Just as an individual becomes unconscious when falling into deep dreamless sleep, because consciousness fails to remain alert except in conditions of differentiation, so too consciousness in a body becomes unconscious and forgetful of its intrinsic nature on higher planes. *Samadhi* aims to restore that essential awareness self-consciously, making the alert meditator capable of altering planes of consciousness without any loss of awareness.

For earnest practitioners, Patanjali taught, *Samadhi* is attained in several distinct but interrelated ways – through *shraddha* (faith), *virya* (energy), *smriti* (retentiveness) and *prajna* (intellectual insight) – which are vital prerequisites for the metapsychological *yoga* of *Samadhi.* *Shraddha* is the calm and confident conviction that *yoga* is efficacious, coupled with the wholehearted orientation of one's psychic, moral and mental nature towards experiential confirmation. Undistracted *shraddha* of this sort leads naturally to *virya,* energy which releases the resolve to reach the goal and the resourceful courage needed to persist in seeking it. In *The Voice of the Silence,* an ancient text of spiritual discipline, *virya* is viewed as the fifth of seven keys required to unlock seven portals on the path to wisdom. In this text, *virya* follows upon *dana, shila, kshanti* and *viraga (vairagya)* – charity, harmony in conduct, patience, and detachment in regard to the fruits of action – all suggesting the hidden depths of *shraddha* which can release dauntless energy in the pursuit of Truth.

Smriti implies the refinement of memory which helps to extract the essential lesson of each experience without the needless elaboration of irrelevancies. It requires the perception of significant connections and the summoning of full recollection, the soul memory stressed by Plato wherein one awakens powers and potentialities transcending the experiences of a lifetime. *Prajna,* released by such inner awakenings, enables consciousness to turn within and cognize the deeper layers of oneself. Seen and strengthened in this manner, one's innate soul-wisdom becomes the basis of one's progressive understanding of the integral connection between freedom and necessity. In time, the 'is' of external facticity becomes a vital pointer to the 'ought' of the spiritual Path and the 'can' of one's true self-hood.

Supreme meditation, the most complete *Samadhi,* is possible for those who can bring clarity, control and imaginative intensity to daily practice. Yet Patanjali's instructions, like those of an athletic coach who guides the gifted but also aids those who show lesser promise, apply to every seeker who sincerely strives to make a modest beginning in the direction of the highest *Samadhi* as well as to those able to make its attainment the constant target of their contemplations. He spoke explicitly of those whose progress is rapid but also of those whose efforts are mild or moderate. An individual's strivings are stimulated to the degree they recognize that they are ever reaching beyond themselves as they have come to think of themselves through habit, convention, weakness and every form of ignorance. Rather than naively thinking that one is suddenly going to surmount every obstacle and obscuration in one's own nature, one can sedulously foster *bhakti,* total devotion and willing surrender to *Ishvara,* the Supreme Spirit immanent in all souls, even if one has hardly begun to grasp one's true self-hood. Such sustained devotion is *ishvarapranidhana,* the potent invocation of the Supreme Self through persistent surrender to It, isomorphic on the plane of consciousness with abnegation of the fruits of all acts to Krishna on the plane of conduct, as taught in the *Bhagavad Gita.*

Ishvara is *saguna brahman,* the supreme repository of all resplendent qualities, in contrast to *nirguna brahman,* the attributeless Absolute.

Ishvara is *Purusha,* "untouched by troubles, actions and their results" (I.24), immanent in all *prakriti.* Cherishing the one source of all is the means by which one moves through degrees of *Samadhi,* culminating in the complete union of the individual and the cosmic, the state of *kaivalya* or isolation. Like *Kether,* the crown in the *Kabbalah, Ishvara* is at once the single motivating force behind the cosmic activity of *prakriti* and the utterly transcendent *(nirguna) Purusha* or pure spirit. What exists in each human soul as the latent bud of omniscience is awakened and it expands into the realm of infinitude in *Ishvara* itself. Untouched by time and therefore untrammelled by ordinary consciousness which is time-bound, *Ishvara* is the supreme Initiator of all, from the ancient *Rishis* to the humble disciple sitting in meditation. *Ishvara* is OM, the primal sound, the basic keynote of all being, the source of the music of the spheres, mirrored in the myriad manifestations of *prakriti.* Surrender to *Ishvara* is aided by the silent repetition of the sacred OM and by deep meditation upon its mystery and meaning. When *bhakti* flows freely in this rapturous rhythm, consciousness readily turns inward and removes all hindrances to progress in *Samadhi.*

Surrender to the luminous core of one's consciousness, which is more powerful than one's strongest proclivities, initiates a mighty countervailing force against the cumulative momentum generated by the *chittavrittis.* As the mind has grown accustomed to indulge, identify with and even cherish ceaseless modifications, any attempt to check those modifications runs against the self-reproducing tenacity of long established habits, impressions and tendencies. The *chittavrittis* are virtually infinite in their discrete manifestations and yet are amenable to broad classification on the basis of essential traits. The hindrances which aggravate mental distraction, fragmented consciousness and continual modification are disease, dullness, doubt, heedlessness, indolence, addiction to objects of sense, distorted perception, and failure to stabilize the mind in any particular state. Though distinct from each other, these distractions are all accompanied by sorrow *(duhkha),* depression, bodily agitation and irregular breathing. They can, however, be most effectively eliminated through *abhyasa,* or constant practice of a single truth or principle. Whilst any profound truth which deeply moves one can be chosen, to the degree that it is true – and so to the degree that it is efficacious over time – it is *ekatattva,* the one principle, which in *Sankhya* philosophy is *Purusha* or pure spirit.

Overcoming mental obstructions through *abhyasa* in respect to one principle requires the progressive purification of the mind, freeing it from the froth and dross of old patterns fostered by feeble and fickle attention. Most seekers typically find easiest and most effective a concerted effort to expand the feeling of friendliness towards all beings, compassion for every creature, inward gladness and a cool detachment in regard to pleasure and pain, virtue and vice. On the physical plane of human nature, one can learn to make one's breathing calm and even, steady and rhythmical. Through intense concentration, one can begin to awaken subtler perceptions which are not subject to hindrances in the way the ordinary sense-organs are, to an almost grotesque extent. One may even activate a spark of *Buddhi,* pure insight and deep penetration, sensing the vast ocean of supernal cosmic light which interpenetrates and encloses everything. Some seekers will find it more feasible to contemplate the lustrous splendour of a mythic, historical or living being who is a paragon of supreme self-mastery. Others may benefit by brooding on flashes of reminiscence that recur in dreams or come from deep dreamless sleep. Patanjali also pointed out that one could gain mental stability by meditating intently upon what one most ardently desired. In the words of Charles Johnston, "Love is a form of knowledge", when it is profound and sacrificial, constant and unconditional.

All such efforts to surmount the hindrances which distract the mind are aids to deep meditation, and when they have fully worked their benevolent magic, the becalmed mind becomes the effortless master of everything which comes into the horizon of consciousness, from the atomic to the infinite. When all the hindrances disappear, mental modifications cease and the mind "becomes like a transparent crystal, attaining the power of transformation, taking on the colour of what it rests on, whether it be the cognizer, the cognized or the act of cognition" (I.41). When the mind is distracted through discursive trains of thought, it tends to oscillate between passive disorientation and aggressive attempts to conceal its ignorance through contentious and partisan fixations. But when the memory is purged of external traces and encrusted conditionality, and the mind is withdrawn from all limiting conceptions – including even its abstract self-image, thus focussed solely on *ekatattva*, truth alone – it is free from obscuration, unclouded (*nirvitarka*), and sees each truth as a whole. It notices the subtle elements behind shifting appearances, including the noumenal, primordial and undifferentiated sources and causes of all mental modifications. This serene self-emancipation of consciousness is called *sabija Samadhi*, meditation with a seed, the fulcrum for gaining all knowledge. In this sublime condition, the mind has become as pellucid as crystal and mirrors the spiritual light of *Purusha*, whence dawns direct insight (*prajna*) into the ultimate Truth.

Unlike other methods of cognizing truth – which concern this or that and hence are involved with *samvritti satya*, relative truths, though truths nonetheless – *prajna* has but one single object for its focus, the Supreme Truth itself (*paramartha satya*). Its power displaces and transcends all lesser forms of truth, exiling them permanently from consciousness. Beyond this lies only that indescribable state called *nirbija Samadhi*, meditation without a seed, wherein the mind lets go of even Truth itself as an object. When the mind ceases to function, the *Yogabhashya* teaches, *Purusha* becomes isolated, pure and liberated. Mind has become the pure instrument that guides the soul ever closer to that threshold where, when reached, spirit steps from false finitude into inconceivable infinitude, leaving the mind behind, passing into *kaivalya*, total isolation or supreme freedom. The last psychic veil is drawn aside and the spiritual man stands with unveiled vision. As M.N. Dvivedi commented, "The mind thus having nothing to rest upon exhausts itself. . . and *Purusha* alone shines in perfect bliss and peace." "The Light", I.K. Taimni remarked, "which was up to this stage illuminating other objects now illuminates Itself, for it has withdrawn beyond the realm of these objects. The Seer is now established in his own Self."

Having depicted the entire path leading from ignorance and bewilderment to beatific illumination, Patanjali saw only two tasks remaining: (1) to explain in detail the diverse means for attaining concentration and meditation, and (2) to elucidate the idea of *kaivalya* or isolation, insofar as it is possible to convey it through words.

Hermes, February 1989

YOGA SUTRAS – BOOK II:
SADHANA PADA

tapah-svadhyayeshvara-pranidhanani kriya-yogah

1. Austerity, self-study and devoted self-surrender to the Lord constitute the practice of yoga. (52)

Samadhi-bhavanarthah klesha-tanukaranarthash cha

2. This is for the sake of shrinking afflictions and inducing meditative absorption (*Samadhi*). (53)

avidyasmita-raga-dveshabhiniveshah kleshah

3. The afflictions are ignorance, egoism, attachment, aversion and the tenacious clinging to existence. (54)

avidya kshetram uttaresham prasupta-tanu-vichchinnodaranam

4. Ignorance is the originating field for the others, whether they be dormant, tenuous, dispersed or activated. (55)

anityashuchi-duhkhanatmasu nitya-shuchi-sukhatmakhyatir avidya

5. Ignorance is the belief that the impermanent, the impure, the painful, are the permanent, the pure, the pleasurable, that the non-Self is the Self. (56)

drig-darshana-shaktyor ekatmatevasmita

6. Egoism (*asmita*) is the delusive or apparent identification of the potency of the Seer with the power of sight. (57)

sukhanushayi ragah

7. Attachment accompanies and pursues pleasure. (58)

duhkhanushayi dveshah

8. Aversion accompanies and dwells upon pain. (59)

svarasavahi vidusho 'pi tatha rudho 'bhiniveshah

9. The tenacious clinging to existence, sustained by its own energy, is so rooted even in the learned. (60)

te pratiprasava-heyah sukshmah

10. These subtle afflictions can be destroyed by inverse propagation (*pratiprasava*), involution or reabsorption into their causal origins. (61)

dhyana-heyas tad-vrittayah

11. Their mental modifications are destroyed by deep meditation (*dhyana*). (62)

klesha-mulah karmashayo drishtadrishta-janma-vedaniyah

12. The mental deposits of *karma* have their roots in the afflictions (*kleshas*) and their fruitage in experiences seen in this life, or in a future life now unseen. (63)

sati mule tad-vipako jaty-ayur-bhogah

13. So long as the roots remain, there must be their fructification in the form of class, length of life and the experience of pleasures and pains. (64)

te hlada-paritapa-phalah punyapunya-hetutvat

14. They have joy or sorrow as their fruit, by reason of virtue or vice. (65)

parinama-tapa-sanskara-duhkhair guna-vritti-virodhach cha
duhkham eva sarvam vivekinah

15. To the discerning, all is sorrowful owing to the miseries brought by change, anxiety and acquired impressions, and also because of the conflict between the propensities (*gunas*) of Nature and mental modifications (*vritti*). (66)

heyam duhkham anagatam

16. The misery which has not yet come must be avoided. (67)

drashtri-drishyayoh sanyogo heya-hetuh

17. The conjunction of the Seer and the seen is the cause of that which is to be avoided. (68)

prakasha-kriya-sthiti-shilam bhutendriyatmakam
bhogapavargarthem drishyam

18. Having the properties of luminosity, motion and inertia, the objective world of visible Nature consists of the elements and the sense-organs, all for the sake of experience and emancipation. (69)

visheshavishesha-lingamatralingani gunaparvani

19. The states and stages of the propensities (*gunas*) are the particularized, the archetypal, the distinctly differentiated, and the signless, irresolvable, undifferentiated. (70)

drashta dristhimatrah shuddho 'pi pratyayanupashyah

20. The Seer is simply pure vision, and yet, though pure, he perceives ideas seemingly through the mind. (71)

tad-artha eva drishyasyatma

21. The very essence of the visible is that it exists for the sake of the Seer, the Self alone. (72)

kritartham prati nashtam apy anashtam tad-anya-sadharanatvat

22. Although it has vanished for him whose purpose is accomplished, it has not ceased to be for others, owing to its very commonality. (73)

sva-svami-shaktyoh svarupopalabdhi-hetah sanyogah

23. The conjunction of the potencies of the Seer and the seen is the reason for the apprehension of his own form and his experience of the true nature of things seen. (74)

tasya hetur avidya

24. Its effective cause is ignorance. (75)

tad-abhavat sanyogabhavo hanam tad drisheh kaivalyam

25. In its absence, the conjunction disappears, and its avoidance is the real remedy; that is the isolation and liberation, the absolute freedom (*kaivalya*), of the Seer. (76)

viveka-khyatir aviplava hanopayah

26. Unbroken discriminative cognition is the means of emancipation. (77)

tasya saptadha pranta-bhumih prajna

27. His awakening of perfect cognition is sevenfold, attained in successive stages. (78)

yoganganushthanad ashuddhikshaye jnanadiptir a viveka-khyateh

28. Through the practice of the component parts of yoga, as impurity is gradually destroyed, the light of wisdom shines forth, leading to discriminative cognition of Reality. (79)

yama-niyamasana-pranayama-pratyahara-dharana-dhyana-samadhyayo 'shtavangani

29. Restraint (*yama*), binding observance (*niyama*), posture (*asana*), regulation of breath (*pranayama*), abstraction and sense-withdrawal (*pratyahara*), concentration (*dharana*), contemplation (*dhyana*) and perfect meditative absorption (*Samadhi*) are the eight limbs of yoga. (80)

tatra ahimsa-satyasteya-brahmacharyaparigraha yamah

30. Of these, non-violence (*ahimsa*), truthfulness (*satya*), non-stealing (*asteya*), continence (*brahmacharya*) and non-possessiveness (*aparigraha*) are the five forms of restraint (*yamas*). (81)

ete jati-desha-kala-samayanavachchimah sarvabhauma mahavratam

31. These are not conditioned or qualified by class or country, time or circumstance, and apply to all spheres and stages, thus constituting the Great Vow. (82)

shaucha-santosha-tapah-svadhyayeshvara-pranidhanani niyamah

32. Purity, contentment, austerity, self-study and devoted self-surrender to the Lord are the five observances (*niyamas*). (83)

vitarka badhane pratipaksha bhavanam

33. When the mind is oppressed by perverse thoughts, it must summon and sustain their opposites. (84)

vitarka himsadayah krita-karitanumodita lobha-krodha-moha-purvaka mridu-madhyadhimatra duhkhajnananantaphala iti pratipaksha-bhavanam

34. Perverse thoughts of a violent and destructive nature, whether enacted, abetted or endorsed, whether induced by avarice, anger or delusion, whether mild, moderately present or intensely indulged, result in endless misery and folly; consequently, their opposites must be nurtured and nourished. (85)

ahimsa-pratishthayam tat-sanniddhau vairatyagah

35. When one is firmly grounded in non-violence (*ahimsa*), all hostility is given up in one's presence. (86)

satya-pratishthayam kriya-phalashrayatvam

36. When one is firmly grounded in truth (*satya*), all acts gestated bear fruit dependably. (87)

asteya-pratishthayam sarva-ratnopasthanam

37. When one is firmly grounded in non-stealing (*asteya*), all sorts of precious jewels present themselves. (88)

brahmacharya-pratishthayam virya-labhah

38. When one is firmly grounded in celibacy in consciousness and conduct (*brahmacharya*), one gains vigour, vitality and strength. (89)

aparigraha-sthairye janma-kathanta-sanbodhah

39. When one is established in non-possessiveness (*aparigraha*), one gains luminous insight in relation to the process and purposes, the meaning and significance, of the succession of births. (90)

shauchat svanga-jugupsa parair asansargah

40. Through internal purity and external purification, one gains bodily protection and freedom from pollution in contacts with others. (91)

sattvashuddhi-saumanasyaikagryendriyajayatma-darshana-yogyatvani cha

41. Through the cleansing of consciousness and purity of motivation, one gains mental serenity, one-pointedness, control of the sense-organs, as well as fitness for soul-vision and direct apprehension of the Self. (92)

santoshad anuttamah sukha-labhah

42. Through joyous contentment, one gains supreme happiness. (93)

kayendriya-siddhir ashuddhi-kshayat tapasah

43. Through the elimination of pollution, the practice of penance (*tapas*) brings about the perfection of the body and the sense-organs. (94)

svadhyayad ishta-devata-sanprayogah

44. Through self-study comes communion with the chosen deity. (95)

Samadhi-siddhir ishvara-pranidhanat

45. Through persevering devotion to the Lord comes perfection in meditative absorption (*Samadhi*). (96)

sthira-sukham asanam

46. The posture must be firm and pleasant. (97)

prayatna-shaithilyananta-samapattibhyam

47. This is gained by release of tension and serene contemplation upon the boundless infinite. (98)

tato dvandvanabhighatah

48. Thus arises freedom from assault by the pairs of opposites. (99)

tasmin sati shvasa-prashvasayor gativichchedah pranayamah

49. When this is attained, there comes *pranayama*, the regulation of breath, the restraint of inhalation and exhalation. (100)

bahyabhyantara-stambha-vrittir deshakala-sankhyabhih
paridrishto dirghasukshmah

50. These modifications are external, internal or wholly suspended; they are regulated according to space, time or number, whether protracted or attenuated. (101)

bahyabhyantara-vishayakshepi chaturthah

51. The fourth modification goes beyond the external-internal range. (102)

tatah kshiyate prakashavaranam

52. Thus is worn away the veil which obscures the light. (103)

dharanasu cha yogyata manasah

53. And thus the mind gains fitness for concentration. (104)

sva-vishayasanprayoge chitta-svarupanukara ivendriyanam pratyaharah

54. *Pratyahara*, abstraction or dissociation, is the disjoining of the sense-organs from their respective objects, assuming, as it were, the nature of the mind itself. (105)

tatah parama vashyatendriyanam

55. Thence comes supreme control of the senses. (106)

Hermes, June 1987

SADHANA PADA

A person without self-discipline cannot attain perfection in Yoga. An undisturbed course of self-purificatory conduct should be practised.

Yogabhashya

Patanjali initiated his teaching concerning *praxis* by calling attention to the three chief elements in the discipline of *Yoga: tapas,* austerity, self-restraint and eventually self-mastery; *svadhyaya,* self-study, self-examination, including calm contemplation of *Purusha,* the Supreme Self; and *ishvarapranidhana,* self-surrender to the Lord, the omnipresent divine spirit within the secret heart. The threefold practice or *Sadhana* can remove the *kleshas* or afflictions which imprison *Purusha* and thus facilitate *Samadhi* or meditative absorption. This arduous alchemical effort was summed up succinctly by Shankaracharya: "Right vision *(samyagdarshana)* is the means to transcendental aloneness *(kaivalya)....* *Yoga* practice, being the means to right vision, comes before it.... Ignorance is destroyed when directly confronted by right vision." The *kleshas,* though varied in their myriad manifestations, are essentially five: *avidya,* ignorance; *asmita,* egoism; *raga,* attachment; *dvesha,* aversion; and *abhinivesha,* tenacious clinging to mundane existence. Ignorance, however, is the broad field in which all the other *kleshas* arise, because they are no more than distinct specializations of ignorance.

Ignorance is a fundamental inverted confusion which mistakes *prakriti* for *Purusha,* the false for the true, the impure for the pure, and the painful for the pleasurable a persisting malaise which might have been difficult to comprehend in the past but which is now a familiar condition in contemporary psychology. Springing from fundamental ignorance, egoism *(asmita)* confuses the potency of the Seer *(Purusha)* with the power of sight *(Buddhi).* Attachment *(raga)* is the pursuit of what is mistaken to be pleasurable, whilst aversion *(dvesha)* flees from what is believed to be painful. These two constitute the primary pair of opposites on the psychological level in the field of ignorance, and all other pairs of opposites are derived from them. Clinging to phenomenal existence *(abhinivesha)* is the logical outcome of the operation of ignorance, and once aroused is self-sustaining through the inertia of habit, so that countervailing measures are needed to eradicate it, together with the other *kleshas*.

Through ignorance *(avidya)* there is an obscuration of the cosmic Self *(Purusha)*, a fundamental misidentification of what is real, a persistent misconception which carries its own distinct logic within the complex dialectic of *maya*.

Since the *kleshas* are engendered by a persistent error, at root mistaking *prakriti* for *Purusha*, or attributing the essential characteristics of *Purusha* to one or another aspect of *prakriti*, they can be eliminated only by a radical reversal of the downward tendency of alienation and retreat from truth. This fundamental correction, as far reaching as the entrenched habit of inversion which necessitates it, is *dhyana*, meditation, together with the mental and moral exercises which strengthen it. To say, as Hindu and Buddhist thinkers alike assert, that *karma* is rooted in *avidya* is to imply that the ramifying results of karma now experienced, or yet to be experienced in a future incarnation, are all rooted in the *kleshas*.

In the graphic language of spiritual physiology, the *kleshas* constitute a psychic colouring or peculiar obsession which forms a persisting matrix of *karma*, the results of which must eventually be experienced, and also creates mental deposits which channel mental energies into repeatedly reinforcing the *kleshas*. *Dhyana* alone can effectively eradicate these mental deposits while providing the clear detachment *(vairagya)* and cool patience *(kshanti)* to exhaust and dissolve the karmic matrix over time. As long as the *kleshas* remain, involuntary incarnation into bodies captive to the pleasure-pain principle is inescapable. Elation and depression are the inevitable effects of such embodiment. Since these are the product of egoism and the polarity of attraction and aversion, rooted in ignorance and resulting in the tenacious clinging to mundane existence, the discerning *yogin* comes to see that the truth of spiritual freedom and the rapture of limitless love transcend the *kleshas* entirely.

All *karma* brings discord and distress, including the insistent pains of loss and gain, growth and decay.

Karma means *parinama*, change, and this invariably induces the longing to recover what is receding, to enhance what is emerging, or to sustain a static balance where no thing can endure. To be drawn to some objects and conditions and to be disinclined towards others is indeed to foster *tapa*, anxious brooding over what might be lost or what one might be forced to encounter. All experiences leave residual impressions, *samskaras*, which agitate the mind and stimulate desires to have or to avoid possible future experiences. In general, the *gunas* or root qualities of *prakriti* – *sattva*, *rajas* and *tamas*: luminosity, action and inertia; purity, restlessness and languor; or harmony, volatility and fixity – persist in ceaselessly shifting permutations which continually modify the uncontrolled mind. For these reasons, Patanjali taught, all life without spiritual freedom is fraught with sorrow. Through *Yoga*, it is not possible to avoid consequences already set in motion, but it is feasible to destroy the *kleshas* and thereby remove the causal chain of suffering.

Metaphysically, *Buddhi*, intuitive intellect, is closer to *Purusha* than any other aspect of *prakriti*. Nonetheless, *Buddhi* is still what is seen by *Purusha*, the Perceiver, and it is through confounding the Perceiver with what is perceived at the super-sensuous level that suffering arises. *Prakriti*, consisting of the *gunas*, is the entire field, enclosing the objective world and the organs of sensation. It exists solely for the sake of the soul's education and emancipation. The *Yogabhashya* teaches that identification of the Perceiver with the seen constitutes experience, "whilst realizing the true nature of *Purusha* is emancipation." In the realm of *prakriti*, wherein the Perceiver is captive to the ever-changing panorama of Nature, the *gunas*, which may be construed as the properties of perceptible objects but which are really propensities from the standpoint of psycho-mental faculties, act at every level of conscious awareness.

At the level of differentiated consciousness, *vitarka*, wherein the mind scrutinizes specific objects and features, the *gunas* are particularized (*vishesha*). When consciousness apprehends archetypes, laws and abstract concepts (*vichara*), the *gunas* are archetypal (*avishesha*). When the *gunas* are discerned as signs and signatures *(linga)*, objects are resolved into symbols of differentiation in a universal field of complete objectivity, and consciousness experiences ecstasy *(ananda)*. Though discrete, objects are no longer distinguished in contrast to one another or through divergent characteristics; they are distinct but seen as parts of a single whole. They are apprehended through *Buddhi* or intuitive insight.

The *gunas* are *alinga* – signless, irresolvable, undifferentiated – and lose their distinction from consciousness itself when objects dissolve in the recognition that consciousness and its modifications alone constitute the noumenal and phenomenal world. Hence, pure consciousness *(lingamatra)*, which is the simple, unqualified sense of 'I', subsists in a pristine noumenal condition *(alinga)* wherein it does not witness the ceaseless operation of the *gunas*. This divine consciousness is the highest state of meditative absorption, beyond which lies complete emancipation, *Purusha* without any tincture of *prakriti*. The Perceiver is pure vision, apprehending ideas seemingly through the mind. Once final emancipation, which is the ultimate aim and purpose of all experience, is attained, *Purusha* no longer encounters the confusion of spirit and matter through mental modifications. As experience, correctly understood, culminates in eventual self-emancipation, *kaivalya*, Patanjali held that "the very essence of the visible is that it exists for the sake of the Seer, the Self alone" (II.21).

The world does not vanish for all others when a man of meditation attains *kaivalya*; they remain in confusion until they also attain the same utterly transcendent state of awareness. Here *Yoga* philosophy exhausts its conceptual and descriptive vocabulary. Whether one asserts that there is an indefinite number of *purushas*, each capable of attaining *kaivalya*, or one states that *Purusha* attains *kaivalya* in this instance but not that, is a matter of indifference, for one perforce invokes enumeration, time and space terms properly applying to *prakriti* alone to characterize a wholly transcendent reality. The pervasive existential fact is that *prakriti* persists so long as there are beings trapped through ignorance, and the vital psychological truth is that no being who attains the transcendent *(taraka)* reality of unqualified, pure *Purusha* can do so vicariously for another. Through their hard-won wisdom and compassion, emancipated seers and sages can point the way with unerring accuracy. They know how to make their magnanimous guidance most effective for every human being, but each seeker must make the ascent unaided.

If the cosmos as considered in contemporary physics resolved itself into a condition of undisturbed entropy, or if, in the language of *Sankhya*, the *gunas* achieved total and enduring equilibrium, Nature (*prakriti*) would cease to exist, since there would be nothing to be perceived. Ignorance and its inseparable concomitant, suffering, arise from a broken symmetry in Nature. In contemporary thought there is no adequate explanation for the origin of that 'cosmic disaster', for the emergence of sentience is said to occur *within* the broken symmetry. If the scientific community were trained to use the language of *Sankhya* and *Yoga* philosophy, it would have to speak of the origin of *Purusha*, consciousness, within the evolutionary permutations and convolutions of *prakriti*. *Sankhya* and *Yoga* teach, however, that *Purusha*, sempiternal and independent, perceives *prakriti* and indirectly gives rise to the broken symmetry itself, the anti-entropic condition which is the activity of the *gunas*. For Patanjali, *prakriti* must necessarily exist, for it is through experience conjunction with *prakriti* that *Purusha* knows itself as it is. But when *Purusha* wrongly apprehends *prakriti*, as it must until it knows itself truly as it is, ignorance and all the entangling *kleshas* arise. When *Purusha* attains *kaivalya*, emancipation, it sees without error, and this is gained through experience in self-correction and self-mastery. From the highest standpoint, this means that *Purusha* preserves its freedom and intrinsic purity by avoiding mistaken assumptions and false conclusions. From the standpoint of any individual involved in *prakriti*, unbroken discriminative cognition (*vivekakhyati*) is the sole means to emancipation, for it releases the abiding sense of reality (*Purusha*) in him. The dual process of removing the *kleshas* and reflecting on the Self (*Purusha*) assures the progressive and climactic attainment of emancipation (*kaivalya*) such that ignorance does not arise again.

Having delineated the path to *kaivalya*, Patanjali discoursed in some detail on the seven successive stages of *Yoga* which lead to *Samadhi*, full meditative absorption, but he insisted that, even though each stage must be passed in succession, truth and wisdom dawn progressively upon the aspirant to stimulate his endeavour. *Yoga* is successive, gradual and recursive, the path of ascent which alone leads from darkness to light, from ignorance to transcendental wisdom, from death and recurring rebirth to conscious immortality and universal self-consciousness. Although the stages through which consciousness must ascend are sequential in one sense, the practice of *Taraka Raja Yoga* involves eight limbs or aspects which are logically successive but ethically and psychologically simultaneous. In fact, one can hardly pursue one part of Patanjali's eight-limbed *Yoga (ashtangayoga)* without also attending to its other divisions. Just as a human being, despite his ignorance, is an integrated whole, so too *ashtangayoga*, despite its logical sequence, is an integral unity. Patanjali enumerated the eight *(ashta)* limbs *(anga)* of this *Taraka Raja Yoga* as five which concern *karma* and lay the foundation for meditation, and three which constitute meditation itself: restraint *(yama)*, binding observance *(niyama)*, posture *(asana)*, regulation of breath *(pranayama)*, abstraction and withdrawal from the senses *(pratyahara)*; concentration *(dharana)*, contemplation *(dhyana)* and complete meditative absorption *(Samadhi)*.

The *yamas* or restraints are five, constituting a firm ethical foundation for spiritual growth, starting with *ahimsa* (nonviolence) and including *satya* (truth), *asteya* (nonstealing), *brahmacharya* (continence) and *aparigraha* (nonpossession). Shankaracharya held that *ahimsa* – nonviolence, harmlessness, defencelessness in Shelley's phrase – is the most important of the *yamas* and *niyamas*, and is the root of restraint. Like all constraints and observances, *ahimsa* must not be interpreted narrowly but should be seen in its widest sense. For Shankaracharya, this meant that *ahimsa* should be practised in body, speech and mind so that one avoids harming others in any way, even through an unkind thought. *Ahimsa* can be taken to include the classical Greek sense of *sophrosyne*, a sense of proportion which voids all excess, the state of mind which can avoid even unintentional harm to a single being in the cosmos. In employing *ahimsa* as a talismanic tool of political and social reform, Gandhi exemplified the central importance and far-reaching scope of *ahimsa*. For Patanjali, however, *ahimsa* and the other *yamas* and *niyamas* constitute the daily moral discipline needed to pursue *Taraka Raja Yoga*. *Taraka Raja Yoga* is not a narrowly technical or specialized practice to be added to other instrumental activities in the world; it is rather the indispensable means for radically transforming one's essential perception of, and therefore one's entire relation to, the world. From the standpoint of Self-knowledge, which is ultimate *gnosis*, there are no greater disciplines. Hence the *yamas* are not altered by condition and circumstance, social class or nationality, nor by time nor the actual level of spiritual attainment. Together they constitute the awesome *mahavrata* or Great Vow, the first crucial step to true spiritual freedom.

The *niyamas* or binding observances are also five, constituting the positive dimension of ethical probity. They are *shaucha* (purity), *santosha* (contentment), *tapas* (austerity, self-discipline), *svadhyaya* (self-study) and *ishvarapranidhana* (surrender to the Lord). Like the *yamas,* the *niyamas* cannot be fully grasped as specific and bounded concepts. First of all, they should be seen as evolving conceptions – for example, purity of thought is deepened through purity of conduct – and then they will rapidly unfold subtler levels of meaning as the aspirant attains more intensive depths of meditation. Purity of volition is thus ever enriched and refined. The greatest obstacles to the restraints and binding observances are those thoughts which run in the opposite direction – thinking of impure things or acts, wishing to do harm for a perceived injustice, self-indulgence, self-deception and self-assertion. Such illicit and destructive thoughts are perverse precisely because they belie and defeat the initial commitment to the *yamas* and *niyamas.* Instead of suppressing such scattered thoughts or wallowing in hideous self-pity, one must firmly and deliberately insert into the mind their potent opposites – love for hate, tenderness for temerity, sweetness for spite, virile confidence for the devilry of self-doubt, authentic self-conquest for compulsive self-indulgence. Thus what begins as a shrewd defence against deleterious thoughts becomes a deft substitution of one kind of thought for another and results in sublimation, the skilful transformation of the tonality and texture of consciousness. Strict and consistent measures are needed to deal with subversive thoughts, not in order to repress them or to hide guilt for having them, but only because they induce depression and self-loathing, with predictable and pathetic consequences. Facing unworthy thoughts firmly, and thereby exorcising them, is to free oneself from their nefarious spell.

When any object is forcibly confined, it exerts crude pressure against its external constraints. In the ethical realm, effortless self-restraint produces a powerful glow of well-being which others can appreciate and even emulate. When, for example, one is established in *ahimsa*, others do become aware of an encompassing and inclusive love, and latent or overt hostility dissolves around one's radius of benevolence. *Satya*, truth, is the path of least resistance amongst the shifting ratios of the *gunas*, and when one is clearly established in truth, the predictable consequences of thought, word and deed are constructive and consistent. Similarly, strengthening oneself through *asteya* (nonstealing), one desists from every form of misappropriation, even on the plane of thought and feeling, and discovers what is apposite on all sides. Nature protects and even provides for those who do not appropriate its abundant resources. *Brahmacharya*, selfless continence in thought and conduct, fosters vitality and vigour. *Aparigraha*, nonpossessiveness, promotes noetic insight into the deeper meaning and purpose of one's probationary sojourn on earth.

Expansiveness too has its compelling effects. *Shaucha*, inward and outer purity, protects the mind and body from moral and magnetic pollution, and prevents one from tarnishing or misusing others. One acquires a dependable degree of serenity, control of the senses and one-pointedness in concentration, thus preparing oneself for the direct apprehension of *Purusha*, the Self. *Santosha*, deep contentment, assures satisfaction not through the gratification of wants (which can at most provide a temporary escape from frustration), but rather through the progressive cessation of craving and its prolific yearnings and regrets. *Tapas*, austerity, penance or self-discipline, removes pollution inherited from one's own past and releases the full potentials of mind, senses and body, including those psychic faculties mistakenly called supernormal only because seldom developed. *Svadhyaya*, self-study, calls for careful study and calm reflection, including the diligent recitation and deep contemplation of texts, thus giving voice to potent *mantras* and sacred utterances. It achieves its apotheosis through direct communion with the *ishtadevata*, the chosen deity upon whom one has concentrated one's complete attention, will and imagination. This exalted state readily leads to *ishvarapranidhana*, one-pointed and single-hearted devotion to the Lord. Such devotion soon deepens until one enters the succeeding stages of meditative absorption *(Samadhi)*.

With the firm foundation of *yamas* and *niyamas*, one can begin to benefit from the noetic discipline of intense meditation and become modestly proficient in it over a lifetime of service to humanity. Since the untrained mind is easily distracted by external and internal disturbance, real meditation is aided by an alert and relaxed bodily vesture. To this end, a steady posture *(asana)* is chosen, not to indulge the acrobatic antics of the shallow *Hatha Yogin*, but rather to subdue and command the body, whilst retaining its alertness and resilience. The correct posture will be firm and flexible without violating the mind's vigorous concentration and precise focus. Once the appropriate *asana* is assumed by each neophyte, the mind is becalmed and turned towards the Infinite, becoming wholly impervious to bodily movement and change, immersed in the boundless space of the akashic empyrean. Thus the impact of the oscillating pairs of opposites upon the volatile brain mind, captivated by sharp contrasts and idle speculations, and the agitation of the body through recurring sensations are at least temporarily muted. In this state of serene peace, the effortless regulation of rhythmic breath *(pranayama)* becomes as natural as floating on the waters of space. Just as the mind and body are intimately interlinked at every point, such that even holding a firm physical posture aids the calming of the mind, so too *pranayama* points to silent mental breathing as well as smooth respiration.

Prana, which includes the solar life-breath, is the efflux of the constant flow of cosmic energy, regulated by the ideation of *Purusha* and radiating from the luminous substance of pure *prakriti*. From the *nadabrahman* the Divine Resonance and perpetual motion of absolute Spirit and the global respiration of the earth reverberating at its hidden core, its slowly rolling mantle and its shifting crust, to the inspiration and expiration of every creature in the cosmos, the ocean of *prana* permeates and purifies all planes of being. In the human constitution, irregular, spasmodic or strained, uneven breathing can disturb the homeostatic equilibrium of the body and cause fragmented, uncoordinated modes of awareness. Proper breathing oxygenates the physical system optimally, and also aids the mind in maintaining a steady rhythm of unbroken ideation, fusing thought, will and energy. *Pranayama* begins with deliberate exhalation, so that the lungs are generously emptied and the unusable matter expelled into them is made to exit the bodily temple. Thereupon, slow inbreathing invites oxygen to permeate the entire lung system and penetrate the blood, arteries, nerves and cells. Holding the breath in a benevolent pause permits the respiratory system to adjust gently to the next phase of oxygenation and detoxification. When these rhythmic movements are marked by due measure and proportion, mantramically fused into the inaudible OM, there is a distinct improvement in psychophysical health and a remarkable increase of vigilance and vigour.

The fourth step in *pranayama* transcends the physiological dimensions of respiration for which they are a preparation. The highest *pranayama* becomes possible when one has gained sufficient sensitivity through the earlier stages of *pranayama* to sense and direct the divine flow of *prana* throughout one's entropic psychophysical system. Then one may, through mental volition alone, fuse mental serenity and single-mindedness with psychophysical equilibrium, and also convey subtle pranic currents, charged with selfless ideation, to various *padmas* or vital centres (*chakras*) in the body. Since each of the seven *padmas* is precisely correlated with the corresponding state of concentrated consciousness, the fearless equipoise needed to activate these magnetic centres and the benevolent *siddhis* or theurgic powers thereby released requires the commensurate and controlled alteration in the tonality and texture of consciousness. When the highest *padma* is effortlessly and gently touched by mind-directed *prana,* nonviolent consciousness simultaneously attains full *Samadhi.* "Thus is worn away," said Patanjali, "the veil which obscures the light" (II. 52), thereby pointing to the subduing of the *kleshas* and the neutralization of *karma* through the progressive awakening of discriminative insight and intuitive wisdom.

The process of purification is not an end in itself, but the necessary condition to prepare the mind for *dharana,* complete concentration. *Pranayama,* delusive and dangerous when misappropriated for selfish purposes pursued through subtle enslavement by the *kleshas,* is hereby integrated into Patanjali's eight-fold *Yoga* as a preliminary step towards subduing the restless mind, freeing it to become the servant of the immortal soul, seeking greater wisdom, self-mastery and universal self-consciousness. *Pratyahara,* abstraction and disassociation of sensory perception from sense-objects, is now accessible. Withdrawal of the senses from their objects of attraction does not destroy them. Rather, the subtler senses take on the plastic and fluidic nature of the serene mind itself. Without the myriad distractions of familiar and strange sense-objects, the senses become subtilized and pliant, no longer pulling consciousness towards internal images, external objects or captivating sense data. Instead, the noetic mind firmly expels images and subdues impulses, gaining sovereign mastery over them. Patanjali ended the second *pada* here, having shown the pathway to proper preparation for profound meditation. The significance of the last three interconnected *angas* or stages of *Yoga* is indicated by the fact that Patanjali set them apart in the third *pada* for his authoritative exposition.

The preparatory discipline or *Sadhana* of the second *pada* has been thus strikingly extolled by Rishi Vasishtha:

> He engaged in the practice of Raja Yoga, remaining silent and graceful in countenance. He abstracted his senses from their objects as the oil is separated from the sesamum seed, withdrawing their organs within himself as the turtle contracts his limbs under his hard shell.
>
> With his steady mind he cast all external sensations far off from himself, as a rich and brilliant gem, shedding a coating of dust, then scattered its rays to a distance. Without coming in contact with them, he compressed his sensations within himself, as a tree in the cold season compresses its sap within its bark . . . .
>
> He confined his subdued mind in the cave of his heart, as a great elephant is imprisoned in a cavern of the Vindhya Mountain when it has been brought by stratagem under subjection. When his soul had gained its clarity, resembling the serenity of the autumnal sky, it forsook all unsteadiness, like the calm ocean unagitated by any winds.

Yoga Vasishtha Maharamayana

YOGA SUTRAS – BOOK III:
VIBHUTI PADA

desha-bandhash chittasya dharana

1. *Dharana*, concentration, is the fixing or focussing of consciousness on a particular point or place. (107)

tatra pratyayaikatanata dhyanam

2. *Dhyana*, meditation, is the continuous, uninterrupted flow of consciousness towards the chosen object. (108)

tad evarthamatra-nirbhasam svarupa-shunyam iva samadhih

3. *Samadhi*, meditative absorption or ecstasy, arises when the object of meditation shines forth alone, as if emptied of the form of the agent. (109)

trayam ekatra sanyamah

4. The three together constitute *sanyama,* constraint. (110)

taj-jayat prajnalokah

5. Through mastery of it comes the light of cognitive insight (*prajna*). (111)

tasya bhumishu viniyogah

6. Its application is by stages. (112)

trayam antarangam purvebhyah

7. The three together are more interior than the preceding. (113)

tad api bahirangam nirbijasya

8. Even these are exterior to seedless *Samadhi,* or soul vision. (114)

*vyutthana-nirodha-sanskarayor abhibhava-pradhurbhavan
nirodha-kshana-chittanvayo nirodha-parinamah*

9. *Nirodhaparinama* is that mental transformation through restraint
   wherein the consciousness becomes permeated by that
   condition which intervenes momentarily between fading
   impressions and emerging potencies. (115)

tasya prashanta-vahita sanskarat

10. Its flow becomes serene and steady through habituation. (116)

*sarvarthataikagratayoh kshayodayau chittasya Samadhi-
parinamah*

11. *Samadhiparinama,* meditative transformation, is the dwindling of
    distractions and the emergence of unitary consciousness or one-
    pointedness (*ekagrata*). (117)

*tatah punah shantoditau tulya-pratyayau chittasyaikagrata-
parinamah*

12. Thence again comes *ekagrataparinama,* the development of
    one-pointedness, wherein the two states of consciousness, the
    quiescent or subsided and the active or uprisen, are exactly
    similar and balanced. (118)

*etena bhutendriyeshu dharma-lakshanavastha-parinama
vyakhyatah*

13. Thus are explained the transformations of intrinsic properties,
    secondary qualities and states of being in the objective elements
    and instrumental sense-organs. (119)

shantoditavyapadeshya-dharmanupati dharmi

14. The substratum is that which is common to the properties, whether quiescent, active or unmanifest. (120)

kramanyatvam parinamanyatve hetuh

15. The variation in sequence or succession is the cause of the difference and distinctness in transformation. (121)

parinama-traya-sanyamad atitanagata-jnanam

16. Through *sanyama*, perfectly concentrated meditative constraint, comes knowledge of past and future. (122)

shabdartha-pratyayanam itaretaradhyasat sankaras tat-pravibhaga-sanyamat sarva-bhuta-ruta-jnanam

17. The sound, the meaning and the idea called up by a word are confounded owing to their indistinct superimposition. Through *sanyama* on their separation and resolution there comes a cognitive comprehension of the sounds uttered by all sentient beings. (123)

sanskara-sakshatkaranat purva-jatijnanam

18. By bringing latent impressions into consciousness there comes the knowledge of former births. (124)

pratyayasya para-chitta-jnanam

19. Through concentrated perception of mental images comes the knowledge of other minds. (125)

na cha tat salambanam tasyavishayi-bhutatvat

20. The mental supports are not perceived, for that is not the object of observation. (126)

kaya-rupa-sanyamat tad-grahya-shakti-stambhe chakshuh-prakashasanprayoge 'ntardhanam

21. Through *sanyama* on the form and colour of the body, by suspending its power of perceptibility and thereby disconnecting the light from the body and the sight of others, there comes the power to make the body invisible. (127)

etena sthabdady antardhanam uktam

22. Thus can also be explained the power of concealment of sound, touch, taste and smell. (128)

sopakramam nirupakramam cha karma tat-sanyamad aparanta-jnanam arishtebhyo va

23. Through *sanyama* on *karma*, which is either fast or slow in fruition, active or dormant, one gains knowledge of the time of death and also of omens and portents. (129)

maitry-adishu balani

24. Through *sanyama* on kindliness (*maitri*) and similar graces one gains mental, moral and spiritual strength. (130)

baleshu hasti-baladini

25. Through *sanyama* on various powers one gains the strength of an elephant. (131)

pravritty-aloka-nyasat sukshma-vyavahita-viprakrishta-jnanam

26. Through *sanyama* on the shining, effulgent light one gains knowledge of the small and subtle, the hidden and veiled, and the remote. (132)

bhavana-jnanam surye sanyamat

27. Through *sanyama* on the sun there comes knowledge of the solar system, cosmic evolution and involution. (133)

chandre tara-vyuha-jnanam

28. Through *sanyama* on the moon there comes knowledge concerning the arrangement of stars. (134)

dhruve tad-gati-jnanam

29. Through *sanyama* on the pole-star comes knowledge of the relative motions and positions of the stars. (135)

nabhi-chakre kaya-vyuha-jnanam

30. Through *sanyama* on the solar plexus comes knowledge of the structure and organization of the body. (136)

kantha-kupe kshut-pipasa-nivrittih

31. Through *sanyama* on the pit of the throat there comes cessation of hunger and thirst. (137)

kurma-nadyam sthairyam

32. Through *sanyama* on the nerve-centre called the 'tortoise' duct there comes steadiness. (138)

murdha-jyotishi siddha-darshanam

33. Through *sanyama* on the light in the head comes the vision of perfected beings. (139)

pratibhad va sarvam

34. Through *sanyama* on the effulgent light of intuition comes all knowledge. (140)

hridaye chitta-sanvit

35. Through *sanyama* on the heart comes knowledge of cosmic intellection. (141)

sattva-purushayor atyantasankirnayoh pratyayavishesho bhogah pararthat svartha-sanyamat Purusha-jnanam

36. Indulgence in experience is the result of the inability to distinguish between the Self (*Purusha*) and the principle of understanding (*sattva*), though they are utterly distinct. Self-knowledge results from *sanyama* on the Self-existent, which is apart from the non-self. (142)

tatah pratibha-shravana-vedanadarshasvada-vartta jayante

37. Thence are produced intuitional, extra-sensory hearing, touch, sight, taste and smell. (143)

te samadhav upasarga vkyutthane siddhayah

38. They are obstacles to meditative absorption (*sanyama*) but are powerful aids when the mind is turned outwards. (144)

bandha-karana-shaithilyat prachara-sanvedanach cha chittasya para-shariraveshah

39. The mind can enter another's body through the suspension of the causes of bondage and through knowledge of the mental channels. (145)

udana-jayaj jala-panka-kantakadishvasanga utkrantisth cha

40. Through mastery over the vital energy called *udana* comes imperviousness to water and mud, thorn and the rest, levitation and victory over death. (146)

samana-jayaj jvalanam

41. Through mastery over the vital energy called *sanyama* comes blazing radiance. (147)

shrotrakashayoh sanbandha-sanyamad divyam shrotram

42. Through *sanyama* on the connection between the ear and the

ether (*Akasha*) comes divine hearing. (148)

kayakashayoh sanbandha-sanyamat laghu-tula-samapattesth chakashagamanam

43. Through *sanyama* on the connection between the body and the ether (*Akasha*) comes lightness like cotton and the attainment of levitation in space. (149)

bahir akalpita vrittir maha-videha tatah prakashavarana-kshayah

44. *Mahavideha* is the power of invoking the incorporeal state of consciousness which is beyond the intellect and therefore inconceivable. Thus is destroyed the obscuring veil over the light. (150)

sthula-svarupa-sukshmanvayarthavattva-sanyamad bhuta-jayah

45. Through *sanyama* on gross matter, its essential form, its subtle qualities, its concomitant compounds and molecules and their functions, comes mastery over the elements. (151)

tato 'nimadi-pradurbhavah kaya-sanpat tad-dharmanabhighatash cha

46. Thence comes the manifestation of the powers of minuteness and the rest, as well as the perfection of the body and the realization of the indestructibility of the elements. (152)

rupa-lavanya-bala-vajra-sanhananatvani kaya-sanpat

47. Perfection of the body consists in beauty, grace, strength and adamantine hardness. (153)

grahana-svarupasmitanvayarthavattva-sanyamad indriya-jayah

48. Mastery over the sense-organs comes through *sanyama* on their power of apprehension, their real nature, egoism, concomitance and specific functions. (154)

tato manojavitam vikarana-bhavah pradhana-jayash cha

49. Thence comes instantaneous cognition, independent of instruments, and the complete mastery of *pradhana*, the chief common principle throughout Nature. (155)

sattva-purushanyata-khyati-matrasya sarvabhavadhishthatritvam sarvajnatritvam cha

50. Only through the knowledge of the distinction between the principle of understanding (*sattva*) and the Self (*Purusha*) comes supremacy over all states of existence and omniscience. (156)

tad-vairagyad api dosha-bija-kshaye kaivalyam

51. Through non-attachment even to that comes the destruction of the seeds of bondage and the state of emancipation (*kaivalya*). (157)

sthany-upanimantrane sangha-smayakaranam punar anishta-prasangat

52. There must be avoidance of attachment or amazement on encountering celestial beings, owing to the possible recurrence of the undesirable. (158)

kshana-tat-kramayoh sanyamad vivekajam jnanam

53. Through *sanyama* on indivisible moments and their order of succession comes discriminative knowledge. (159)

jati-lakshana-deshair anyatanavachchedat tulyayos tatah pratipattih

54. Therefrom comes the discernment of two similar events and of things whose distinctness cannot be measured or distinguished by class, property or position. (160)

tarakam sarva-vishayam sarvatha-vishayam akramam cheti vivekajam jnanam

55. Transcendental discriminative knowledge is that which simultaneously encompasses all objects and all possible processes, reaching beyond all endings. (161)

sattva-purushayoh shuddhi-samye kaivalyam

56. Emancipation (*kaivalya*) is attained when there is equalization of purity between the principle of understanding (*sattva*) and the Self (*Purusha*). (162)

Hermes, July 1987

VIBHUTI PADA

Attention is the first and indispensable step in all knowledge.
Attention to spiritual things is the first step to spiritual knowledge.

Charles Johnston

Patanjali commenced the third *pada* of the *Yoga Sutras* with a compelling distinction between three phases of meditation. *Dharana* is full concentration, the focussing of consciousness on a particular point, which may be any object in the world or a subject chosen by the mind. The ability to fix attention is strengthened by the practice of the first five *angas* of Patanjali's *ashtangayoga*, for without some cultivation of them the mind tends to meander and drift in every direction. *Dhyana* is meditation in the technical sense of the term, meaning the calm sustaining of focussed attention. In *dhyana*, consciousness still encounters some modifications, but they all flow in one direction and are not disturbed by other fluctuations of any sort. Rather like iron – consisting of molecules clustered together in various ways, their axes oriented in different directions – undergoes a shift of alignment of all molecules in a single direction when magnetized, so too consciousness can become unidirectional through experiencing a current of continuity in time.

Samadhi, broadly characterized as 'meditative absorption' or 'full meditation', signifies the deepening of *dhyana* until the chosen object of meditation stands alone and consciousness is no longer aware of itself as contemplating an object. In *Samadhi* consciousness loses the sense of separateness from what is contemplated and, in effect, becomes one with it. Like a person wholly lost in their work, "the object stands by itself," in the words of the *Yogabhashya*, as if there were only the object itself. Although these three phases can be viewed as separate and successive, when they occur together in one simultaneous act they constitute *sanyama*, serene constraint or luminous concentration. The novice who nonetheless is capable of entering *Samadhi* may take a long

86

time to move from *dharana* to deep *Samadhi*, because he experiences the entire movement as a radical change in consciousness. But the adept in *sanyama* can include all three in a virtually instantaneous act, thus arousing the ability to move from one object of contemplation to another almost effortlessly.

Prajna, cognitive insight, the resplendent light of wisdom, or intuitive apprehension, comes as a result of mastering *sanyama*. Although *prajna* is the highest level of knowledge to which philosophy can aspire, it is not the supreme state, for it halts at the threshold of *vivekakhyati*, pristine awareness of Reality, which can be neither articulated nor elucidated. *Sanyama*, Patanjali taught, is not completely mastered all at once. Rather, once *sanyama is* attained, it is strengthened in stages by deft application to different objects and levels of being. Each such application reveals the divine light as it manifests in that context, until the adept practitioner of exalted *sanyama* can focus entirely on *Purusha* itself. In *sanyama* the patient aspirant glimpses the divine radiance, the resplendent reflection of *Purusha*, wherever he focusses attention, but in time he will behold only *Purusha*. In the *Bhagavad Gita*, Krishna asked Arjuna to see Himself in all things, but in the climactic cosmic vision, Arjuna witnessed the cosmic form *(vishvarupa)* of the Lord. *Sanyama* is wholly internal, whilst the first five *yoga* practices are external. Though all the *angas* are crucial to *yoga*, the last three, harmoniously synthesized in *sanyama*, constitute *yoga* proper. Since this is the central aim of everything stated so far in the *Yoga Sutras*, *sanyama* received considerable emphasis from Patanjali.

Nirodha, restraint, cessation or interception, is essential to *sanyama* because it is concerned neither with different states nor objects of consciousness, but chiefly with the process of transformation or replacement of the contents of consciousness. In *sanyama* the definite shift from one object of attention to another – and these can be wholly abstract and mental objects – involves a change of mental impression. As an object fades from mental view, another appears on the mental horizon to take its place. But like the pregnant moment just before dawn, when night is fleeing and the first light of day is sensed but has not yet shown itself, there is a suspended moment when what is fading has receded and the new object of focus is yet to appear. This is *nirodhaparinama*, the moment, however fleeting, between successive modifications when, according to the *Yogabhashya*, "the mind has nothing but subliminal impressions" (III .9). Should the mind lose its alertness at just that point, it would fall into a somnolent state, for in *sanyama*, consciousness is wholly absorbed in the object of consciousness, whilst in *nirodhaparinama* that object has vanished. But if it remains fully awake, it gains a powerful glimpse of the tranquil state of nonmodification, and may thus pass through the *laya* or still point of equilibrium to enter into a higher plane. With sufficient practice, the *yogin* learns to extend *nirodha* and abide in it long enough to initiate this transition. The less accomplished, if they do not get caught in the torpor of the penultimate void, may notice the passage of *nirodha* as a missed opportunity. With persistent effort, the *yogin* learns to remain in *nirodha*, relishing the peaceful, smooth flow of cosmic consciousness and reaching the highest *Samadhi*.

Samadhiparinama, meditative transformation, occurs when *nirodha* is experienced not simply as a negation of objects of consciousness but rather as a positive meditation on nothingness. One-pointedness of consciousness has been so mastered through the progressive displacement of all distractions that *ekagrata*, one-pointedness, alone subsists, and this becomes *ekagrataparinama*, total one-pointedness. It is as if the seed of meditation, first sought and recovered every single time the mind wandered and was sharply brought back to a focus, then firmly fixed in focus, had been split asunder until nothing remained but the empty core upon which the mind settles peacefully. Here the besetting tendency to fluctuate has become feeble, whilst the propensity to apply restraint is strong. Since all states of consciousness are necessarily correlated with states of matter, both being products of the *gunas* stimulated to action by the presence of *Purusha*, the depiction of consciousness also pertains to matter. The powerful transformation of consciousness is precisely matched in the continual transformations of matter, though the ordinary eye fails to apprehend the critical states in the transformation of matter, just as it remains largely unaware of *nirodha*. Nonetheless, there is a single substratum, *dharmin*, which underlies all change, whether in consciousness or in matter, and this is *prakriti*, the primeval root of all phenomena. For Patanjali, this means that all transformations are phenomenal in respect to *prakriti* the *prima materia* in its essential nature, and, like *Purusha*, ever unmodified. The ceaseless fluctuations of mind and world are merely countless variations of succession owing to alterations of cause. Realizing this, the *yogin* who has mastered *sanyama,* and thereby controls the mind at will, can equally control all processes of gestation and growth.

Having elucidated the nature of concentration as the sole means for discovering and transforming consciousness at all levels, Patanjali turned to the remarkable phenomenal effects possible through *sanyama.* Any fundamental change in consciousness initiates a corresponding change in and around one's vestures. A decisive shift in the operation and balance of the *gunas,* in thought, focus and awareness, reverberates throughout the oscillating ratios between the *gunas* everywhere. Since any significant refocussing of the mind produces dazzling insights and diverse phenomena, Patanjali conveyed their range and scope. For *yoga* they are not important in themselves because the goal is *kaivalya,* liberation, but they are vitally important as aids or obstacles on the way to achieving the goal. Patanjali could not dismiss or overlook them, since they are real enough and inescapable, and so he delineated them clearly, knowing fully that all such arcane information can be abused. One who willingly uses such knowledge to stray off the arduous path to emancipation brings misery upon himself. One who would use this knowledge wisely needs to understand the many ways one can be misled into wasting the abundant resources accessible to the *yogin.* Profound alterations in states of consciousness through *sanyama* can bring about awakened powers called *siddhis,* attainments, many of which may seem to be supernatural and supernormal to the average person. They are, however, neither miraculous nor supernatural, since they suspend, circumvent or violate no laws. Rather, they merely indicate the immense powers of controlled consciousness within the perspective of great Nature, powers that are largely latent, untapped and dormant in most human beings. They are suggestive parameters of the operation of the vast scope and potency of consciousness in diverse arenas of *prakriti.*

Sanyama, the electric fusion of *dharana, dhyana* and *Samadhi,* can release preternatural knowledge of past and future; the *yogin* gains profound insight into the metaphysical mystery of time. The future is ever conditioned by the past, and the past is accurately reflected in every aspect of the future. The present is strictly not a period of time; it is that ceaselessly moving point which marks the continual transition from future to past. Comprehending causality, seeing the effect in the cause, like the tree in the seed, the *yogin* perceives past and future alike by concentrating on the three phases of transformation experienced in the present and which, at the critical points of transformation, indicate the eternal, changeless substratum hidden behind them. Once conscious awareness is fixed beyond the temporal succession of states of consciousness, causality ceases to be experienced as a series of interrelated events – since the succession is itself the operation of past *karma* – and is perceived as an integrated whole in the timeless present. Thus past and future are seen from the same transcendent perspective as the timeless present. Freeing oneself from captivity to the mechanical succession of moments in clock time, one can rise beyond temporality and grasp causality noetically rather than phenomenally.

Although language is often viewed as an arbitrary and conventional system of communication, interpersonal understanding and mental telepathy as well as rapport between receptive and congenial minds are based on more than mere convention. Just as time is experienced as internal to the subject when the mind is mechanical, whilst causality is not necessarily time-bound, the evolution of language cannot dispense with intersubjectivity, shared clusters of concepts, rites and rituals, habits and customs, races and cultures. The deepest meaning of sounds is subtle and elusive, dissolving meanings and expectations. The linkage connected to the possibility of speech as well as to the potency of the primordial OM, the secret name of *Ishvara*, is *sphota*, the ineffable and inscrutable meaning intimated by sounds and speech. Through *sanyama*, the *yogin* can so deftly discern sound, meaning and idea that he instantly grasps the meaning, whatever the utterance of any person. Not only does he readily understand what is said by anyone, however awkward, disingenuous or deceptive the utterance, but he also apprehends the meaning of any sound uttered by any sentient being, whether birds and beasts, insects, trees or aquatic creatures.

The focussing power of *sanyama* enables the *yogin* to explore the subtlest impressions retained on the mental screen, and in so doing he can summon them into the light of consciousness. In this way, he can examine his entire mental inheritance and even discern previous lives. Knowing the exact correlations between states of consciousness and external conditions, he can recognize the linkage between latent memories and the traumas they induce, as well as the integral connection between past impressions and their inevitable karmic effects, thereby recollecting the patterns of previous incarnations. Similarly, by directing his yogic focus on the *pratyaya* or content of any mind functioning through a set of vestures, he can cognize that mental condition. Since all such mental contents are mirrored in the features and gestures of another, he can read the thoughts of another by looking at the person, and he can make the same determination by examining any portion of the expressed thought of another. Rather like a hologram, each and every aspect of an individual reflects the evolving structure of the whole being. Through *sanyama*, any facet of the person can reveal his psychic and mental make-up. Such attention will not, however, unveil the underlying structure of another's deepest consciousness, since that is hidden even to the person scrutinized. To discover the inward depths of the person, the *yogin* has to take the subject as the sole object of his sustained concentration and not merely that subject's mental contents. The ultimate question "Who are you?" can be resolved only in the way the question "Who am I?" is taken as a theme of intense meditation.

For Patanjali, as for different schools of Indian thought and for Plato (*Republic*, Book VI), seeing is a positive act and not merely a passive reception of light refracted from an object in the line of sight. Seeing involves the confluence of light (an aspect of *sattvaguna*) from the object of sight and the light from the eye of the seer, an active power (another aspect of *sattva*). The *yogin* can direct *sanyama* to the form and colour of his own body and draw in the light radiating from it, centring it wholly within his mind, *manas*, so that the *sattva* from the eye of another cannot fuse with it. Thus the body of the *yogin* cannot be seen, for he has made himself invisible. Similarly, by meditation upon the ultimate basis of any sensory power, the element essential to that sense, and its corresponding sense-organ, the *yogin* can become soundless, intangible and beyond the limited range of all the bodily senses. With the proper inversion of the process, he can dampen or delete any sense image, like glaring lights or background noise, either converting them into mild sensations or blanketing them entirely.

If the *yogin* should choose to practise *sanyama* on his past *karma*, he can obtain unerring insight into every causal chain he once initiated. Recognizing which tendencies are being expended and at what rates, as well as those lines of force which cannot bear fruit in this life, he may discern the time of his death – that point wherein the fruition of *karma* ensures the complete cessation of vital bodily functions. At the same time, such knowledge readily gives warnings of future events, all of which are the inevitable fruition of *karma*, and thus the *yogin* readily sees in each moment signs and portents of the future. He does not perceive, in such instances, something that is present only to his penetrating gaze. Rather, he is only reading correctly the futurity which ever lurks in present events, just as gold ore inheres in the dull rock even though only the trained eye of the prospector can see it and know it for what it is. Whilst such practical wisdom allows the *yogin* to foresee mental and physical conditions, he can also discern more fundamental changes which are due to the inexorable working of overlapping cycles, and, even more, he can focus on those critical points which trace the curve of potentiality for permanent spiritual change, or *metanoia*.

By focussing on *maitri*, kindliness, or any similar grace of character, the *yogin* can fortify that virtue in himself, thereby increasing his mental and moral strength and becoming the shining exemplar and serene repository of a host of spiritual graces. The *yogin* can activate and master any power manifest in Nature and mirrored in the human microcosm, refining its operation through his vestures, honing his inward poise and inimitable timeliness in its benevolent use. Thus, by contemplating the *sattva* or light within, discarding the reflected lights imperfectly and intermittently transmitted through the sensory apparatus, the *yogin* can investigate and come to cognize every subtle thing, whether small, hidden, veiled or very distant. He can discern the atom (*anu*) by deploying the light within, for all light is ultimately one. Should he choose to practise *sanyama* in respect to the sun, he can come to know the harmonies of the solar system from the standpoint of its hidden structure as a matrix of solar energies. Further, he can know all solar systems by analogy with ours, and so his comprehension of cosmic forces expressed in, through and around the sun is more than mere familiarity with the structure of a physical system. He also grasps the architectonics – psychic, mental and spiritual – of all such systems. Similarly, his concentration on the moon yields insights into the intricate arrangements of the stars, since, like the moon, they are all in motion around multiple centres. By concentrating on the pole-star – whose arcane significance is far more than what is commonly assumed on the basis of its visible locus in the sidereal vault – he discerns the motions of the stars in relation to one another, not just on the physical plane but also as the shimmering veil of *Ishvara*, the manifested *Logos* of the cosmos.

Directing the power of *sanyama* upon the soul's vestures, the *yogin* can calmly concentrate on the solar plexus, connected with the pivotal *chakra* or psycho-spiritual centre in the human constitution, and thus thoroughly grasp the structure and dynamics of the physical body. By concentrating on the pit of the throat, connected with the trachea, he can control hunger and thirst. Since hunger and thirst are physical expressions at one level of being which have corresponding correlates and functions at every level, his concentration can also affect mental and psychic cravings, since he has mastered the *prana* or vital energy flowing from this particular *chakra*. More specifically, by concentrating on the *nadi*, or nerve centre called the 'tortoise', below the trachea, the *yogin* gains mental, psychic and physical steadiness, facilitating enormous feats of strength.

If *sanyama* is directed to the divine light in the head, the *yogin* can come to see *siddhas*, perfected beings. This supple light is hidden in the central *sushumna* nerve in the spinal column, and emanates that pristine vibration *(suddhasattva)* which is magnetically linked to the sun and is transmitted through the moon. Concentrating on that supernal light, the *yogin* can perceive those perfected beings whose luminous and translucent vestures are irradiated by the light of the *Logos (daiviprakriti)*. Similarly, concentration on the laser light of spiritual intuition, *kundalini* released by *Buddhi*, results in flashes of inward illumination. This light emanates from *pratibha*, the pure intellect which is self-luminous and omnidirectional, constant and complete, unconnected with earthly aims and objects. Focussing on its radiance releases *taraka jnana*, the transcendental *gnosis* which has been aptly termed 'the knowledge that saves'. This primeval wisdom is wholly unconditioned by any temporal concern for self or the external world, is self- validating and self-shining, the ultimate goal of *Taraka Raja Yoga*. It puts one in close communion with *Ishvara* whilst preserving a vital link, like a silver thread, with the world of woe, illusion and ignorance. *Pratibha* is that crystalline intellection exemplified by *Bodhisattvas* who have transcended all conditionality, yet seek to serve ceaselessly all souls trapped in the chains of bondage. By concentration on the secret, spiritual heart – the *anahata chakra* – the *yogin* becomes attuned to cosmic intellection, for the *anahata* is man's sacred connection with cosmic consciousness, reverberating until near death with the inaudible yet ever pulsating OM.

Should the *yogin* master all these marvellous *siddhis*, he would still remain ensnared in the world which is pervaded by pain and nescience, until he is prepared to take the next, absolutely vital step in the mastery of *taraka jnana*. Any individual involuntarily participates in the stream of sensory experience by blindly assenting to the pleasure-pain principle. This will last as long as he cannot discriminate between *Purusha*, the cosmic Self, and the individuating principle of spiritual insight, *sattva*. Even the subtlest light shining in the incomprehensible darkness of pure Spirit, *Purusha*, must be transcended. The *Yogabhashya* states the central issue: "It has therefore been asked in the *Upanishad*: By what means can the Knower be known?" *Sanyama* must be entirely directed to *Purusha* so that it is perfectly mirrored in the serene light of noetic understanding (*sattva*). *Buddhi*, that intuitive faculty of divine discernment through which the highest *sattva* expresses itself, becomes a pellucid mirror for *Purusha*. Just as *Purusha*, cosmically and individually, penetrates and comprehends *prakriti*, so too the highest *prakriti* now becomes the indispensable means for apprehending *Purusha*. This is the basis for *svasamvedana*, ultimate self-knowledge, the paradigm for all possible self-study at any and every level of consciousness and being. Once this fundamental revolution has occurred, self-consciousness can turn back to the world of objects – which once plunged it into a state of delusion and later gave rise to a series of obstacles to be surmounted – and adopt a steadfast, universal standpoint flowing from all-potent, pure awareness. What once needed various mental and psychophysical mechanisms can now be accomplished without adventitious aids, thereby dispensing altogether with all conditionality and systemic error.

In practice, the *yogin* can now freely and directly exercise the powers commonly connected with the lower sense-organs, without dependence on sensory data. Hence his sight, hearing, smell, taste and especially touch are extrasensory, far greater in range and reach than ever before, precisely because there is no longer reliance on imperfect sensory mechanisms conditioned by physical space and psychological time. What were once obstructions to the deepest meditation (*Samadhi*) can now serve as talismanic aids in benefitting both Nature and Humanity. The *yogin* can, for example, choose at will to enter another's body with full consent, because his mind is no longer entangled with a physical or astral vesture and because he knows the precise conduits through which minds are tethered to bodies. Having risen above any and all temptation to gratify the thirst for sensation or the craving for experience, he can employ his extraordinary powers and extra-sensory faculties solely for the sake of universal enlightenment and the welfare of the weak.

Having gained complete self-mastery, the *yogin* can now exercise benevolent control over invisible and visible Nature (*prakriti*) for the *Agathon*, the greatest good of all. Since even his own vestures are now viewed as external to him, his relation to them has become wholly isomorphic with his conscious connection to the vital centres in the Great Macrocosm. By mastering *udana*, one of the five currents of *prana*, chiefly connected with vertical motion, the *yogin* makes his body essentially impervious to external influences, including the presence of gravity and the inevitability of death. By mastering *samana*, the current of *prana* which governs metabolic and systemic processes, he can render his body self-luminous and radiant, as Jesus did during his climactic transfiguration and as Moses is said to have done during his salvific descent from Mount Sinai. Knowing the integral connection between the inner ear and *Akasha*, the supple light and etheric empyrean in invisible space, the trained *yogin* can hear anything that ever impressed itself, however distantly, upon that universal, homogeneous and supersensuous medium. Similarly, knowing the vital connection between the astral body and *Akasha*, he can make his body light and even weightless, and also as pliable and versatile as a superb musical instrument.

From the standpoint of self-consciousness, the *yogin* who has
mastered *taraka jnana* can practise *mahavideha*, the power of making
the mind wholly incorporeal, so that it abides in pure and perfect
awareness beyond even *Buddhi*. Such a state of cosmic consciousness
is indescribable, though it can be identified as that exalted condition
in which no light anywhere is absent from his mental horizon. From
the standpoint of Nature, the perfected *yogin* has total control of matter
and can fully comprehend it in its subtlest and most minute forms. He
can manifest through his vestures the entire spectrum of possibilities of
universal self-consciousness and effortless control over matter – merging
into the atom, magnifying himself into the galactic sphere, making the
human temple worthy of every perfection, including grace, beauty,
strength, porosity, malleability and rock-like hardness. Controlling
the seven sense-organs, the masterly *yogin* knows precisely how they
function on the spiritual, mental, moral and physical planes, and he
can instantaneously cognize anything he chooses. Comprehending and
controlling *pradhana*, the common principle and substratum of invisible
Nature, he can direct every change and mutation in material *prakriti*. He
is no longer subject to the instruments he employs, for the entire cosmos
has become his aeolian harp and sounding-board.

The *yogin's* total grasp of the elusive and ever-shifting distinction
between *Purusha* and *prakriti*, especially between the universal Self and
the individuating principle of understanding *(sattva)*, between subject and
object at all levels, becomes the basis for his unostentatious sovereignty
over every possible state of existence. His complete comprehension of
the Soundless Sound (OM), of the Sound in the Light and the Light in
the Sound, results in what is tantamount to serene omnipotence and
silent omniscience. Yet although the perfected *yogin* is a *Magus*, a Master
of *gnosis*, wholly lifted out of the sphere of *prakriti* and supremely free,
self-existent and self-conquered, he does not allow even the shadow of
attachment to transcendental joy to stain his sphere of benevolence to
all. Complete and invulnerable non-attachment, *vairagya*, can destroy the
lurking seeds of self-concern and susceptibility to delusion, and he may
thus approach the threshold of *kaivalya*, supreme self-emancipation. If,
however, he is enthralled by the glorious deities and celestial wonders

he encounters in the spiritual empyrean, he could rekindle the dormant yearning for terrestrial life, with its fast-proliferating chain of earthly entanglements. But if he steadfastly practises *sanyama* on the *kalachakra*, the Wheel of Time, and even more, penetrates the last veil of *kala*, the mystery of Being, Becoming and Beness, the infinitude of the Eternal Now hidden within the infinitesimal core of the passing moment, he can dissolve without trace the divine *yogamaya* of conditioned space-time. Such unfathomable depths of consciousness transcend the very boundaries of *gnosis* and cannot be conveyed in any language, conceptual or ontological.

The purest and most perfect awareness is indistinguishable from the direct apprehension of ultimate Reality wherein, in the words of Shankaracharya, the very distinctions between seer, seeing and sight, or knower, knowing and known, wholly vanish. Here, for example, the Leibnizian principle of the identity of indiscernibles collapses in thought and language. Knowing eternity in time in its irreducible moments, even indistinguishable events or objects can be instantaneously separated in an ecstatic, simultaneous apprehension of the One without a second, of the One mirrored in the many, of the many co-present in the One, of the tree of knowledge within the tree of life. And yet nothing is known by species, genus or class: each thing is known by its instantaneous co-presence. *Taraka jnana* is thus not only omniscient in its range but simultaneous in its scope. The *yogin* knows at once all that can possibly be known, in a world of commonalities, comparisons and contrasts, and infinitesimal parts within infinite wholes.

Supreme emancipation, *kaivalya*, dawns only when *Purusha* shines unhindered and *sattva* receives the full measure of light. *Purusha* is no longer veiled, obscured or mirrored by the faculties and functions of *prakriti* and *Buddhi* becomes unconditional, untainted by any teleological or temporal trace. There is no more any consciousness of seeking the light, which the aspirant legitimately entertains, or of radiating the light, which the recently omniscient *yogin* experiences. There is now solely the supernal and omnipresent, ever-existing light of *Purusha*, abiding in its intrinsic splendour of supreme freedom, and this is *kaivalya*, the supreme state of being "aloof and unattached, like *Akasha*" (*Srimad Bhagavatam* VI). Since this is the ultimate goal of *Taraka Raja Yoga*, in terms of which each spiritual potency, skill and striving must be calibrated, Patanjali devoted the concluding fourth *pada* to this exalted theme.

In the memorable words of the Sage Kapila to Devahuti, the daughter of *Manu*:

> The moment his mind ceases to discriminate, by reason of the activities of the senses, between objects which are not intrinsically different, looking upon some as pleasant, on others as not, that moment he sees with his own mind his own SELF, equable and self-luminous, free from likes and dislikes, and completely aloof, serenely established in the intuition of transcendental rapture. Pure Consciousness is spoken of variously as *parabrahm, Paramatman, Ishvara* or *Purusha*. The Lord, the One without a second, masquerades as the multiplicity of seer, seen and so on. The one goal of all *yoga*, practised perfectly with all its ancillary disciplines, is the attainment by the *yogin* of total detachment from the world.... At the same time he should learn to see the SELF in all creatures, and all creatures in the SELF, making no difference between them, even as in all creatures he recognizes the presence of the gross elements. Just as fire looks different in the diverse logs that it burns, owing to the difference between the logs, so too does the SELF seem different in the varied bodies it indwells. The *yogin*, vanquishing thus the inscrutable *maya* of the Lord, which deludes the *jiva* and is the cause of the phenomenal world, rests secure in his own true state.

> *Srimad Bhagavatam*

Hermes, April 1989

YOGA SUTRAS - BOOK IV:
KAIVALYA PADA

janmaushadhi-mantra-tapah-samadhijah siddhayah

1. Spiritual powers (*siddhis*) are inborn and activated by herbs, incantations, austerities or meditative absorption (*Samadhi*). (163)

jaty-antara-parinamah prakrity-apurat

2. Transformation from one species or state of existence into another is made possible through the overflow of natural tendencies and forces. (164)

nimittam aprayojakam prakritinam varanabhedas tu tatah kshetrikavat

3. The instrumental cause does not produce the essential modification or movement of natural tendencies; it merely pierces through obstructions, just like the farmer in the field. (165)

nirmana-chittany asmita-matrat

4. Many minds are produced solely by the power of egoism or selfhood. (166)

pravritti-bhede prayojakam chittam ekam anekesham

5. The one mind is directing many minds in their multiple activities. (167)

tatra dhyanajam anashayam

6. Of these, the mind born of meditation is devoid of mental

deposits or latent impressions. (168)

karmashuklakrishnam yoginas trividham itaresham

7. The actions of *yogins* are neither white nor black, while those of others are of three kinds. (169)

tatas tad-vipakanugunanam evabhivyaktir vasananam

8. From these, only those tendencies are manifested for which the conditions are favourable for fruition. (170)

jati-desha-kala-vyavahitanam apy anantaryam smriti-sanskarayor ekarupatvat

9. Although separated by class, locality and time, there is an immediate succession of memories and tendencies which are identical in form. (171)

tasam anaditvam chashisho nityatvat

10. And there is no temporal beginning for those tendencies, owing to the constant persistence of desire or the will to live. (172)

hetu-phalashrayalambanaih sangrihitatvad esham abhave tad-abhavah

11. As they are bound together by cause and effect, substratum and support, they cease to exist when these disappear. (173)

atitanagatam svarupato 'sty adhva-bhedad dharmanam

12. The past and the future subsist in their true nature, while the variation in properties is owing to differences of phase and direction. (174)

te vyakta-sukshmah gunatmanah

13. They, whether manifest or unmanifest, are of the nature of *gunas* or potencies. (175)

parinamaikatvad vastu-tattvam

14. The essential nature of the object consists in the identity and uniqueness of the transformation. (176)

vastu-samye chitta-bhedat tayor vibhaktah panthah

15. Though the object is the same, the cognition is different, owing to the diversity and distinctness of states of being. (177)

na chaika-chitta-tantram vastu tad-apramanakam tada kim syat

16. Nor is an object dependent on one mind. What would become of it when not cognized by that mind? (178)

tad-uparagapekshitvach chittasya vastu jnatajnatam

17. An object is known or not known according as the mind is coloured and attracted by it or not. (179)

sada jnatasth chitta-vrittayas tat-prabhoh purushasyaparinamitvat

18. The modifications of the mind are always known to its master, owing to the immutability of the Self (*Purusha*). (180)

na tat svabhasam drishyatvat

19. Nor is the mind self-luminous, since it can be seen as an object. (181)

eka-samaye chobhayanavadharanam

20. Nor can it be both cognizer and cognized at the same time. (182)

chittantara-drishye Buddhi-buddher atiprasangah smriti-sanskarah cha

21. If the mind were to be seen by another within, there would be an endless series of perceiving minds and a commingling of memories. (183)

chiter apratisankramayas tad-akarapattau svabuddhi-sanvedanam

22. Knowledge of its own nature through self-cognition comes when consciousness assumes that form in which it does not move from place to place. (184)

drashtri-drishyoparaktam chittam sarvartham

23. Consciousness, coloured by the Seer and the seen, is all-comprehensive. (185)

tad asankhyeya-vasanabhish chitram api parartham sanhatya-karitvat

24. Though variegated by countless impressions, the mind exists for another (*Purusha*), for it acts in association. (186)

vishesha-darshina atma-bhava-bhavana-vinivrittih

25. For the discerning Seer there is complete cessation of identification of mental states with the consciousness of the Self (*atman*). (187)

tada hi viveka-nimnam kaivalya-pragbharam chittam

26. Verily, then, the mind becomes serenely bent towards discrimination and is borne onwards towards total emancipation (*kaivalya*). (188)

tach-chidreshu pratyayantarani sanskarebhyah

27. During intervals other thoughts will arise through the force of former impressions. (189)

hanam esham kleshavad uktam

28. Their removal is like that of the afflictions (*kleshas*) already mentioned. (190)

prasankhyane 'py akusidasya sarvatha viveka-khyater dharma-

meghah samadhih

29. From constant and continuous discriminative knowledge, without any selfish attachment even towards the highest illumination, comes the meditative absorption (*Samadhi*) known as the rain-cloud of righteousness (*dharma-megha*). (191)

tatah klesha-karma-nivrittih

30. Then comes the cessation of afflictions (*kleshas*) and works (*karma*). (192)

tada sarvavarana-malapetasya jnanasyanantyaj jneyam alpam

31. Then all veils and stains being removed, his knowledge becoming infinite, little remains to be known. (193)

tatah kritarthanam parinama-krama-samaptir gunanam

32. Then the three *gunas* having fulfilled their purpose, the process of transformation comes to an end. (194)

kshana-pratiyogi parinamaparanta-nirgrahyah kramah

33. Succession is the uninterrupted sequence of moments and is fully apprehended at the final stage. (195)

purushartha-shunyanam gunanam pratiprasavah kaivalyam svarupa-pratishtha va chiti-shakter iti

34. Emancipation (*kaivalya*) comes when the *gunas*, becoming devoid of any motive for action for the Self (*Purusha*), are reabsorbed into latency. In this state the Self (*Purusha*) is established in its own nature, which is the energy of pure consciousness or cosmic ideation. (196)

kaivalya nirvanayoh purnaikyam

35. There is complete identity of emancipation (*kaivalya*) and supreme peace (*nirvana*). (197)

kaivalyam dharman dharminah purushasya

36. Emancipation (*kaivalya*) is the state which subsists in the Self (*Purusha*). (198)

kaivalye akhile vishve Purusha-darshanam purushe chakhila vishva-darshanam

37. In the state of emancipation there is the vision of the Self in the entire cosmos and of the cosmos in the Self. (199)

sagunam satchidanandam nirgunam chatatah param tatvam iti

38. Absolute Existence, Consciousness and Bliss constitute the plenitude of the Self, and beyond these is the Attributeless Self. (200).

Hermes, August 1987

KAIVALYA PADA

With the fulfillment of their twofold purpose, the experience and
the emancipation of the SELF, and with the cessation of mutations,
the gunas cannot manifest even for a moment.

Yogabhashya

Patanjali provided a vast perspective on consciousness and its varied
levels, as well as the necessary and sufficient conditions for sustained
meditation. He set forth the essential prerequisites to meditation, the
persisting obstacles to be overcome by the conscientious seeker, and
the awesome powers and exhilarating experiences resulting from
the progressive attainment of *Samadhi*. In the fourth *pada*, the heart
of which is *kaivalya*, the ultimate aim and transcendental culmination
of the discipline of *Taraka Raja Yoga*, Patanjali epitomized the entire
process from the standpoint of the adept *yogin* in meditation. He was
thus able to offer a rounded exposition which might otherwise remain
obscure. The *Yoga Sutras* is for daily use, and not dilettantish perusal.
Its compelling logic is intrinsically self-validating as well as capable of
continuous self-testing. Its reasonableness and efficacy are endorsed by
a long succession of accredited seers and seekers.

The *siddhis*, or arcane, supernormal and spiritual powers, may be
inborn in any incarnation. Although they may appear spontaneous
or superfluous to the superficial eye, they are strictly the products
of profound meditations in previous lives, as they depend for their
development on mastery of the mind and its myriad correlations amongst
the manifold elements in the cosmos. Since individual consciousness
may have undergone such strenuous discipline in prior incarnations but
not in the present life, the imprint of these practices in the immortal soul
can be retained without conscious remembrance of the fact. If, however,
it is not supported and strengthened by conscious discipline (*abhyasa*) in
this life, the manifestation of unusual mental capacities and uncommon

siddhis may be sporadic, relatively uncontrolled and precariously inconstant. Furthermore, because all knowledge is recollection, in a Platonic sense, and the residues of the past linger in the present, *siddhis* can sometimes be stimulated by hallucinogenic drugs and herbs like verbena, or by sacred chants and time-honoured incantations, although the effects of external aids are notoriously uneven and ever unpredictable. Systematic austerities (*tapas*) may also release something of the attainments of previous incarnations, but true *Samadhi* alone provides the rigorous, progressive and reliable pathway to self-mastery and sovereignty over the subtle forces of Nature. With such complete command of the *gunas* or modes of *prakriti* as it manifests in the mind and in the external world, the adept *yogin* can alter his nature from one class of being (the human) to another (a *deva* or god, in a broad sense of the term), if the karmic conditions in life are congenial and conducive to rapid development. Even then, the wise practitioner would not pursue this discipline except from the highest of motives, for anything less would hinder *prakrityapurat*, the 'flow of *prakriti*' needed for its safe and smooth accomplishment.

No significant change of human nature would be possible if it merely depended upon instrumental causes, for these can only rearrange components or unveil hidden but pre-existent features. Hence, doing good deeds cannot transform one's composite nature, nor need they bear that burden, for one's inmost nature is *Purusha*, Self alone, and this is reflected by pure consciousness, *Buddhi*. Right conduct on the moral and mental planes can remove various obstructions to the rapid unfoldment of the vast potential of consciousness and that complete realization of *Purusha* known as self-emancipation (*kaivalya*). To the *yogin*, his mind serves as the director of any number of mental matrices or emanated minds which can carry out semi-independent functions under its supervision. Just as the presence of *Purusha* quickens and facilitates the fertile expansion of consciousness, so too the controlled mind of the *yogin* stimulates intellection everywhere. The *yogin* can work through the receptive minds of mature disciples, aiding all humanity by strengthening its spiritual aspirations. Whether mental aspects of the *yogin* or the sympathetic minds of others, no matrix of consciousness is free of *samskaras* or mental deposits, save the *yogin*'s mind born of meditation. Only the consciousness integrated by pure *dhyana* is devoid of all impediment.

The *yogin* is above good and evil acts, not because he has become indifferent to the consequences of action, but rather because he is naturally disposed to remove all obstructions and mental deposits. Good conduct as well as bad bears fruit for the doer, but the *yogin* acts in such complete accord with Nature that what he does responds to necessity, being neither pure (*sattva*) nor polluted (*tamas*) nor mixed, like that of most human beings. His conduct follows a fourth course, that of *nishkama* or desirelessness, so that he cannot be said to do what he wishes, but rather he only does what needs to be done. *Nishkama karma*, the fruition of pure desireless action, neither returns nor clings to the *yogin*. Being one with Nature, he ceases to be a separative centre of focus or agency, and his actions, strictly speaking, are no longer 'his', being the spontaneous play of *prakriti* before *Purusha*. Hence, he leaves no impressions or residues in his consciousness even whilst doing his duty with single-minded precision, since he acts as the willing instrument of *Purusha* immanent in *prakriti*. He has only former mental deposits, resulting from past *karma*, which he meticulously removes to attain total freedom.

The *yogin's* assiduously nurtured capacities disallow the emergence of fresh *karma*, the results of which could adhere to him because he is no longer subject to *vasana*, the force of craving and the unchecked impulse for life in form, with its attendant consequences. But he cannot instantly dissolve *karma* generated long ago, for whatever was the result of *vasana* in the past must inevitably linger, although the *yogin* is aware of its antecedents and does not become distracted or discouraged by it. In addition to the results that are already manifest, the force of craving and the *vasanas* (identifiable traces of unfulfilled longings and the cumulative *karma* they rapidly engender) deposit unconscious residues in the mind. These are more difficult to discern, for they are not recurring modifications of consciousness such as those induced by specific objects of desire, but are subtle tinctures or discolorations in the lens of cognition, hard to detect, recognize and remove. Being unconscious, and unknown to the thinker, they will appear only when conditions are ripe, and the *yogin* must patiently wait for their emergence in order to eliminate them. Even though immense periods of time and many incarnations may intervene between the initial insertion of the *vasanas* into consciousness and their eventual emergence, they are neither dissolved nor transformed, for they are retained in a stream of soul reminiscence which is not brain dependent, and which indeed provides a basis of continuity. This stream of latent reminiscence is revealed in the sometimes sudden appearance of surprising tendencies that seem out of character, but are nonetheless inescapable in the strict operation of *karma*.

Although any specific *vasana* could, in principle, be traced to a particular point in time – some previous incarnation – when the stream of consciousness encountered a similar cluster of thoughts, feelings or acts, *vasana* or desire in general is atemporal. It is coeval with mind (*chitta*) and with the cosmos. Whilst any distinct *vasana* could first appear only when a congenial psychophysical structure arose to make its manifestation possible, *vasana* as a force is an inextricable element in the matrices of differentiated matter. Just because the propensity to enjoyment or self-indulgence is an integral aspect of the cosmic process – the captivating dance of *prakriti* before *Purusha* – the overcoming of all such propensities demands a deliberate choice maintained over time through *Taraka Raja Yoga*, the discipline of transcendental detachment. *Vasana* finds its support in the mutable mind, which is the action of *prakriti* owing to the proximity of *Purusha*. Only when the mind is fully awake, wholly focussed and serenely steadfast will *vasana* vanish. This is equivalent to the potential ability of *prakriti* to behold *Purusha* qua *Purusha* without wavering, and this is only possible as a deliberate act – *Buddhi* reflecting *Purusha* without distortion or fluctuation.

Considered from the temporal standpoint, the protracted continuity of *vasana* as a strong force and the specific *vasanas* as persisting matrices of memory suggest the arbitrariness of the divisions of time into past, present and future. Each *vasana* is but a seed which inevitably grows into a plant and bears appropriate fruit: knowing the seed, one can cognize all future states of development. In the present lie latent the past and the future, just as the present was contained in the future and will remain until it slides speedily into the past. The underlying reality cannot be understood without seeing the present as no more than a moving phase through the limitless continuum of time, all of which is latent save for the swiftly passing moment. When all the *vasanas* have been consigned to the past, and when even the very basis of desire ceases to bother consciousness, *kaivalya* alone abides. All continuous change and the ramifying consequences of change are the tumultuous activity of the *gunas*, and when that relentless activity belongs to the past, no longer swaying the mind of the *yogin*, the *gunas* have ceased their incessant interplay in the stream of consciousness. Becoming latent, they have ceased to manifest and have become dormant or homogeneous, leaving intact the luminous vision of serene self emancipation *(kaivalya)*.

An object is what it is, not because of some unique substratum, for the ultimate substratum of everything is the same. An object is distinct only because of the complex configuration of the *gunas*, the ceaseless interplay of which constitutes its nature. The fluid geometry of Nature, with the shifting ratios of *gunas*, permits some objects to persist longer than others, but the principle remains the same and endurance is merely relative. Even though an object survives for a time, the mutual activity of the *gunas* which constitutes each mind is different and alters at varying rates. Hence each person cognizes the object distinctively. The object is independent of each and every mind, though all apprehension of the object is entirely mind-dependent. Whether an object is known or not is the result of whether or not a particular mind is attracted to it. *Purusha*, however, cannot be a mental object. Rather, it is seen directly when the mind remains focussed upon it and does not move. Significantly, direct awareness of *Purusha* occurs when the mind ceases to act, which in *Sankhya* philosophy is equivalent to saying that the mind ceases to be what it is. *Purusha* witnesses all mental modifications and is the true Knower precisely because it does not alter or waver.

The mind is not self-luminous and cannot know itself by its own effort. Subject to change, it can be seen as an object by another, and ceaselessly changing, it cannot know itself, for change cannot discern change, just as relativities cannot calibrate relativities. *Purusha*, the ever changeless, is alone the Knower, whose reflection is cast upon consciousness, which then knows derivatively. Since the mind moves from moment to moment, it cannot both function as that which cognizes and that which is cognized. Hence, that which cognizes the mind whilst it cognizes objects (and so undergoes modification) is above the mind. Since consciousness operates on many levels, the level of awareness which apprehends consciousness necessarily transcends the level of the apprehended consciousness. Ultimately, *Purusha* comprehends all consciousness. One cannot speak of one mind knowing another within itself, as if the human being were constituted by many minds – an erroneous view encouraged by the limitations of descriptive and conceptual languages; one would have to posit an infinite regress of such minds, each knowing the one 'below' or 'in front of' itself, since none could know itself. The absurdity of an infinite series of minds within the consciousness of each individual is shown clearly by the problem of memory. Which mind would then remember? All of them? An infinitude of interacting memories would result in utter confusion of consciousness.

Self-cognition is possible when the relativating nature of the mind – its constant fluctuation which is the activity of the *gunas* – ceases. Pure consciousness desists from deploying the mind and so can know it, and when it does so, it ceases to be involved in any sort of movement from moment to moment. "The self-knowledge spoken of here", W. Q. Judge wrote, "is that interior illumination desired by all mystics, and is not merely a knowledge of self in the ordinary sense." Likening consciousness to light and the mind to a globe, I. K. Taimini suggested a striking metaphor: "If a light is enclosed within a translucent globe, it reveals the globe. If the globe is removed, the light reveals itself." This revelation is not knowledge in any ordinary sense, because within it there is no subject/object distinction, no separation of perceiver, perceived and perception; there is only the eternal Reality of the Self-illuminated *Purusha*. Although the mind, acted upon by the *gunas* and so consisting wholly of *prakriti*, is not consciousness, it is tinctured by *Purusha* and receives its luminous hue from it, even whilst suffused with the gaudier colours of the world of objects. It seems to be both conscious and nonconscious, and so those who do not know *Purusha* but experience its effects in *prakriti* mistake the mind, an instrument, for consciousness itself, when in fact the true cognizer of objects impressed upon the mind is *Purusha*. This root error – mistaking the organ of perception for the power of perception – is the origin of all ignorance, illusion and sorrow.

"The mind, which is essentially an assemblage," the *Yogabhashya* teaches, "cannot act on its own to serve its own interests" (IV.24). Modified by a chaotic series of new impressions and weighed down by myriad deposits from past impressions, the mind cannot act for itself even though it thinks it does. From a teleological standpoint, the mind exists solely for *Purusha*, and despite an individual's deep-seated, ignorant confusion – the inexorable cause of sorrow – all mental activity arises in association with the Self, which it unknowingly seeks. Impressions engender a *maya* of independent activity which is dispelled in *Samadhi* wherein the nature of the mind is discerned. When the Perceiver, *Purusha*, sees beyond the confusion of ordinary cerebrations, there is no identification of the power of sight with the instrument of seeing, and it is entirely unaffected by the attributes, tendencies and images of the mind. The fully awakened, alert and tranquil mind, settled in the supreme stillness of *Samadhi*, speedily learns correct cognition and moves steadily in the direction of *kaivalya*, self-emancipation. In fact, it is *Purusha* hidden behind the gossamer veils of intellection whose light illumines the way, but, in the apt analogy of I. K. Taimini, like the magnet attracting iron filings, the mind seems to move towards the magnetic *Purusha*, when in truth the invisible power of *Purusha* draws the mind to itself. At this exalted stage, the individual seeks nothing except the total freedom of self emancipation. Even when the mind, like a guided missile locked on to its target, moves without the slightest wavering or change of course towards the luminous *Purusha*, old impressions will cyclically reassert themselves, owing to their unspent momentum. They can be eliminated by the same methods developed for dissolving the *kleshas* or afflictions, except that here the *yogin* knows them already for what they are and can instantaneously destroy them, or return them to complete dormancy, through undisturbed discernment (*vivekakhyati*) of the True Self (*Purusha*).

When the *yogin* abides in this peaceful state wherein *Purusha* alone stands at the focal point of his entire consciousness, he verges on *prasankhyana*, omniscience or complete illumination. Since any lurking attachment can be a hindrance to self-realization, he must renounce even the desire for the highest illumination, save insofar as it may elevate all existence. From the inception of his spiritual quest in lives long past, *viveka* (discrimination) and *vairagya* (detachment) have been crucial to his endeavours. As *viveka* culminates in *vivekakhyati* (discernment of the Real), so too *vairagya* culminates in *paravairagya*, supreme detachment towards the highest conceivable fruit of effort, *prasankhyana*. When this occurs, *Samadhi* becomes *dharmamegha*, the rain cloud of righteousness, which is perpetual discernment of *Purusha* or unending enlightenment. The circle is closed, the line returns upon itself, and the *yogin* passes from linear time into the omnidirectional realization of *Purusha*, the Self, rising above time to the Eternal Now, which transcends every moment though implicit in temporal succession. All the residues of the afflictions *(kleshas)* simply drop away as water runs off an impervious surface, and the *yogin* finds self-emancipation even in embodied life. *Dharmamegha Samadhi* destroys the residuum of *karma* and the *kleshas* at the root, so that they can never arise again. The *yogin* has attained that supreme felicity from which there is no falling away.

The *yogin's* cognition becomes infinite and without any limit whatsoever, for of the three *gunas*, *rajas* and *tamas* have ceased to be active. But even this cognition is transcended, for the stilling of *rajas* and *tamas* deprives *sattva* of a contrasting field for expression, and so all three *gunas* become quiescent. This can be conceived as their merger into homogeneous latency or as their cessation, for they no longer sustain the process of ceaseless transformation. Without such transformation, there is no existence as evident in Nature (*prakriti*), and yet since they remain latent they still exist for all those who live in ignorance. As all knowledge depends upon transformations of consciousness which occur through the succession of moments (*kshanas*), knowledge is limited by the discontinuity of moments. For the *yogin* who has reached the threshold of *kaivalya*, the succession of moments is seen as a discrete continuum and is wholly transcended. His knowledge is no longer bound by temporal succession because he beholds the process as a whole. Rather than being subject to the transformations of the world, he sees them as an endless succession of discrete states, whilst his transcendental (*taraka*) knowledge is continuous and complete. He is now the Perceiver (*Purusha*), utterly unaffected by the passing show of phenomenal Nature (*prakriti*).

The *gunas*, no longer stirred to activity by the presence of *Purusha*, are reabsorbed into absolute latency, and *Purusha* abides in its own essential nature, without any trace of ignorance, misconception, confusion and sorrow. For the *yogin*, experience comes to an end, for he has become one with his true nature, which is *Purusha*, the energy of pure consciousness – devoid of moments – which is cosmic ideation, upon which all noumena and phenomena depend. This is complete emancipation, *kaivalya*, and supreme peace, *nirvana*. *Kaivalya* is the ineffable state of stillness – though such terms are wholly inadequate, metaphysically and metapsychologically – which is the self-existence of *Purusha* in and as itself. The *yogin* is no longer captive to the central duality postulated in *Sankhya* philosophy, for he beholds *Purusha*, which is himself, in the entire cosmos, and the entire cosmos, which is also himself, in *Purusha*. For him, as in *Mahayana* mysticism, *nirvana* is *samsara* and vice versa. Since there is no separation between the two, there is no room for even the subtlest error, and so sin and sorrow vanish forever. *Sat-chit-ananda*, Being, Consciousness and Bliss, constitute for him the fullness of *Purusha*, which nonetheless abides beyond them as the attributeless Self.

What, one might ask, does the *yogin* do now? Does he abide forever in unalloyed bliss? Such questions cannot be raised, for the *yogin* is no longer a creature of time and space. Rather than being now or doing then, he always was, is and will be, for he lives in the Eternal Now. Even though consciousness, bound by time, change and error, makes of such an inconceivable condition a frozen ecstasy, no picture of it can be anything but a fantasy rooted in ignorance. The *yogin* is entirely free and moves through sublime states of awareness which the unenlightened mind can neither imagine nor articulate, and therefore Patanjali, a true Sage, remained silent. When the *yogin* ceases to be a part of the temporal process and becomes indistinguishable from it – on the principle of the identity of indiscernibles – he becomes its creator. He was there in the beginning and he is its *eschaton*, the end and goal beyond which there is only Silence.

In the memorable words of *Shrimad Bhagavatam*, Book XI:

> The *yogin*, having discarded the notions of 'good' and 'bad', though experiencing the objects of the senses in all their diversity, is no more addicted to them than the wind to the places where it happens to blow. The *yogin* who has realized the SELF, though he seems to identify with the properties of the material vesture he inhabits, is no more attached to them than the breeze is attached to the fragrant scent it carries. Even whilst remaining in the body, the Sage should think of his soul as unattached to the body and the like, and unlimited just as the sky is, not only because it is present in all Nature, animate and inanimate, as the invariable concomitant, but being identical with the Supreme, it is also all pervading . . . .

Pure and kind-hearted by nature, the Sage is like water, in that he is a sanctifying influence in the lives of those who purify themselves by seeing, touching or speaking of him. Radiating power, enhanced by austerities, possessing nothing, yet imperturbable, the *yogin* who has steadied his mind remains unsoiled like the fire, regardless of what he may consume. While the creation and destruction of the bodies that the SELF assumes proceeds every moment at the hands of Time, which rushes like a swift stream, the SELF remains unnoticed, like the emergence and subsidence of tongues of flame in a burning fire.

Hermes, May 1989

MEDITATION AND SELF-STUDY

Atmanam atmana pasya

Meditation and self-study are of immeasurable importance to every single person. They concern the longest journey of the soul, the divine discontent in human life. The quest for true meditation and the yearning for real self-knowledge are as old as thinking man. Today, more than ever before in recorded history, there is a widespread hunger for teaching and instruction concerning meditation and concentration. Some seek even more, longing for a way of life irradiated by the inward peace and joyous strength of contemplation. Ours is an age of acute, almost obsessive, self-consciousness. Everyone is oppressed by the ego-games endemic to contemporary culture, the thought-forms and speech habits, the paranoid, loveless and competitive modes seemingly required merely to keep body and soul together. We are tempted to think that there is some inescapable necessity to assert ourselves to survive, to protect ourselves from being exploited, engulfed or drowned. At the same time, we look in many directions, to ancient and modern as well as to new-fangled schools of psychological health, hoping to enhance our capacity for self-analysis, mental clarification, and minimum control over our personal lives.

The hunger for authentic knowledge and reliable techniques of meditation, and the poignant concern for self-definition, are paramount needs of our time. They are more fundamental, more lasting and more bewildering than all other clamorous claims. But they appear to move in opposite directions. The impulse toward meditation seems to be towards opting out of the world – the world of illusion – or at least the decaying structure of any society. It suggests liberation, an escape from the great wheel of birth and death and the whole life-process. It involves the desire for an equivalent to the conventional concepts of heaven. Images of eternal, nirvanic and absolute self-transcendence are often analogous to the perpetual and perfect release which men desperately seek and fail to find on the physical plane of the lower *eros*. On the other hand, the entire concern for self-analysis and self-understanding is bound up with the need to improve our relation to our fellow men, our capacity for survival, the abject dependence on acceptance and love. It is so much directed to a re-entry into the world that self-study and meditation seem to represent poles that fly off in opposite directions. And in both cases there are more teachers than disciples. There are so many schools, so many sects, such a vast range of panaceas that there is something absurd and also deeply sad about the ferment on the threshold of the 1975 cycle.

If we think for a moment of another age, a distant time in which men sought for supreme wisdom concerning the immortality of the Self and the ultimate joys of contemplation, we may discern that there were men and women who gave their whole lives to a sustained and desperate search. They consecrated everything they had for the sake of finding some answer by which they could live, and from which they could gain a more fundamental insight, a more permanent solution, not only for themselves, but also in relation to the intense human predicament, the malaise of mankind. Today we certainly do not find anything comparable to the exacting demands and the aristocratic sense in which many are called, few persist, fewer are chosen, and very few succeed. There is a tantalizing statistic in the *Bhagavad Gita* suggesting that one man in a million succeeds in the quest for immortality. When we think of that exalted perspective upon the journey, in an age where there is an almost universal concern, and if we consider it in impersonal terms, for the sake of all and not only for ourselves, we are bound to feel deeply puzzled. Something is going wrong. Yet there must be a legitimacy in what is happening. How can one understand this? Where can one find the true wisdom and teaching? Where are the real teachers? Where are those authentic men of meditation who can by their compassion consecrate the whole endeavour, showing not only discrimination in the choice of deserving disciples, but also a supreme justice befitting the total need of the world as a whole? The more we ask questions of this kind, the more we must retreat, if we are honest, into a cleansing confession of absolute ignorance.

We do not know whether there is in the world any knowledge, of which there are external signs that are absolutely certain, in relation to a sovereign method. The conditions, the requirements and the object of the quest are obscure to us. Viewing the immense need of our age, we are uncertain whether there is anything that could adequately serve the diverse needs of vast numbers of varied kinds of human agony, sickness and pain. We might think we are in the Dark Ages, that the Wise Men have gone, and that there is no longer access to the highest conception of wisdom in relation to meditation or self-knowledge. This answer would come naturally to a humble and honest man in the context of the immemorial tradition of the East. In the West one might be inclined either to argue that having no way of knowing whether the whole thing is a distraction, it is better not to look in any direction, or, to see our plight in terms of the messianic religious traditions of the Piscean Age.

Thus there is a restless intensity to the search for a technique or formula, which is not merely a surefire method of meditation or of self-study, but which is in fact a panacea for salvation. Those who are not only concerned for themselves, but share a sense of awareness of the common needs of men, think less in terms of a mere panacea than of a mandate for universal salvation. They seek what is not only supremely valid, decisive and certain, but what could also be made available to all and is capable of ready use by human beings as they are – with all their fallibilities, limitations and imperfections – whether as apprentices and beginners, or merely for the sake of avoiding the slide into self-destruction. They are looking for what can in fact be widely marketed and made available. Put in another language, the idea of a mandate for salvation becomes more understandable, and can be lent a certain minimal dignity. It is as if one says that one wants, for any ordinary person in the street, not the knowledge he needs for him to become a saint or a sage, or a man of meditation perfected in self-knowledge, but simply the knowledge that would enable him to have what he cannot find in any pill or potion, and cannot get from any physician or psychiatrist.

It is the knowledge that will help him to balance his life and to gain, in a chaotic time, enough calm and sufficient continuity of will-energy, to be able to survive without succumbing to the constant threat and danger of disintegration, ever looming large like a nightmare. What is needed is the ability to avoid the dreadful decline along an inclined slope tending towards an awful abyss of annihilation and nothingness. On that inclined slope are steps that are very painful and readily recognisable, not only by oneself but by each other. They represent the weakening of the will and the progressive inability to reinforce the will, especially amidst the breakdown of all those collectivised goals of societies and men in terms of which one was once able to generate a kind of extraordinary will-energy. In our Promethean or Faustian culture individuals simply do not have the will-energy required for the most minimal notions of survival. When we put the subject in this agonizing contemporary context, and not in a classical context seemingly removed from our time, we are entitled to ask whether there is any Theosophical text on meditation and self-study worthy of scrutiny and deeply relevant in one's life, which is in principle capable of universalization and could have the widest relevance to our contemporary condition.

Here one may turn to the meticulous and enigmatic wisdom of that immensely compassionate and extraordinary human being whom we know as Helena Petrovna Blavatsky. She chose, though only at the very end of her life, to give to the world and yet dedicate to the few, a translation from unknown Tibetan sources of stanzas, still chanted in monasteries and sanctuaries of initiation, which she called *The Voice of the Silence*. This beautiful book was blessed in her time by the man whose karmic privilege it was to assume the custodianship of all the orders and schools in Tibet, the Dalai Lama of her day. Early in this century it was published in a Peking edition that had a preface from the Panchen Lama. It is a book that has been blessed by the visible representatives of the authentic tradition of Tibet. For those who have read the book and compared it to the *Bhagavad Gita*, and to the classical

Indian texts on meditation and the Self, either going back to Patanjali or Shankaracharya or coming down to modern representatives of the old tradition – to those who have done this at even some elementary level, it is clear that the book is extremely difficult but also that it is an invitation and a challenge.

There are those who have actually taken very seriously, on trust, the words of H.P. Blavatsky on the very first page of the book – "Chosen Fragments from the Book of the Golden Precepts, for the Daily Use of Lanoos." Only wishing to become a *lanoo* or a disciple, they aspire to a discipline that is divine but which must be practised every single day. Those who are simple enough, like God's fools, to have this kind of response to the book, and who use it, soon find themselves in the position of asking whether they really understand what is being taught and whether these instructions are living and relevant realities in their lives. No doubt there may be moods in which the text may seem to be empty words, but over a period does it honestly make a difference to one's consciousness, one's daily life, one's capacity for calm self-control and growth in self-knowledge? When a person applies these tests to himself, all that can be said in advance is that people who have so used the book have found it of sufficient help to them to become immeasurably grateful to those responsible for giving the world this version of an old and traditional discipline, which we associate with the Theosophical Movement. Indeed, there must surely be a few for whom the book ultimately ceases to be a book, and for whom the very pathway of ascent through portals becomes a supreme reality in their lives. For them the problem becomes not one of questioning this reality, but one of relating it to the so-called realities of the world in which we live. How do we live this life, not in some secluded and protected spot on earth, but here and now? In crowded cities, among lowly human beings, everything seems to drown and crowd out the message of this book. Anyone who wishes may consider meditation and self-study in the context of the teaching in *The Voice of the Silence*. It seems only appropriate that Theosophical students should avail themselves of the privilege of doing this, not only for their own increasing benefit, but also out of a genuine wish to share with those who may not have had the opportunity to give themselves a chance to use this teaching and this book. Minimally, one could say that this would be no worse than anything else they could think of. But each one must decide on his own.

If we do approach the subject in this context, we might ask how this book, even what one knows of it, helps to link up the contemporary agony with the supreme flights of meditation of the classical past. Astonishingly, both are in the book – at the beginning and at the end. Early in the book we are told about the immense tragedy of the human condition – "Behold the Hosts of Souls. Watch how they hover o'er the stormy sea of human life, and how, exhausted, bleeding, broken-winged, they drop one after other on the swelling waves. Tossed by the fierce winds, chased by the gale, they drift into the eddies and disappear within the first great vortex." The crisis of identity, the psychological terror, the desperate struggle for survival and for a minimum meaning to be attached to one's life – these are all around us. At best we can only imagine the boundless compassion of beings so much greater than ourselves who are capable of comprehending the enormity of the anguish. At the same time, the book tells us what the ideal man of meditation would be like. It gives us a moving and compelling picture, a vibrant image of the man of meditation. It shows how he is mightier than the gods, that he is so strong that he "holdeth life and death in his strong hand." His mind, "like a becalmed and boundless ocean, spreadeth out in shoreless space. So great is the emergence of such a Being, at any time or place hidden in the obscurity of the secret history of mankind, that it is known and recorded and receives a symphonic celebration in all the kingdoms of nature. The whole of nature "thrills with joyous awe and feels subdued."

The text evokes in us memories of a forgotten past, of mythic conceptions, of golden ages that are gone, when men, like children, sat in an atmosphere of trust and peace, with abundant leisure, under the shade of trees. While some came for shelter, some to fall asleep, some to sit and learn, and some to sit and chat about everything ranging from the most metaphysical to the most practical, still others came for the sake of the existential embodiment of the discipline of a life of contemplation. Images of this kind come into our minds, while at the same time we perhaps see that there is a continuity within the agony of mankind throughout history. There is a deeper anguish, a divine discontent at the very core of the human condition, which is as old as man and which is as strikingly pertinent as all the accounts of the needs of our age. Somewhere there is a connection between the tremendous consummation of the Supreme Master of meditation and light – he who has become one with the universe, who has become a living mirror of the glory of the garment of God, of the universe as a whole, of the Self of all creatures – somewhere there is a connection between that Being, if he is a part of the family of man, and all those who are on the verge of disintegration.

There is in every single human being the embryo of this ideal man of meditation, and we can at least imagine what it would be like for such a being to be present somewhere in our midst, if not in ourselves. We also can recognize that we have our own share in the desperate demand for psychological survival. In this way we restore an integrity to our own quest and are somewhat deserving of that illumination which will take hold in our consciousness in relation to the great and priceless teaching. We might begin to wonder whether perhaps there is a golden chord that connects the golden sphere of a man of meditation and the complex intermediary realms in which he must, by pain and anguish and awakening, by knitting together minute golden moments rescued from a great deal of froth and self-deception, come to know himself. If there were not a fundamental connection between meditation and self-study, something of the uniquely precious wisdom in this great text would be lost to us. When we begin to realize this in our lives, we come to appreciate that, while we may not be in a position to make judgments about teachers and schools in a vast and largely unrecorded history or in our own time, nonetheless we do know that there is something profoundly important in stressing both meditation and self-study, in bringing the two together. We must reconcile what looked like a pair of opposites and get beyond despair to something else which allows an existential and dynamic balance between meditation and self-study. This is the quality of compassion. It is in the heart of every human being in his response to human pain, and brings him truly into the fellowship of those Beings of Boundless Compassion.

A man is a Buddha before he seeks to become a Buddha. He is a Buddha potentially. The Buddha at one time must have had a desire to become a Buddha, to understand human pain. The Buddha vow is holy because it is a vow taken on behalf of all. There is in everyone the capacity to want something for the sake of all, and also honestly to want it for oneself. In this there is an authentic mirroring, in every human heart, of the highest, the holiest and the most pregnant of beginnings of the quest. There are many beginnings, many failures, and many seeming endings. The quest itself, since it applies to all beings and not only to any one man, is beginningless and endless. It is universal, since any individual quest in this direction becomes at some point merged into the collective quest. Put in poetical form, or recognized in the simplest feelings, there is something metaphysically important and philosophically fundamental to the connection between meditation or self-transcendence, and the kind of self-study which makes true self-actualization possible. There is a way in which a man can both be out of this world and in this world, can forget himself and yet be more truly himself. These paradoxes of language are difficult to explain at one level and yet we all know them to be the paradoxes of our very lives. In our moments of greatest loneliness we suddenly find a surprising capacity to come closer to beings far removed from us, men of different races and alienated groups in pain. Then we come to feel a brotherhood that is so profound that it could never be secured in any other way. These are part of the everyday experience of mankind.

Here we touch on a crucial emphasis, maintained sedulously by the *Gelukpa* tradition of Tibet, which affirms that unless you spend sufficient time in refining, studying and purifying your motive, in using compassion as fuel to generate the energy needed to take off and land, you should not begin to rush into meditation. It is a slow school, but it greets the aspirant in the name of all. It scorns powers and the notion of one man becoming a superman in isolation from the quest of other men. Making no promises or claims, it does not insult our intelligence by promising us something to be attained without effort.

Are we not old enough in history to be somewhat apprehensive of schools that promise too much and too soon, when we know that this does not work in any sphere of life? Would we go to some local, loud-talking musician who tells us that he could make us as good as Casals in a week? Would we even take him seriously? We might go to him out of fun or sympathy or curiosity. Why in the most sacred of all realms should we be misled? Is it because of our impatience, our feeling of unworthiness, an advance fear of failure? These questions throw us back upon ourselves. In raising them, in probing our own standpoint at the original moment of the beginning of the quest, we make discoveries about ourselves. They are very profound and important, as they may sum up for us a great deal of the past. They would also be crucial in the future where we may come to sense the supreme relevance all along the way, when it is hard and rough, of what Merlin said to Arthur: "Go back to the original moment." If one could understand the fullness of what is anticipated in that original moment of our quest, one could trace the whole curve of our growth that is likely to emerge, with its ups and downs. Yet it cannot tell all as long as there are unknown depths of potentiality and free will in a human being.

A statement in *The Morning of the Magicians* suggests that as long as men want something for nothing, money without work, knowledge without study, power without knowledge, virtue without some form of asceticism, so long will a thousand pseudo-initiatory societies flourish, imitating the truly secret language of the 'technicians of the sacred.' There must be some reason why the integrity of the quest requires that no false flattery be made to the weaker side in every man. *The Voice of the Silence* tells us early on: "Give up thy life, if thou would'st live." That side of you which is afraid, which wants to be cajoled and flattered and promised, which would like an insurance policy, must go, must die. It is only in that dying that you will discover yourself. We all limit ourselves. We engage in a collective act of daily self-denigration of mankind. We impose, in addition to our tangible problems, imaginary and insurmountable difficulties owing to our dogmatic insistence on the finality of our limitations.

The Wisdom-Religion is transmitted so as to restore in the human being, and collectively in the world, the reality of the perfectibility of man, the assurance that men are gods, that any man is capable of reaching the apex, and that the difference between a Buddha or a Christ and any one of us is a difference of degree and not of kind. At the same time it shows that the slaying of the dragon, the putting of the demon under the foot, the command of the sovereign will of the Adept, "Get thee behind me, Satan," are heroic deeds every one of us could accomplish. Potential gods could also become kings. Every man could be a king in his own republic, but he can only become a king and eventually a god if he first experiences the thrill of affirming what it is to be a man – man *qua* man, one who partakes of the glory, the potentiality, the promise and the excellence of human nature, one who shares points of contact with the mightiest man of meditation. He must understand what the power of his thought can do, and discern a connection between the imagination of children and the disciplined imagination of perfected teachers.

With this exalted view of the individual embodiment of the collective potentialities of man, a person can say, "I'm proud to be a man and man enough to give myself a minimum of dignity. I'm willing to be tried, to be tough, to go through a discipline. I'm willing to become a disciple, and dissipate that portion of myself which is pretentious, but which is also my problem and my burden – like the donkey the man carries on his back in the Japanese fable – instead of making it an ever-lengthening shadow by walking away from the sun. I can make that shadow shrink by walking towards the sun, the *Logos* reflected in the great teachers, which is real and in me and every single living being." This is a great affirmation. To make it is profoundly important. It is to affirm in this day and age that it is meaningful for a man to give up lesser pretensions and engage in what may look like presumption, but is really an assertion in his life that he can appreciate the prerogative of what it is to be a *manushya*, a man, a self-conscious being. That is a great step on the path of progressive steps in meditation and self-study.

So far all that has been said is about beginnings, but this really is an arena where the first step seems to be the most difficult. Also, it is a matter of how you define the first step. An analogy may be made here with our experience in the engineering of flying machines. The designs were there; the diagrams were there; the equations were there; the knowledge of what is involved in maintaining a jet engine at high altitudes was there. The tough part was the take-off and landing problem. We now know more widely, in an age when people turn in desperation to a variety of drugs, that it is very difficult to have control over entry into the higher states of consciousness in a manner that will assure a smooth re-entry into ordinary life. It is because of the take-off and landing problem that we need both to be very clear about our beginnings and also to see the whole quest as a re-sharpening of the integrity of the beginning, in relation to meditation and self-study.

In the *Gelukpa* schools one would be told to spend a lot of time expanding compassion but also meditating on meditation. What is one going to meditate on? Meditate on meditation itself. Meditate on men of meditation. In other words, the more you try to meditate, the more you realize that meditation is elusive. But this is an insight that protects you from self-deception. Ultimately, the entire universe is an embodiment of collective mind. Meditation in its fullness is that creative power of the Platonic Demiurge, of the Hindu Visvakarman, of the *Logos* of the Gnostics, which could initiate a whole world. That initiation or inauguration of a world is a representation of the mighty power of meditation. You can become, says *The Voice of the Silence*, one with the power of All-Thought, but you cannot do so until you have expelled every particular thought from your mind-soul. Here is the philosophical and cosmic basis of meditation in its fullness. All meditations can only be stepping stones towards a larger meditation. What will give us a gauge of the quality, strength and meaningfulness of our power to meditate, and of our particular meditations, is our ability to harvest in the realm of self-knowledge that which can be tested in our knowledge and understanding of all other selves. To put this in another way, if to love one person unconditionally is so difficult for us, how extraordinarily remote from us seems to be the conception of those beings who can unconditionally love all living beings. We cannot do it even with one. Now someone might say, "No, but I can do it with one or a few sufficiently to understand in principle what it would be like to do it for all." Someone else might say, "Oh, when I look at my life I find that I don't know what it is fully to love any one, but I do know that somewhere in my loneliness and pain I feel the closeness of anonymous faces, a silent bond of brotherhood between myself and many others.

There are different ways by which we could see in ourselves the embryo of that boundless love and compassion which is the fruit of self-knowledge at its height, where a man becomes self-consciously a universal embodiment of the *Logos*, having no sense of identity except in the very act of mirroring universal light. There must be a tremendous integrity to a teaching and discipline which says that every step counts, that every failure can be used, and that the ashes of your failures will be useful in regrafting and rejuvenating what is like a frail tree that has to be replanted again and again. But the tree one is planting is the tree of immortality. One is trying to bring down into the lesser vehicles of the more differentiated planes of matter the glorious vesture of immortality, which showed more clearly when one was a baby, which one saluted in the first cry of birth, and of which one becomes somewhat aware at the moment of death.

There is a hint at the moments of birth and death, something like an intimation of the hidden glory of man, but during life one is not so awake. This becomes a problem of memory and forgetfulness. The chain of decline is started. It was classically stated in the second chapter of the *Gita*: "He who attendeth to the inclinations of the senses, in them hath a concern; from this concern is created passion, from passion anger, from anger is produced delusion, from delusion a loss of the memory, from the loss of memory loss of discrimination, and from loss of discrimination, loss of all!" Every man is fragmenting himself, spending himself, limiting himself, finitizing himself, localizing himself, to such a degree, with such an intensity and irregularity, and such a frenetic, feverish restlessness, that he is consuming himself. Physiologically we know that we cannot beat the clocktime processes of the changes in the physical body. Therefore we cannot expect to find the elixir of immortality on the physical plane. But we all know that by attending to the very process of growth and change, and by awareness of what happens to us in sickness, that we do have some control and can make a difference by our very attitude and acceptance of the process. If you are very ill, by worrying about it you are going to make yourself worse, but there are people who are really quite ill, who by acceptance have gained something of the aroma of well-being.

These are everyday facts having analogues and roots in a causal realm of ideation and creative imagination which gives shape and form to the subtle vehicle, through which a transmission could take place of the immortal, indestructible and inexhaustible light of the *Logos* which is in every man and came into the world with every child. It is the radiance of Shekinah, the *nur* of Allah, the light of St. John. It is a light that looks like darkness and is not to be mistaken for those things that have a glamour on the sensory plane. To bring it down or make it transmit through the causal realm and become a living *tejas* or light-energy issuing forth from the fingers and all the windows and apertures of the human body is, of course, asking for a great deal. But what one is asking is meaningful, and we have got to try to understand.

It is so important in this quest to keep asking questions, both about apprenticeship in meditation and the repeated attempts and failures at gaining self-knowledge, that this in itself brings about a great discovery. There is a critical factor or determining role that may be assigned to what *The Voice of the Silence* calls the principle of sifting. "'Great Sifter' is the name of the 'Heart Doctrine.'" The ratio between meaning and experience, which in Plato's definition of insight is the learning capacity of the human soul, is that which enables one man to learn from one experience what another man will not learn in a lifetime. We see this all around us. We often see ourselves repeating the same mistakes and at other points we are relieved that we finally learnt something sufficiently well. That is the x-factor, the mystery of each human being, the capacity to be a learner when it is tough, to say, "I don't want to kid myself." In this way a man builds a raised platform of confidence that is authentic and stable because the man at the height of the quest is a man of such supreme confidence that it is no longer personal. It is the confidence of the universe, and he embodies it. He becomes a conscious agent of the collective and creative will in the universe. What this means in another sense is spontaneous forgetfulness of self. He is so assured that he doesn't have to claim anything. He can forget name and form. He can totally afford not to think of the small self, the little 'me,' because he has accepted and inherited, come to embody, renounce and enjoy, the entirety of a universe of infinite possibilities. He acquires the psychological capacity to maintain a meaningful relationship between a universe of ontological plenty, analogous to a realm of illimitable light where giving does not deplete, and a universe of scarcity, a region of finite matter where there are hard choices to be made and where to move in one direction is to negate another, to take one thing is to give up something else, and to use time or energy in one way is to deny their use in other ways. Not to see the latter is to be a fool. Not to see the former is to deny oneself the opportunity to enjoy and actualize the potentiality and plenty of the universe in every man.

Instead of being depressed that we cannot really do more than meditate in small ways and that we are liable again and again to get into the cuckoo cloud of fantasy which we have to give up, we must say, "I will persist." What is important in meditation is continuity of consciousness. All attempts at meditation are merely fumbling attempts at building a line of life's meditation. A being who does this fully, like the Buddha, could say when asked whether he was a man or a god, "I am awake." To be fully awake is difficult. We are partly awake and partly asleep. One only fully meditates when one is fully awake and one cannot be fully awake except in relation to the One which is hidden, the supreme reality which has no form, which will never show its face, and yet which can include all faces and assume all forms. One is fully awake only when one can know proportionality, and accurately assign relative reality to everything. One must be able to say, "Yes, that's true. I can understand Eichmann. I know there is that in me which can be the embryo of a Hitler. I also know there is that in me which makes me feel close to Christ." A man can then expand his conception of the Self, so that nothing outside annoys or attracts him of which he cannot see in himself exact and genuine analogues. He can also say, "Somewhere

I understand, at the very root of my nature, what it would be like to visualize the Golden Age where all men are consciously and continually bathing in the noon-day glory of the Divine." As Paul Hazard said: "As long as there are children, there will be a Golden Age." All of us can attempt to make mental images of the Golden Age, and to do so is deeply therapeutic, individually and collectively.

The *Gelukpa* tradition, which seems so demanding, has points of contact for all of us with our daily lives. One could say that to meditate is to remove hindrances to continuity of consciousness caused by the modifications of the mind. We do have to go on doing this again and again. You do it much better when you sit down to it and prepare for it properly, but above all you do it best when you meditate on universal good, as Plato taught. When you sit down to meditate on universal good – which you cannot conceptualize and which includes and transcends all conceptions of welfare and particular goods – you can free yourself from a great deal of tension. But you cannot stay there very long without the danger of falling asleep, of becoming passive, of fantasizing. You have to pull out at the right time. You do not want to dilly-dally, least of all to be anxious and settle for imitations. You want the real thing even if for a moment. The more you do this, the more it becomes like breathing. You do not have control over breathing, but fortunately most of the time your breathing can take care of itself.

What about mental breathing? That is where discipline is needed in regard to meditation. You can do something about the disordered, unregulated mental breathing, the way in which you receive the world of objects and in which you forget that awareness which you do have of the One that is hidden. Unless you can regulate this mental breathing, you cannot authentically laugh at and look at the absurdities and weaknesses of your lower self and make it genuinely meaningful for you to say, "I am more than you think. I am more than anyone else understands. And so is everyone else." Not only that, but this can be extended. One can be convinced in one's darkest hour, like men in concentration camps, that there is something profoundly precious to one's own individual sense of being human. One can be proud of what one somewhere knows one has to give to the world, which can be an authentic gift to the whole of mankind. When one can legitimately be proud of that, and increase the content of that knowledge, it ceases to be a feeling. Then one is not afraid of anything in oneself. Then one can understand and rejoice in the statement in the *Light on the Path*:". . . no man is your enemy, no man is your friend. All alike are your teachers."

Life is a school. There is an eternal learning and at any given time you alone can determine how much improved you are as a learner. One comes to see that while the whole of life is a teacher of concentration, that the whole of life also makes it difficult for you to retain the power needed to become continuous in your consciousness. This means that you are both immortal and mortal. To recover immortality while you are aware that you are mortal is not easy. You can do it at one level in one way at one time. You can feel it at some other time in a certain mood. To really do it, however, you have to know it in the classical sense defined by Plotinus – by reason, by experience, and by illumination, independently and by each. You have only half-knowledge otherwise. Knowing it mentally is not enough, though it is important. Knowing it in terms of a peak experience, though very grand, is not adequate to the demands of life. That we may fail to know independently by an appeal to illumination, reason and experience is to say that we know nothing. Yet, what we seek potentially includes all knowledge. These are paradoxes which become realities, truths about consciousness, because consciousness knows no limitations. The power of identification, the power of projection, the power of making yourself, of self-analyzing reflection or *svasamvedana*, is immense. You can play roles and if you can play every role, you can also play the role of the Christ. You can play the role of the Buddha. But you cannot begin to understand what this means unless you can also recognize what it is to play the role of a Hitler, and furthermore, what it means to be the *Kutastha*, he who plays no role whatsoever.

There is an integrity to this quest which is coeval with the whole of life. No one can reduce it to a technique. It is a very beautiful teaching. There never could be enough time, nor could there be any meaningfulness in assuming that anyone could ever fully tell anyone else what is involved. In the end each has to plunge into the stream. Every attempt at meditation within the context of universal meditation, and every attempt at self-knowledge within the context of the fullest concept of self-knowledge, is a meaningful stepping-stone. It can be carried forward in a ceaseless process of alchemy. Once we decide not to settle for the easier way out, once we taste the joy of the toughness of the Path, then we also find it is fun. It is enjoyable. One can truly say that he even enjoys knowing his failures. Then one may fall into another trap. One may too much enjoy being aware, but if one does, life will correct. We will suddenly look and find that we are ready to plunge into the abyss again.

All of these are representations of what in reality is a process of building, out of the repeated dyings of our vehicles, that fabric of stable, subtle, radiant matter which can be inhabited by ceaseless ideation and universal contemplation, so that one can be a man of meditation who can live as and for every other being. You are a *Bodhisattva*. You can become a Buddha. It is not possible for any of us to say this to ourselves except in the context of some genuine understanding. Otherwise it is false. Hence, of course, we need teachers. The best Teachers give us the confidence that we have access, each uniquely but within ourselves, to that triadic sanctuary within, which becomes the gateway to the cosmic triad. We can then say, as did the ancient Aryans, *Atmanam Atmana pasya*: "See the universal self through your own immortal self." The issue is one of reaffirmation but it is a reaffirmation we can receive only from those who, as they affirm it, can make us believe. Of this we could never be judges, because we would never know whether the problem was in us or in them. But if we are sufficiently in earnest we will know, even though we will make mistakes. We will say, "This is real. This not only speaks to me; this speaks within me. I am hearing a voice which is the voice of my own Self." When this becomes real for a man, then indeed he is blessed. He enters that kind of initiation and reaches that threshold beyond which the quest will be extremely challenging, but from which he cannot fall back.

There is such a point. To reach that point is possible. This is the great priceless boon of learning the truth about meditation and the Self that all the great texts give, which was for long periods of time used as the basis of a discipline in secret sanctuaries of initiation, and which we have in *The Voice of the Silence*, the voice of *Brahma Vach*. It is possible for any person to make the wisdom of this book a living power in his life. Then he does not have to be wasting energy and time as to what he thinks of someone else, because that no longer matters, since there is no longer any 'someone else.' He has become the One. The seeker has become the object of his quest. There is no gap between himself as a knower and the known and the knowledge. The three are in one. They are all in one at the beginning, but unconsciously to him. Self-consciously they become one again. Until he reaches that point, or until he makes a proper beginning, let him not waste time running around in circles, expending energy, asking all those kinds of questions which are really the questions of the man who is never going to climb mountains, who is never going to swim, who is never going to walk. The lame cannot be made to walk unless they want to walk upon this path. The sick cannot be healed unless they wish to be healed. Therefore we are profoundly grateful to all those Teachers of *Gupta Vidya* who once again gave us the knowledge and the assurance, the faith and the conviction, that we are the Path, that we can heal ourselves, and that we can become what we may now think is impossible. We can become that, not for our own sake, but for the sake of all and thereby become guides and exemplars to those who need our help.

Toronto
October 9, 1971
Hermes, March 1976

GLOSSARY

The Yoga Sutras of Patanjali

A

Absoluteness. When predicated of the UNIVERSAL PRINCIPLE, it denotes an abstract noun, which is more correct and logical than to apply the adjective "absolute " to that which has neither attributes nor limitations, nor can IT have any.

Adam (*Heb.*). In the *Kabalah* Adam is the "only-begotten", and means also "red earth". (See "Adam-Adami" in the *S.D.* II p. 452.) It is almost identical with *Athamas* or *Thomas*, and is rendered into Greek by *Didumos*, the "twin"– Adam, "the first", in chap. 1 of *Genesis,* being shown, "male-female."

Adam Kadmon (*Heb.*). Archetypal Man; Humanity. The "Heavenly Man" not fallen into sin; Kabalists refer it to the Ten Sephiroth on the plane of human perception. [w.w.w.]

In the *Kabalah* Adam Kadmon is the manifested Logos corresponding to our *Third* Logos; the Unmanifested being the first paradigmic ideal Man, and symbolizing the Universe in *abscondito*, or in its "privation" in the Aristotelean sense. The First Logos is the "Light of the World", the Second and the Third – its gradually deepening shadows.

Adept (*Lat.*). *Adeptus*, "He who has obtained." In Occultism one who has reached the stage of Initiation, and become a Master in the science of Esoteric philosophy.

Âditi (*Sk.*). The Vedic name for the *Mûlaprakriti* of the Vedantists; the abstract aspect of Parabrahman, though both unmanifested and unknowable. In the *Vedas* Âditi is the "Mother-Goddess", her terrestrial symbol being infinite and shoreless space.

Adwaita (*Sk.*). A Vedânta sect. The non-dualistic (A-dwaita) school of Vedântic philosophy founded by Sankarâchârya, the greatest of the historical Brahmin sages. The two other schools are the Dwaita (dualistic) and the Visishtadwaita; all the three call themselves Vedântic.

Adwaitin (*Sk.*). A follower of the said school.

Æther (*Gr.*). With the ancients the divine luminiferous substance which pervades the whole universe, the "garment" of the Supreme Deity, Zeus, or Jupiter. With the moderns, Ether, for the meaning of which in physics and chemistry see Webster's *Dictionary* or any other. In esotericism Æther is the third principle of the Kosmic Septenary; the Earth being the lowest, then the Astral light, Ether and *Âkâsa* (phonetically *Âkâsha*) the highest.

Agathodæmon (*Gr.*). The beneficent, good Spirit as contrasted with the bad one, Kakodæmon. The "Brazen Serpent" of the Bible is the former; the flying serpents of fire are an aspect of Kakodæmon. The Ophites called Agathodæmon the Logos and Divine Wisdom, which in the Bacchanalian Mysteries was represented by a serpent erect on a pole.

Agathon (*Gr.*). Plato's Supreme Deity. Lit., "The Good", our ALAYA, or "Universal Soul".

Agni (*Sk.*). The God of Fire in the Veda; the oldest and the most revered of Gods in India. He is one of the three great deities: Agni, Vâyu and Sûrya, and also all the three, as he is the triple aspect of fire; in heaven as the Sun; in the atmosphere or air (Vâyu), as Lightning; on. earth, as ordinary Fire. Agni belonged to the earlier Vedic *Trimûrti* before Vishnu was given a place of honour and before Brahmâ and Siva were invented.

Agnishwattas (*Sk.*). A class of Pitris, the creators of the first ethereal race of men. Our solar ancestors as contrasted with the *Barhishads,* the "lunar" Pitris or ancestors, though otherwise explained in the *Purânas.*

Aham (*Sk.*). "I" – the basis of *Ahankâra*, Self-hood.

Ahankâra (*Sk.*). The conception of "I", Self-consciousness or Self-identity; the "I", the egotistical and *mâyâvic* principle in man, due to our ignorance which separates our "I" from the Universal ONE-SELF Personality, Egoism.

Ain Soph (*Heb.*). The "Boundless" or Limitless; Deity emanating and extending. [w.w.w.]

Ain Soph is also written *En Soph* and *Ain Suph*, no one, not even Rabbis, being sure of their vowels. In the religious metaphysics of the old Hebrew philosophers, the ONE Principle was an abstraction, like Parabrahmam, though modern Kabbalists have succeeded now, by dint of mere sophistry and paradoxes, in making a "Supreme God" of it and nothing higher. But with the early Chaldean Kabbalists Ain Soph is "without form or being", having "no likeness with anything else" (Franck, *Die Kabbala*, p. 126). That Ain Soph has never been considered as the "Creator" is proved by even such an orthodox Jew as Philo calling the "Creator" the *Logos*, who stands next the "Limitless One", and the "Second God". "The Second God is its (Ain Soph's) wisdom", says Philo

(*Quaest. et Solut.*). Deity is NO-THING; it is nameless, and therefore called Ain Soph; the word *Ain* meaning NOTHING. (See Franck's *Kabbala*, p. 153 ff.)

Aitareya (*Sk.*). The name of an Aranyaka (Brâhmana) and a Upanishad of the *Rig Veda*. Some of its portions are purely Vedântic.

Akâsa (*Sk.*). The subtle, supersensuous spiritual essence which pervades all space; the primordial substance erroneously identified with Ether. But it is to Ether what Spirit is to Matter, or *Âtmâ* to *Kâma-rûpa*. It is, in fact, the Universal Space in which lies inherent the eternal Ideation of the Universe in its ever-changing aspects on the planes of matter and objectivity, and from which radiates the *First Logos*, or expressed thought. This is why it is stated in the *Purânas* that Âkâsa has but one attribute, namely sound, for sound is but the translated symbol of Logos – "Speech" in its mystic sense. In the same sacrifice (*the Jyotishtoma Agnishtoma*) it is called the "God Âkâsa". In these sacrificial mysteries Âkâsa is the all-directing 'and omnipotent Deva who plays the part of Sadasya, the superintendent over the magical effects of the religious performance, and it had its own appointed Hotri (priest) in days of old, who took its name. The Âkâsa is the indispensable agent of every *Krityâ* (magical performance) religious or profane. The expression "to stir up the Brahmâ", means to stir up the power which lies latent at the bottom of every magical operation, Vedic sacrifices being in fact nothing if not ceremonial magic. This power is the Âkâsa – in another aspect, *Kundalini* – occult electricity, the alkahest of the alchemists in one sense, or the universal solvent, the same *anima mundi* on the higher plane as the *astral light* is on the lower. "At the moment of the sacrifice the priest becomes imbued with the spirit of Brahmâ, is, for the time being, Brahmâ himself". (*Isis Unveiled*).

Alaya (*Sk.*). The Universal Soul (See *Secret Doctrine* Vol. I. pp. 47 *et seq.*). The name belongs to the Tibetan system of the contemplative *Mahâyâna* School. Identical with *Âkâsa* in its mystic sense, and with *Mulâprâkriti,* in its essence, as it is the basis or root of all things.

Amânasa (*Sk.*). The " Mindless", the early races of this planet; also certain Hindu gods.

Ambhâmsi (*Sk.*). A name of the chief of the Kumâras Sanat-Sujâta, signifying the "waters". This epithet will become more comprehensible when we remember that the later type of Sanat-Sujâta was Michael, the Archangel, who is called in the Talmud "the Prince of *Waters*", and in the Roman Catholic Church is regarded as the patron of gulfs and promontories. Sanat-Sujâta is the immaculate son of the immaculate mother (Ambâ or Aditi, chaos and space) or the "waters" of limitless space. (See *Secret Doctrine*-, Vol. I., p. 460.)

Androgyne Ray (*Esot.*). The first differentiated ray; the Second Logos;

Adam Kadmon in the *Kabalah;* the "male and female created he them", of the first chapter of *Genesis.*

Anima Mundi (*Lat.*). The"Soul of the World", the same as the *Alaya* of the Northern Buddhists; the divine essence which permeates, animates and informs all, from the smallest atom of matter to man and god. It is in a sense the "seven-skinned mother" of the stanzas in the *Secret Doctrine,* the essence of seven planes of sentience, consciousness and differentiation, moral and physical. In its highest aspect it is *Nirvâna,* in its lowest Astral Light. It was feminine with the Gnostics, the early Christians and the Nazarenes; bisexual with other sects, who considered it only in its four lower planes. Of igneous, ethereal nature in the objective world of form (and then ether), and divine and spiritual in its three higher planes. When it is said that every human soul was born by detaching itself from the *Anima Mundi,* it means, esoterically, that our higher Egos are of an essence identical with It, which is a radiation of the ever unknown Universal ABSOLUTE.

Annamaya Kosha (*Sk.*). A Vedantic term. The same as *Sthûla Sharîra* or the physical body. It is the first "sheath" of the *five* sheaths accepted by the Vedantins, a sheath being the same as that which is called "principle" in Theosophy.

Anoia (*Gr.*). "Want of understanding", "folly". *Anoia* is the name given by Plato and others to the lower Manas when too closely allied with Kâma, which is irrational (*agnoia*). The Greek word agnoia is evidently a derivation from and cognate to the Sanskrit word *ajnâna* (phonetically, *agnyana*) or ignorance, irrationality, absence of knowledge. (See "Agnoia" and "Agnostic".)

Antahkarana (*Sk.*), or Antaskarana. The term has various meanings, which differ with every school of philosophy and sect. Thus Sankârachârya renders the word as "understanding"; others, as "the internal instrument, the Soul, formed by the thinking principle and egoism"; whereas the Occultists explain it as the *path* or bridge between the Higher and the Lower Manas, the divine *Ego,* and the *personal* Soul of man. It serves as a medium of communication between the two, and conveys from the Lower to the Higher Ego all those personal impressions and thoughts of men which can, by their nature, be assimilated and stored by the undying Entity, and be thus made immortal with it, these being the only elements of the evanescent *Personality* that survive death and time. It thus stands to reason that only that which is noble, spiritual and divine in man can testify in Eternity to his having lived.

Anthropomorphism (*Gr.*). From "*anthropos*" meaning man. The act of endowing god or gods with a human form and human attributes or qualities.

Anugîtâ (*Sk.*). One of the *Upanishads.* A very occult treatise. (*See The sacred Books of the East.*)

Anupâdaka (*Sk.*). Anupapâdaka, also Aupapâduka; means parentless", "self-existing", born without any parents or progenitors. A term applied to certain self-created gods, and the Dhyâni Buddhas.

Arjuna (*Sk.*). Lit., the "white". The third of the five Brothers Pandu or the reputed Sons of Indra (esoterically the same as Orpheus). A disciple of Krishna, who visited him and married Su-bhadrâ, his sister, besides many other wives, according to the allegory. During the fratricidal war between the *Kauravas* and the *Pândavas,* Krishna instructed him in the highest philosophy, while serving as his charioteer. (*See Bhagavad Gîtâ.*)

Arûpa (*Sk.*). "Bodiless", formless, as opposed to *rûpa*, "body", or form.

Arvâksrotas (*Sk.*). The *seventh* creation, that of man, in the *Vishnu Purâna.*

Âryasangha (*Sk.*). The Founder of the *first* Yogâchârya School. This Arhat, a direct disciple of Gautama, the Buddha, is most unaccountably mixed up and confounded with a personage of the same name, who is said to have lived in Ayôdhya (Oude) about the fifth or sixth century of our era, and taught Tântrika worship in addition to the Yogâchârya system. Those who sought to make it popular, claimed that he was the same Âryasangha, that had been a follower of Sâkyamuni, and that he was 1,000 years old. Internal evidence alone is sufficient to show that the works written by him and translated about the year 600 of our era, works full of Tantra worship, ritualism, and tenets followed now considerably by the "red-cap" sects in Sikhim, Bhutan, and Little Tibet, cannot be the same as the lofty system of the early Yogâcharya school of pure Buddhism, which is neither northern nor southern, but absolutely esoteric. Though none of the genunine Yogâchârya books (the *Narjol chodpa*) have ever been made public or marketable, yet one finds in the *Yogâchârya Bhûmi Shâstra* of the *pseudo-*Âryasangha a great deal from the older system, into the tenets of which he may have been initiated. It is, however, so mixed up with Sivaism and Tantrika magic and superstitions, that the work defeats its own end, notwithstanding its remarkable dialectical subtilty. (See the *Theosophical Glossary*)

Asakrit Samâdhi (*Sk.*). A certain degree of ecstatic contemplation. A stage in *Samâdhi.*

Âsana (*Sk.*). The third stage of *Hatha Yoga*, one of the prescribed postures of meditation.

Ashta Siddhis (*Sk.*). The eight consummations in the practice of Hatha Yoga.

Astral Body, or Astral "Double". The ethereal counterpart or shadow of man or animal. The ***Linga Sharira,*** the "Doppelgäinger". The reader must not confuse it with the ASTRAL SOUL, another name for the lower Manas, or Kama-Manas so-called, the reflection of the HIGHER EGO.

Astral Light (*Occult.*). The invisible region that surrounds our globe, as it does every other, and corresponding as the second Principle of Kosmos (the third being Life, of which it is the vehicle) to the *Linga Sharira* or the Astral Double in man. A subtle Essence visible only to a clairvoyant eye, and the lowest but one (*viz.*, the earth), of the Seven Akâsic or Kosmic Principles. Eliphas Levi calls it the great Serpent and the Dragon from which radiates on Humanity every evil influence. This is so; but why not add that the Astral Light gives out nothing but what it has received; that it is the great terrestrial crucible, in which the vile emanations of the earth (moral and physical) upon which the Astral Light is fed, are all converted into their subtlest essence, and radiated back intensified, thus becoming epidemics – moral, psychic and physical. Finally, the Astral Light is the same as the *Sidereal Light* of Paracelsus and other Hermetic philosophers. "Physically, it is the ether of modern science. Metaphysically, and in its spiritual, or occult sense, ether is a great deal more than is often imagined. In occult physics, and alchemy, it is well demonstrated to enclose within its shoreless waves not only Mr. Tyndall's *'promise* and potency of every quality of life', but also the *realization* of the potency of every quality of spirit. Alchemists and Hermetists believe that their *astral*, or sidereal ether, besides the above properties of sulphur, and white and red magnesia, or *magnes*, is the *anima mundi*, the workshop of Nature and of all the Kosmos, spiritually, as well as physically. The 'grand magisterium' asserts itself in the phenomenon of mesmerism, in the 'levitation' of human and inert objects; and may be called the ether from its spiritual aspect. The designation *astral* is ancient, and was used by some of the Neo-platonists, although it is claimed by some that the word was coined by the Martinists. Porphyry describes the celestial body which is always joined with the soul as 'immortal, luminous, and star-like'. The root of this word may be found, perhaps, in the Scythic *Aist-aer* – which means star, or the Assyrian *Istar*, which, according to Burnouf has the same sense." (*Isis Unveiled.*)

Asuras (*Sk.*). Exoterically, elementals and evil, gods – considered maleficent; demons, and *no* gods. But esoterically – the reverse. For in the most ancient portions of the *Rig Veda*, the term is used for the Supreme Spirit, and therefore the Asuras are spiritual and divine It is only in the last book of the *Rig Veda*, its latest part, and in the *Atharva Veda*, and the *Brâhmanas*, that the epithet, which had been given to Agni, the greatest Vedic Deity, to Indra and Varuna, has come to signify the reverse of gods. *Asu* means breath, and it is with his breath that Prajâpati (Brahmâ) creates the Asuras. When ritualism and dogma got the better of the Wisdom religion, the initial letter **a** was adopted as a negative prefix, and the term ended by signifying "not a god", and Sura only a deity. But in the Vedas the Suras have ever been connected with *Surya*, the sun, and regarded as *inferior* deities, devas.

Aswattha (*Sk.*). The **Bo-tree**, the tree of knowledge, *ficus religiosa*.

Atmâ (or **Atman**) (*Sk.*). The Universal Spirit, the divine Monad, the 7th Principle, so-called, in the septenary constitution of man. The Supreme Soul.

Atma-bhu (*Sk.*). Soul-existence, or existing as soul. (See "*Alaya*".)

Atmabodha (*Sk.*). Lit., "Self-knowledge"; the title of a Vedantic treatise by Sankârachârya.

Atma-jnâni (*Sk.*). The Knower of the World-Soul, or Soul in general.

Atma Vidyâ (*Sk.*). The highest form of spiritual knowledge; lit., "Soul-knowledge".

Atri, Sons of (*Sk.*). A class of Pitris, the "ancestors of man", or the so-called Prâjapâti, "progenitors"; one of the seven Rishis who form the constellation of the Great Bear.

Attavada (*Pali*). The sin of personality.

Aum (*Sk.*). The sacred syllable; the triple-lettered unit; hence the trinity in One.

Avalokiteswara (*Sk.*). "The on-looking Lord" In the exoteric interpretation, he is Padmapâni (the lotus bearer and the lotus-born) in Tibet, the first divine ancestor of the Tibetans, the complete incarnation or Avatar of Avalokiteswara; but in esoteric philosophy Avaloki, the "on-looker", is the Higher Self, while Padmapâni is the Higher Ego or Manas. The mystic formula "Om mani padme hum" is specially used to invoke their joint help. While popular fancy claims for Avalokiteswara many incarnations on earth, and sees in him, not very wrongly, the spiritual guide of every believer, the esoteric interpretation sees in him the Logos, both celestial and human. Therefore, when the Yogâchârya School has declared Avalokiteswara as Padmâpani "to be the Dhyâni Bodhisattva of Amitâbha Buddha", it is indeed, because the former is *the spiritual reflex in the world of forms* of the latter, both being one – one in heaven, the other on earth.

Avatâra (*Sk.*). Divine incarnation. The descent of a god or some exalted Being, who has progressed beyond the necessity of Rebirths, into the body of a simple mortal. Krishna was an avatar of Vishnu. The Dalai Lama is regarded as an avatar of Avalokiteswara, and the Teschu Lama as one of Tson-kha-pa, or Amitâbha. There are two kinds of avatars: those born from woman, and the parentless, the *anupapâdaka*.

Avidyâ (*Sk.*). Opposed to *Vidyâ*, Knowledge. Ignorance which proceeds from, and is produced by the illusion of the Senses or *Viparyaya*.

B.

Barhishad (*Sk.*). A class of the "lunar" Pitris or "Ancestors", Fathers, who are believed in popular superstition to have kept up in their past incarnations the household sacred flame and made fire-offerings. Esoterically the Pitris who evolved their shadows or *chhayas* to make there-with the first man. (See *Secret Doctrine*, Vol. II.)

Bhagavad-Gita (*Sk.*). Lit., "the Lord's Song". A portion of the Mahabharata, the great epic poem of India. It contains a dialogue wherein Krishna—the "Charioteer"—and Arjuna, his Chela, have a discussion upon the highest spiritual philosophy. The work is pre-eminently occult or esoteric.

Bhagavat (*Sk.*). A title of the Buddha and of Krishna. "The Lord" literally.

Bhâshya (*Sk.*). A commentary.

Bodhisattva (*Sk.*). Lit., "he, whose essence (*sattva*) has become intelligence *(bodhi)*"; those who need but one more incarnation to become perfect Buddhas, i.e., to be entitled to Nirvâna. This, as applied to *Manushi* (terrestrial) Buddhas. In the metaphysical sense, *Bodhisattva* is a title given to the sons of the celestial *Dhyâni* Buddhas.

Brahma (*Sk.*). The student must distinguish between Brahma the neuter, and Brahmâ, the male creator of the Indian Pantheon. The former, Brahma or Brahman, is the impersonal, supreme and uncognizable Principle of the Universe from the essence of which all emanates, and into which all returns, which is incorporeal, immaterial, unborn, eternal, beginningless and endless. It is all-pervading, animating the highest god as well as the smallest mineral atom. Brahmâ on the other hand, the male and the alleged Creator, exists periodically in his manifestation only, and then again goes into pralaya, i.e., disappears and is annihilated.

Brahmâ's Day. A period of 2,160,000,000 years during which Brahmâ having emerged out of his golden egg (*Hiranyagarbha*), creates and fashions the material world (being simply the fertilizing and creative force in Nature). After this period, the worlds being destroyed in turn, by fire and water, he vanishes with objective nature, and then comes Brahmâ's Night.

Brahmâ's Night. A period of equal duration, during which Brahmâ is said to be asleep. Upon awakening he recommences the process, and this goes on for an AGE of Brahmâ composed of alternate "Days", and "Nights", and lasting 100 years (of 2,160,000,000 years each). It requires fifteen figures to express the duration of such an age; after the expiration of which the *Mahapralaya* or the Great Dissolution sets in, and lasts in its turn for the same space of fifteen figures.

Brahmâ Vâch (*Sk.*). Male and female Brahmâ. Vâch is also some-times called the female logos; for Vâch means Speech, literally. (See *Manu* Book I., and *Vishnu Purâna*.)

Brahma Vidyâ (*Sk.*). The knowledge, the esoteric science, about the two Brahmas and their true nature.

Brahmâ Virâj (*Sk.*). The same: Brahmâ separating his body into two halves, male and female, creates in them Vâch and Virâj. In plainer terms and *esotericlly* Brahmâ the Universe, differentiating, produced thereby material nature, Virâj, and spiritual intelligent Nature, Vâch – which is the *Logos* of Deity or the manifested expression of the eternal divine Ideation.

Brâhman (*Sk.*). The highest of the four castes in India, one supposed or rather fancying himself, as high among men, as Brahman, the ABSOLUTE of the Vedantins, is high among, or above the gods.

Brahmâputrâs (*Sk.*). The Sons of Brahmâ.

Buddha (*Sk.*). Lit., "The Enlightened". The highest degree of knowledge. To become a Buddha one has to break through the bondage of sense and personality; to acquire a complete perception of the REAL SELF and learn not to separate it from all otherselves; to learn by experience the utter unreality of all phenomena of the visible Kosmos foremost of all; to reach a complete detachment from all that is evanescent and finite, and live while yet on Earth in the immortal and the everlasting alone, in a supreme state of holiness.

Buddhi (*Sk.*). Universal Soul or Mind. *Mahâbuddhi* is a name of Mahat (see "Alaya"); also the spiritual Soul in man (the sixth principle), the vehicle of Atmâ exoterically the seventh.

Buddhism. Buddhism is now split into two distinct Churches : the Southern and the Northern Church. The former is said to be the purer form, as having preserved more religiously the original teachings of the Lord Buddha. It is the religion of Ceylon, Siam, Burmah and other places, while Northern Buddhism is confined to Tibet, China and Nepaul. Such a distinction, however, is incorrect. If the Southern Church is nearer, in that it has not departed, except perhaps in some trifling dogmas due to the many councils held after the death of the Master, from the public or *exoteric* teachings of Sâkyamuni – the Northern Church is the outcome of Siddhârta Buddha's esoteric teachings which he confined to his elect Bhikshus and Arhats. In fact, Buddhism in the present age, cannot he justly judged either by one or the other of its exoteric popular forms. Real Buddhism can be appreciated only by blending the philosophy of the Southern Church and the metaphysics of the Northern Schools. If one seems too iconoclastic and sterile, and the other too metaphysical and transcendental, even to being overgrown with the weeds of Indian exotericism – many of the gods of its Pantheon having been transplanted under new names to Tibetan soil – it is entirely due to the popular expression of Buddhism in both Churches. Correspondentially they stand in their relation to each other as Protestantism to Roman Catholicism. Both err by an excess of zeal and erroneous interpretations, though neither the Southern nor the Northern Buddhist clergy have ever departed from truth consciously, still less have they acted under the dictates of *priestocracy*, ambition, or with an eye to personal gain and power, as the two Christian Churches have.

C

Causal Body. This "body", which is no body either objective or subjective, but *Buddhi*, the Spiritual Soul, is so called because it is the direct cause of the Sushupti condition, leading to the *Turya* state, the highest state of *Samadhi*. It is called *Karanopadhi*, "the basis of the Cause", by the Târaka Raja Yogis; and in the Vedânta system it corresponds to both the *Vignânamaya* and *Anandamaya Kosha*, the latter coming next to Atma, and therefore being the vehicle of the universal Spirit. Buddhi alone could not be called a "Causal Body ", but becomes so in conjunction with Manas, the incarnating Entity or EGO.

Chakra (*Sk.*). A wheel, a disk, or the circle of Vishnu generally. Used also of a cycle of time, and with other meanings.

Chaldeans, or *Kasdim*. At first a tribe, then a caste of learned Kabbalists. They were the *savants,* the magians of Babylonia, astrologers and diviners. The famous Hillel, the precursor of Jesus in philosophy and in ethics, was a Chaldean. Franck in his *Kabbala* points to the close resemblance of the "secret doctrine" found in the *Avesta* and the religious metaphysics of the Chaldees.

Chelâ (*Sk.*). A disciple, the pupil of a Guru or Sage, the follower of some adept of a school of philosophy (*lit.,* child).

Chhâyâ (*Sk.*). "Shade" or " Shadow". The name of a creature produced by Sanjnâ, the wife of Surya, from herself (astral body). Unable to endure the ardour of her husband, Sanjnâ left Chhâyâ in her place as a wife, going herself away to perform austerities. Chhâyâ is the astral image of a person in esoteric philosophy.

Chhaya loka (*Sk.*). The world of Shades; like Hades, the world of the *Eidola* and *Umbræ*. We call it *Kâmaloka*.

Chidâkâsam (*Sk.*). The field, or basis of consciousness.

Chohan (*Tib.*). "Lord" or "Master" ; a chief; thus **Dhyan-Chohan** would answer to "Chief of the Dhyanis", or celestial Lights – which in English would be translated Archangels.

Chréstos (*Gr.*). The early Gnostic form of Christ. It was used in the fifth century B.C. by Æschylus, Herodotus, and others. The *Manteumata pythochresta,* or the "oracles delivered by a Pythian god" "through a pythoness, are mentioned by the former (*Choeph.*901). *Chréstian* is not only "the seat of an oracle", but an offering to, or for, the oracle.

Chréstés is one who explains oracles, "a prophet and soothsayer", and

Chrésterios one who serves an oracle or a god. The earliest Christian writer, Justin Martyr, in his first *Apology* calls his co-religionists Chréstians. It is only through ignorance that men call themselves Christians instead of Chréstians," says Lactantius (lib. iv., cap. vii.). The terms Christ and Christians, spelt originally Chrést and Chréstians, were borrowed from the Temple vocabulary of the Pagans. Chréstos meant in that vocabulary a disciple on probation, a candidate for hierophantship. When he had attained to this through initiation, long trials, and suffering, and had been "*anointed*" (i.e., "rubbed with oil', as were Initiates and even idols of the gods, as the last touch of ritualistic observance), his name was changed into Christos, the "purified", in esoteric or mystery language. In mystic symbology, indeed, *Christés*, or *Christos,* meant that the "Way", the Path, was already trodden and the goal reached ; when the fruits of the arduous labour, uniting the personality of evanescent clay with the indestructible INDIVIDUALITY, transformed it thereby into the immortal EGO. "At the end of the Way stands the *Chréstes"*, the *Purifier,* and the union once accomplished, the *Chrestos,* the "man of sorrow", became *Christos* himself. Paul, the Initiate, knew this, and meant this precisely, when he is made to say, in bad translation : "I travail in birth again until Christ be formed in you" (Gal. iv.19), the true rendering of which is . . . "until ye form the Christos within yourselves" But the profane who knew only that Chréstés was in some way connected with priest and prophet, and knew nothing about the hidden meaning of Christos, insisted, as did Lactantius and Justin Martyr, on being called *Chréstians* instead of Christians. Every good individual, therefore, may find Christ in his "inner man" as Paul expresses it (*Ephes.* iii. 16,17), whether he be Jew, Mussulman, Hindu, or Christian. Kenneth Mackenzie seemed to think that the word *Chréstos* was a synonym of Soter, "an appellation assigned to deities, great kings and heroes," indicating "Saviour," – and he was right. For, as he adds: "It has been applied redundantly to Jesus Christ, whose name Jesus or Joshua bears the same interpretation. The name Jesus, in fact, is rather a title of honour than a name – the true name of the Soter of Christianity being Emmanuel, or God with us (*Matt*.i, 23.).Great divinities among all nations, who are represented as expiatory or self-sacrificing, have been designated by the same title." *(R. M. Cyclop.)* The Asklepios (or Æsculapius) of the Greeks had the title of *Soter.*

Cosmic Gods. Inferior gods, those connected with the formation of matter.

Cosmic ideation (*Occult.*). Eternal thought, impressed on substance or spirit-matter, in the eternity ; thought which becomes active at the beginning of every new life-cycle.

Cycle. From the Greek *Kuklos*. The ancients divided time into end less cycles, wheels within wheels, all such periods being of various durations, and each marking the beginning or the end of some event either cosmic, mundane, physical or metaphysical. There were cycles of only a few years, and cycles of immense duration, the great Orphic cycle, referring to the ethnological change of races, lasting 120,000 years, and the cycle of Cassandrus of 136,000, which brought about a complete change in planetary influences and their correlations between men and gods – a fact entirely lost sight of by modern astrologers.

D

Dæmon (*Gr.*). In the original Hermetic works and ancient classics it has a meaning identical with that of "god", "angel" or "genius". The Dæmon of Socrates is the incorruptible part of the man, or rather the real inner man which we call Nous or the rational divine Ego. At all events the Dæmon (or Daimon of the great Sage was surely not the demon of the Christian Hell or of Christian orthodox theology. The name was given by ancient peoples, and especially the philosophers of the Alexandrian school, to all kinds of spirits, whether good or bad, human or otherwise. The appellation is often synonymous with that of gods or angels. But some philosophers tried, with good reason, to make a just distinction between the many classes.

Daitya Guru (*Sk.*). The instructor of the giants, called *Daityas* (*q.v.*) Allegorically, it is the title given to the planet Venus-Lucifer, or rather to its indwelling Ruler, *Sukra*, a male deity (See *Sec. Doct..* ii. p. 30).

Daityas (*Sk.*). Giants, Titans, and exoterically demons, but in truth identical with certain Asuras, the intellectual gods, the opponents of the useless gods of ritualism and the enemies of *puja* sacrifices.

Daksha (*Sk.*). A form of Brahmâ and his son in the Purânas But the *Rig Veda* states that "Daksha sprang from Aditi, and Aditi from Daksha", which proves him to be a personified correlating Creative Force acting on *all the planes*. The Orientalists seem very much perplexed what to make of him; but Roth is nearer the truth than any, when saying that Daksha is the spiritual power, and at the same time the male energy that generates the gods in eternity, which is represented by Aditi. The Purânas as a matter of course, anthropomorphize the idea, and show Daksha instituting "sexual intercourse on this earth", after trying every other means of procreation. The generative Force, spiritual at the commencement, becomes of course at the most material end of its evolution a procreative Force on the physical plane ; and so far the Purânic allegory is correct, as the Secret Science teaches that our present mode of procreation began towards the end of the third Root-Race.

Dangma (*Sk.*). In Esotericism a purified Soul. A Seer and an Initiate; one who has attained full wisdom.

Darsanas (*Sk.*). The Schools of Indian philosophy, of which there are six;

Shad-darsanas or six demonstrations.

Day of Brahmâ. See "Brahmâ's Day" etc.

Demiurgic Mind. The same as "Universal Mind". Mahat, the first "product" of Brahmâ, or himself.

Demiurgos (*Gr.*). The Demiurge or Artificer; the Supernal Power which built the universe. Freemasons derive from this word their phrase of "Supreme Architect ". With the Occultists it is the third manifested Logos, or Plato's "second god", the second logos being represented by him as the "Father", the only Deity that he dared mention as an Initiate into the Mysteries.

Demon est Deus inversus (*Lat.*). A Kabbalistic axiom; lit., "the devil is god reversed", which means that there is neither evil nor good, but that the forces which create the one create the other, according to the nature of the materials they find to work upon.

Deva (*Sk.*). A god, a "resplendent" deity. Deva-Deus, from the root *div* "to shine". A Deva is a celestial being – whether good, bad, or indifferent. Devas inhabit "the three worlds", which are the *three planes* above us. There are 33 groups or 330 millions of them.

Deva Sarga (*Sk.*). Creation: the origin of the principles, said to be Intelligence born of the qualities or the attributes of nature.

Devachan (*Sk.*). The "dwelling of the gods". A state intermediate between two earth-lives, into which the EGO (Atmâ-Buddhi-Manas, or the Trinity made One) enters, after its separation from Kâma Rupa, and the disintegration of the lower principles on earth.

Devajnânas (*Sk.*). or *Daivajna*. The higher classes of celestial beings, those who possess divine knowledge.

Deva-lôkas (*Sk.*). The abodes of the Gods or Devas in superior spheres. The seven celestial worlds above Meru.

Devamâtri (*Sk.*). Lit., "the mother of the gods". A title of Aditi, Mystic Space.

Dhârana (*Sk.*). That state in Yoga practice when the mind has to be fixed unflinchingly on some object of meditation.

Dhâranî (*Sk.*). In Buddhism—both Southern and Northern—and also in Hinduism, it means simply a *mantra* or *mantras*—sacred verses from the *Rig Veda*. In days of old these mantras or Dhâranî were all considered mystical and practically efficacious in their use. At present, however, it is the Yogâchârya school alone which proves the claim in practice. When chanted according to given instructions a **Dhâranî** produces wonderful effects. Its occult power, however, does not reside in the *words* but in the inflexion or accent given and the resulting sound originated thereby. (See "Mantra" and "Akasa").

Dharma (*Sk.*). The sacred Law; the Buddhist Canon.

Dharmachakra (*Sk.*). Lit., The turning of the "wheel of the Law". The emblem of Buddhism as a system of cycles and rebirths or reincarnations.

Dharmakâya (*Sk.*). Lit., "the glorified spiritual body" called the "Vesture of Bliss". The third, or highest of the *Trikâya* (Three Bodies), the attribute developed by every "Buddha", i.e., every initiate who has crossed or reached the end of what is called the "fourth Path" (in esotericism the sixth "portal" prior to his entry on the seventh). The highest of the *Trikâya*, it is the *fourth* of the *Buddhakchêtra*, or Buddhic planes of consciousness, represented figuratively in Buddhist asceticism as a robe or vesture of luminous Spirituality. In popular Northern Buddhism these vestures or robes are: (1) Nirmanakâya (2) Sambhogakaya (3) and Dharmakâya the last being the highest and most sublimated of all, as it places the ascetic on the threshold of Nirvâna. (See, however, the *Voice of the Silence*, page 96, *Glossary*, for the true *esoteric* meaning.)

Dhyan Chohans (*Sk.*). Lit., "The Lords of Light". The highest gods, answering to the Roman Catholic Archangels. The divine Intelligences charged with the supervision of Kosmos.

Dhyâna (*Sk.*). In Buddhism one of the six Paramitas of perfection, a state of abstraction which carries the ascetic practising it far above this plane of sensuous perception and out of the world of matter. Lit., "contemplation". The six stages of Dhyan differ only in the degrees of abstraction of the personal Ego from sensuous life.

Dhyani Bodhisattyas (*Sk.*). In Buddhism, the five sons of the Dhyani-Buddhas. They have a mystic meaning in Esoteric Philosophy.

Dhyani Buddhas (*Sk.*). They "of the Merciful Heart"; worshipped especially in Nepaul. These have again a secret meaning.

Dianoia (*Gr.*). The same as the Logos. The eternal source of thought, "divine ideation", which is the root of all thought. (See "Ennoia.")

Djnâna (*Sk.*), or *Jnâna*. Lit., Knowledge; esoterically, "supernal or divine knowledge acquired by Yoga". Written also *Gnyana*.

Drakôn (*Gr.*), or Dragon. Now considered a "mythical" monster, perpetuated in the West only on seals,. &c., as a heraldic griffin, and the Devil slain by St. George, &c. In fact an extinct antediluvian monster In Babylonian antiquities it is referred to as the "scaly one" and connected on many gems with Tiamat the sea. "The Dragon of the Sea" is repeatedly mentioned. In Egypt, it is the star of the Dragon (then the North Pole Star), the origin of the connection of almost all the gods with the Dragon. Bel and the Dragon, Apollo and Python, Osiris and Typhon, Sigur and Fafnir, and finally St. George and the Dragon, are the same. They were all solar gods, and wherever we find the Sun there also is the Dragon, the symbol of Wisdom—Thoth-Hermes. The Hierophants of Egypt and of Babylon styled themselves "Sons of the Serpent-God" and "Sons of the Dragon". "I am a Serpent, I am a Druid", said the Druid of the Celto-Britannic regions, for the Serpent and the Dragon were both types of Wisdom, Immortality and Rebirth. As the serpent casts its old skin only to reappear in a new one, so does the immortal Ego cast off one personality but to assume another.

Dwapara Yuga (*Sk.*). The third of the "Four Ages" in Hindu Philosophy; or the second age counted from below.

Dynasties. In India there are two, the Lunar and the Solar, or the *Somavansa* and the *Suryavansa*. In Chaldea and Egypt there were also two distinct kinds of dynasties, the *divine* and the *human.* In both countries people were ruled in the beginning of time by Dynasties of Gods. In Chaldea they reigned one hundred and twenty Sari, or in all 432,000 years; which amounts to the same figures as a Hindu Mahayuga 4,320,000 years. The chronology prefacing the *Book of Genesis* (English translation) is given "Before Christ, 4004". But the figures are a rendering by solar years. In the original Hebrew, which preserved a lunar calculation, the figures are 4,320 years. This "coincidence" is well explained in Occultism.

Dzyan or Dzyn (*Tib.*). Written also *Dzen*. A corruption of the Sanskrit Dhyan and *jnâna* (or *gnyâna* phonetically) – Wisdom, divine knowledge. In Tibetan, learning is called *dzin.*

E

Ego (*Lat.*). " Self" ; the consciousness in man "I am I" – or the feeling of "I-am-ship". Esoteric philosophy teaches the existence of two Egos in man, the mortal or personal, and the Higher, the Divine and the Impersonal, calling the former "personality" and the latter "Individuality Egoity. From the word "Ego". Egoity means "individuality", never "personality", and is the opposite of egoism or "selfishness", the characteristic par excellence of the latter.

Elementals. Spirits of the Elements. The creatures evolved in the four Kingdoms or Elements – earth, air, fire, and water. They are called by the Kabbalists, Gnomes (of the earth), Sylphs (of the air), Salamanders (of the fire), and Undines (of the water). Except a few of the higher kinds, and their rulers, they are rather forces of nature than ethereal men and women. These forces, as the servile agents of the Occultists, may produce various effects; but if employed by" Elementaries" (*q.v.*)_in which case they enslave the mediums – they will deceive the credulous. All the lower invisible beings generated on the 5th 6th, and 7th planes of our terrestrial atmosphere, are called Elementals Peris, Devs, Djins, Sylvans, Satyrs, Fauns, Elves, Dwarfs, Trolls, Kobolds, Brownies, Nixies, Goblins, Pinkies, Banshees, Moss People, White Ladies, Spooks, Fairies, etc., etc., etc.

Elementaries. Properly, the disembodied souls of the depraved; these souls having at some time prior to death separated from themselves their divine spirits, and so lost their chance for immortality; but at the present stage of learning it has been thought best to apply the term to the spooks or phantoms of disembodied persons, in general, to those whose temporary habitation is the Kâma Loka. Eliphas Lévi and some other Kabbalists make little distinction between elementary spirits who have been men, and those beings which people the elements, and are the blind forces of nature. Once divorced from their higher triads and their bodies, these souls remain in their *Kâma-rupic* envelopes, and are irresistibly drawn to the earth amid elements congenial to their gross natures. Their stay in the Kâma Loka varies as to its duration; but ends invariably in disintegration, dissolving like a column of mist, atom by atom, in the surrounding elements.

Elohîm (*Heb.*). Also *Alhim*, the word being variously spelled. Godfrey Higgins, who has written much upon its meaning, always spells it *Aleim*. The Hebrew letters are *aleph, lamed, hé,yod, mem*, and are numerically 1, 30, 5, 10, 40 = 86. It seems to be the plural of the feminine noun *Eloah*, ALH, formed by adding the common plural form IM, a masculine ending; and hence the whole seems to imply the emitted active and passive essences. As a title it is referred to "Binah" the Supernal Mother, as is also the fuller title IHVH ALHIM, Jehovah Elohim. As Binah leads on to seven succeedent Emanations, so " Elohim" has been said to represent a sevenfold power of godhead. [w.w. w.]

Emanation, The Doctrine of. . In its metaphysical meaning, it is opposed to Evolution, yet one with it. Science teaches that evolution is physiologically a mode of generation in which the germ that develops the foetus pre-exists already in the parent, the development and final form and characteristics of that germ being accomplished in nature; and that in cosmology the process takes place blindly through the correlation of the elements, and their various compounds. Occultism answers that this is only the ***apparent*** mode, the real process being Emanation, guided by intelligent Forces under an immutable LAW. Therefore, while the Occultists and Theosophists believe thoroughly in the doctrine of Evolution as given out by Kapila and Manu, they are *Emanationists* rather than *Evolutionists*. The doctrine of Emanation was at one time universal. It was taught by the Alexandrian as well as by the Indian philosophers, by the Egyptian, the Chaldean and Hellenic Hierophants, and also by the Hebrews (in their Kabbala, and even in *Genesis*). For it is only owing to deliberate mistranslation that the Hebrew word asdt has been translated "angels" from the Septuagint, when it means *Emanations, Æons*, precisely as with the Gnostics. Indeed, in Deuteronomy (xxxiii., 2) the word *asdt* or *ashdt* is translated as" fiery law", whilst the correct rendering of the passage should be "from his right hand went [not a fiery law, but a fire according to law "; viz., that the fire of one flame is imparted to, and caught up by another like as in a trail of inflammable substance. This is precisely emanation. As shown in Isis Unveiled : "In Evolution, as it is now beginning to he understood, there is supposed to be in all matter an impulse to take on a higher form – a supposition clearly expressed by Manu and other Hindu philosophers of the highest antiquity. The philosopher's tree illustrates it in the case of the zinc solution. The controversy between the followers of this school and the Emanationists may he briefly stated thus The Evolutionist stops all inquiry at the borders of ' the Unknowable "; the Emanationist believes that nothing can be evolved – or, as the word means, unwombed or born – except it has first been involved, thus indicating that life is from a spiritual potency above the whole."

En (or **Ain**) **Soph** (*Heb.*). The endless, limitless and boundless. The absolute deific Principle, impersonal and unknowable. It means literally "no-thing" i.e., nothing that could be classed with anything else. The word and ideas are equivalent to the Vedantic conceptions of Parabrahmn. [w.w.w.]

Some Western Kabbalists, however, contrive to make of IT, a personal "He", a male deity instead of an impersonal deity.

Epimetheus (*Gr.*). Lit., "He who takes counsel *after*" the event. A brother of Prometheus in Greek Mythology.

Epinoia (*Gr.*). Thought, invention, design. A name adopted by the Gnostics for the first passive Æon.

Eros (*Gr.*). Hesiod makes of the god Eros the third personage of the Hellenic primordial Trinity composed of Ouranos, Gæa and Eros. It is the personified procreative Force in nature in its abstract sense, the propeller to "creation" and procreation. Exoterically, mythology makes of Eros the god of lustful, animal desire, whence the term *erotic* esoterically, it is different. (See " Kâma".)

Esoteric (*Gr.*). Hidden, secret. From the Greek *esotericos*, "inner" concealed.

Esoteric Bodhism. Secret wisdom or intelligence from the Greek *esotericos* "inner", and the Sanskrit *Bodhi*, "knowledge", intelligence – in contradistinction to *Buddhi,* "the *faculty* of knowledge or intelligence" and *Buddhism*, the philosophy or Law of Buddha (the Enlightened). Also written " Budhism", from *Budha* (Intelligence and Wisdom) the Son of Soma.

Ether. Students are but too apt to confuse this with Akâsa and with Astral

Light. It is neither, in the sense in which ether is described by physical Science. Ether is a material agent, though hitherto undetected by any physical apparatus; whereas Akâsa is a distinctly spiritual agent, identical, in one sense, with the Anima Mundi, while the Astral Light is only the seventh and highest principle of the terrestrial atmosphere, as undetectable as Akâsa and real Ether, because it is something quite on another plane. The seventh principle of the earth's atmosphere, as said, the Astral Light, is only the second on the Cosmic scale. The scale of Cosmic Forces, Principles and Planes, of Emanations – on the metaphysical – and Evolutions – on the physical plane – is the Cosmic Serpent biting its own tail, the Serpent reflecting the Higher, and reflected in its turn by the lower Serpent. The Caduceus explains the mystery, and the four-fold Dodecahedron on the model of which the universe is said by Plato to have been built by the manifested Logos – synthesized by the unmanifested First-Born – yields geometrically the key to Cosmogony and its microcosmic reflection – our Earth.

Evolution. The development of higher orders of animals from lower. As said in *Isis Unveiled:* "Modern Science holds but to a one-sided physical evolution, prudently avoiding and ignoring the higher or spiritual evolution, which would force our contemporaries to confess the superiority of the ancient philosophers and psychologists over themselves. The ancient sages, ascending to the UNKNOWABLE, made their starting-point from the first manifestation of the unseen, the unavoidable, and, from a strictly logical reasoning, the absolutely necessary creative Being, the Demiurgos of the universe. Evolution began with them from pure spirit, which descending lower and lower down, assumed at last a visible and comprehensible form, and became matter. Arrived at this point, they speculated in the Darwinian method, but on a far more large and comprehensive basis." (See "Emanation".)

Exoteric. Outward, public; the opposite of esoteric or hidden.

F

First Point. Metaphysically the first point of manifestation, the germ of primeval differentiation, or the point in the infinite Circle "whose centre is everywhere, and circumference nowhere". The Point is the Logos.

Fire *(Living)*. A figure of speech to denote deity, the "One" life. A theurgic term, used later by the Rosicrucians. The symbol of the *living fire* is the sun, *certain of whose rays develope the fire of life in a diseased body, impart the knowledge of the future* to the sluggish mind, and stimulate to active function a certain psychic and generally dormant faculty in man. The meaning is very occult.

Fohat *(Tib.)*. A term used to represent the active (male) potency of the Sakti (female reproductive power) in nature. The essence of cosmic electricity. An occult Tibetan term for *Daiviprakriti* primordial light: and in the universe of manifestation the ever-present electrical energy and ceaseless destructive and formative power. Esoterically, it is the same, Fohat being the universal propelling Vital Force, at once the propeller and the resultant.

G

Gautama (*Sk.*). The Prince of Kapilavastu, son of Sudhôdana, the Sâkya king of a small realm on the borders of Nepaul, born in the seventh century B.c., now called the "Saviour of the World". Gautama or Gôtama was the sacerdotal name of the Sâkya family, and Sidhârtha was Buddha's name before he became a Buddha. Sâkya Muni, means the Saint of the Sâkya family. Born a simple mortal he rose to Buddhaship through his own personal and unaided merit. A man—verily greater than any god!

Gayâtri (*Sk.*), also *Sâvitri*. A most sacred verse, addressed to the Sun, in the Rig -Veda, which the Brahmans have to repeat mentally every morn and eve during their devotions.

Genii (*Lat.*). A name for Æons, or angels, with the Gnostics. The names of their hierarchies and classes are simply legion.

Gnâna (*Sk.*). Knowledge as applied to the esoteric sciences.

Gnân Devas (*Sk.*). Lit., "the gods of knowledge". The higher classes of gods or devas; the "mind-born" sons of Brahmâ, and others including the Manasaputras (the Sons of Intellect). Esoterically, our reincarnating Egos.

Gnânasakti (*Sk.*). The power of true knowledge, one of the seven great forces in Nature (*six,* exoterically).

Gnôsis (*Gr.*). Lit., "knowledge". The technical term used by the schools of religious philosophy, both before and during the first centuries of so-called Christianity, to denote the object of their enquiry. This Spiritual and Sacred Knowledge, the *Gupta Vidya* of the Hindus, could only be obtained by Initiation into Spiritual Mysteries of which the ceremonial "Mysteries" were a type.

Gnostics (*Gr.*). The philosophers who formulated and taught the Gnôsis or Knowledge (*q.v.*). They flourished in the first three centuries of the Christian era: the following were eminent, Valentinus, Basilides, Marcion, Simon Magus, etc. [w.w. w.]

Golden Age. The ancients divided the life cycle into the Golden, Silver, Bronze and Iron Ages. The Golden was an age of primeval purity, simplicity and general happiness.

Great Age. There were several "great ages" mentioned by the ancients.

In India it embraced the whole Maha-manvantara, the "age of Brahmâ", each "Day" of which represents the life cycle of a chain – i.e. it embraces a period of seven Rounds. (See *Esoteric Buddhism,* by A. P. Sinnett.) Thus while a "Day" and a "Night" represent, as Manvantara and Pralaya, 8,640,000,000 years, an "age" lasts through a period of 311,040,000,000,000 years; after which the Pralaya, or dissolution of the universe, becomes universal. With the Egyptians and Greeks the "great age" referred only to the tropical or sidereal year, the duration of which is 25,868 solar years. Of the complete age – that of the gods – they say nothing, as it was a matter to he discussed and divulged only in the Mysteries, during the initiating ceremonies. The "great age" of the Chaldees was the same in figures as that of the Hindus.

Grihastha (*Sk.*). Lit., "a householder", "one who lives in a house with his family". A Brahman " family priest" in popular rendering, and the sarcerdotal hierarchy of the Hindus.

Guardian Wall. A suggestive name given to the host of translated adepts (Narjols) or the Saints collectively, who are supposed to watch over, help and protect Humanity. This is the so-called "Nirmanâkâya" doctrine in Northern mystic Buddhism. (See *Voice of the Silence,* Part III.)

Guhya Vidyâ (*Sk.*). The secret knowledge of mystic Mantras.

Gunas (*Sk.*). Qualities, attributes (See" Triguna") ; a thread, also a cord.

Gupta Vidyâ (*Sk.*). The same as Guhya Vidyâ; Esoteric or Secret Science; knowledge.

Guru (*Sk.*). Spiritual Teacher; a master in metaphysical and ethical doctrines; used also for a teacher of any science.

Guru Deva (*Sk.*). Lit., "divine Master".

H

Hatha Yoga (*Sk.*). The lower form of Yoga practice; one which uses physical means for purposes of spiritual self-development The opposite of *Râja Yoga.*

Hermaphrodite (*Gr.*). Dual-sexed; a male and female Being, whether man or animal.

Hermes Trismegistus (*Gr.*). The "thrice great Hermes", the Egyptian. The mythical personage after whom the Hermetic philosophy was named. In Egypt the God Thoth or Thot. A generic name of many ancient Greek writers on philosophy and Alchemy. Hermes Trismegistus is the name of Hermes or Thoth in his human aspect, as a god he is far more than this. As *Hermes-Thoth-Aah,* he is Thoth, the moon, i.e., his symbol is the bright side of the moon, supposed to contain the essence of creative Wisdom, "the elixir of Hermes ". As such he is associated with the Cynocephalus, the dog-headed monkey, for the same reason as was Anubis, one of the aspects of Thoth. (See " Hermanubis".) The same idea underlies the form of the Hindu God of Wisdom, the elephant-headed Ganesa, or Ganpat, the son of Parvati and Siva. (See "Ganesa".) When he has the head of an *ibis,* he is the sacred scribe of the gods; but even then he wears the crown *atef* and the lunar disk. He is the most mysterious of gods. As a serpent, Hermes Thoth is the divine creative 'Wisdom. The Church Fathers speak at length of Thoth-Hermes. (See "Hermetic".)

Hermetic. Any doctrine or writing connected with the esoteric teachings of Hermes, who, whether as the Egyptian Thoth or the Greek Hermes, was the God of Wisdom with the Ancients and, according to Plato, "discovered numbers, geometry, astronomy and letters". Though mostly considered as spurious, nevertheless the Hermetic writings were highly prized by St. Augustine, Lactantius, Cyril and others. In the words of Mr. J. Bonwick, " They are more or less touched up by the Platonic philosophers among the early Christians (such as Origen and Clemens Alexandrinus) who sought to substantiate their Christian arguments by appeals to these heathen and revered writings, though they could not resist the temptation of making them say a little too much. Though represented by some clever and interested writers as teaching pure monotheism, the Hermetic or Trismegistic books are, nevertheless, purely pantheistic. The Deity referred to in them is defined by Paul as that in *which* "we live, and move and have our being" – notwithstanding the "in Him" of the translators.

Hierophant. From the Greek "Hierophantes"; literally, "One who explains sacred things ". The discloser of sacred learning and the Chief of the Initiates. A title belonging to the highest Adepts in the temples of antiquity, who were the teachers and expounders of the Mysteries and the Initiators into the final great Mysteries. The Hierophant represented the Demiurge, and explained to the postulants for Initiation the various phenomena of Creation that were produced for their tuition. " He was the sole expounder of the esoteric secrets and doctrines. It was forbidden even to pronounce his name before an uninitiated person. He sat in the East, and wore as a symbol of authority a golden globe suspended from the neck. He was also called *Mystagogus*" (Kenneth R. H. Mackenzie, ix., F.T.S., in *The Royal Masonic cyclopædia*). In Hebrew and Chaldaic the term was *Peter,* the opener, discloser; hence the Pope as the successor of the hierophant of the ancient Mysteries, sits in the Pagan chair of St. Peter.

Higher Self. The Supreme Divine Spirit overshadowing man. The crown of the upper spiritual Triad in man – Atmân.

Hochmah (*Heb.*). See "Chochmah".

Hotri (*Sk.*). A priest who recites the hymns from the *Rig Veda*, and makes oblations to the fire.

Hotris (*Sk.*). A symbolical name for the *seven* senses called, in the *Anugita* "the Seven Priests". "The senses supply the fire of mind (i.e., desire) with the oblations of external pleasures." An occult term used metaphysically.

Humanity. Occultly and Kabbalistically, the whole of mankind is symbolised, by Manu in India; by Vajrasattva or Dorjesempa, the head of the Seven Dhyani, in Northern Buddhism; and by Adam Kadmon in the Kabbala. All these represent the totality of mankind whose beginning is in this androgynic protoplast, and whose end is in the Absolute, beyond all these symbols and myths of human origin. Humanity is a great Brotherhood by virtue of the sameness of the material from which it is formed physically and morally. Unless, however, it becomes a Brotherhood also intellectually, it is no better than a superior genus of animals.

I

Ichchha (*Sk.*). Will, or will-power.

Ichchha Sakti (*Sk.*). Will-power; force of desire; one of the occult Forces of nature. That power of the will which, exercised in occult practices, generates the nerve-currents necessary to set certain muscles in motion and to paralyze certain others.

Illusion. In Occultism everything finite (like the universe and all in it) is called illusion or *maya*.

Illuminati (*Lat.*). The "Enlightened", the initiated adepts.

Image. Occultism permits no other image than that of the living image of divine man (the symbol of Humanity) on earth. The *Kabbala* teaches that this divine Image, the copy of the *sublime and holy upper Image* (the Elohim) has now changed into *another similitude*, owing to the development of men's sinful nature. It is only the *upper divine Image* (the Ego) which is the same; the lower (personality) has changed, and man, now fearing the wild beasts, has grown to bear on his face the similitude of many of them. (*Zohar* I. fol. 71a.) In the early period of Egypt there were no images; but later, as Lenormand says, "In the sanctuaries of Egypt they divided the properties of nature and consequently of Divinity (the Elohim, or the Egos), into seven abstract qualities, characterised each by an emblem, which are matter, cohesion, fluxion, coagulation, accumulation, station and division ". These were all attributes symbolized in various images.

Incarnations (*Divine*) or *Avatars*. The Immaculate Conception is as pre-eminently Egyptian as it is Indian. As the author of *Egyptian Belief* has it: "It is not the vulgar, coarse and sensual story as in Greek mythology, but refined, moral and spiritual "; and again the incarnation idea was found revealed on the wall of a Theban temple by Samuel Sharpe, who thus analyzes it: "First the god Thoth . . . as the messenger of the gods, like the Mercury of the Greeks (or the Gabriel of the first Gospel), tells the *maiden* queen Mautmes, that she is to give birth to a son, who is to be king Amunotaph III. Secondly, the god Kneph, the Spirit . . . . and the goddess Hathor (Nature) both take hold of the queen by the hands and put into her mouth the character for life, a cross, which is to be the life of the coming child", etc., etc. Truly divine incarnation, or the *avatar* doctrine, constituted the grandest mystery of every old religious system!

Individuality. One of the names given in Theosophy and Occultism to the Human Higher EGO. We make a distinction between the immortal and divine Ego, and the mortal human Ego which perishes. The latter, or "personality" (personal Ego) survives the dead body only for a time in the Kama Loka; the Individuality prevails forever.

Initiate. From the Latin *Initiatus*. The designation of anyone who was received into and had revealed to him the mysteries and secrets of either Masonry or Occultism. In times of antiquity, those who had been initiated into the arcane knowledge taught by the Hierophants of the Mysteries; and in our modern days those who have been initiated by the adepts of mystic lore into the mysterious knowledge, which, notwithstanding the lapse of ages, has yet a few real votaries on earth.

Initiation. From the same root as the Latin *initia,* which means the basic or first principles of any Science. The practice of initiation or admission into the sacred Mysteries, taught by the Hierophants and learned priests of the Temples, is one of the most ancient customs. This was practised in every old national religion. In Europe it was abolished with the fall of the last pagan temple. There exists at present but one kind of initiation known to the public, namely that into the Masonic rites. Masonry, however, has no more secrets to give out or conceal. In the palmy days of old, the Mysteries, according to the greatest Greek and Roman philosophers, were the most sacred of all solemnities as well as the most beneficent, and greatly promoted virtue. The Mysteries represented the passage from mortal life into finite death, and the experiences of the disembodied Spirit and Soul in the world of subjectivity. In our own day, as the secret is lost, the candidate passes through sundry meaningless ceremonies and is initiated into the solar allegory of Hiram Abiff, the "Widow's Son".

Inner Man. An occult term, used to designate the true and immortal Entity in us, not the outward and mortal form of clay that we call our body. The term applies, strictly speaking, only to the Higher Ego, the "astral man" being the appellation of the Double and of Kâma Rupa (*q.v.*) or the surviving *eidolon*.

Intercosmic gods. The Planetary Spirits, Dhyan-Chohans, Devas of various degrees of spirituality, and "Archangels" in general.

Isis. In Egyptian *Issa*, the goddess Virgin-Mother; personified nature. In Egyptian or Koptic *Uasari*, the female reflection of *Uasar* or Osiris. She is the "woman clothed with the sun" of the land of Chemi. Isis Latona is the Roman Isis.

Iswara (*Sk.*). The "Lord" or the personal god – *divine Spirit in man. Lit.*, sovereign (independent) existence. A title given to Siva and other gods in India. Siva is also called Iswaradeva, or sovereign deva.

J

Jhâna (*Sk.*). or *Jnana*. Knowledge; Occult Wisdom.

Jiva (*Sk.*). Life, as the Absolute; the Monad also or "Atma-Buddhi".

Jivanmukta (*Sk.*). An adept or yogi who has reached the ultimate state of holiness, and separated himself from matter; a Mahatma, or *Nirvânee*, a "dweller in bliss" and emancipation. Virtually one who has reached Nirvâna during life.

Jivatma (*Sk.*). The ONE universal life, generally; but also the divine Spirit in Man.

Jnânam (*Sk.*). The same as "Gnâna", etc., the same as "Jhâna" (*q.v.*).

Jnânendriyas (*Sk.*). The five channels of knowledge.

Jnâna Sakti (*Sk.*). The power of intellect.

K

Kadmon (*Heb.*). Archetypal man. See."Adam Kadmon".

Kaliyuga (*Sk.*). The fourth, the black or iron age, our present period, the duration of which us 432,000 years. The last of the ages into which the evolutionary period of man is divided by a series of such ages. It began 3,102 years B.C. at the moment of Krishna's death, and the first cycle of 5,000 years will end between the years 1897 and 1898.

Kalpa (*Sk.*). The period of a mundane revolution, generally a cycle of time, but usually, it represents a "day" and "night" of Brahmâ, a period of 4,320,000,000 years.

Kama (*Sk.*). Evil desire, lust, volition; the cleaving to existence. Kama is generally identified with *Mara* the tempter.

Kamadeva (*Sk.*). In the popular notions the god of love, a Visva-deva, in the Hindu Pantheon. As the *Eros* of Hesiod, degraded into Cupid by exoteric law, and still more degraded by a later popular sense attributed to the term, so is Kama a most mysterious and metaphysical subject. The earlier Vedic description of Kama alone gives the key-note to what he emblematizes. Kama is the first conscious, *all embracing desire* for universal good, love, and for all that lives and feels, needs help and kindness, the first feeling of infinite tender compassion and mercy that arose in the consciousness of the creative ONE Force, as soon as it came into life and being as a ray from the ABSOLUTE. Says the *Rig Veda*, "Desire first arose in IT, which was the primal germ of mind, and which Sages, searching with their intellect, have discovered in their heart to be the bond which connects Entity with non-Entity", or *Manas* with pure *Atma-Buddhi*. There is no idea of sexual love in the conception. Kama is pre-eminently the divine desire of creating happiness and love; and it is only ages later, as mankind began to materialize by anthropomorphization its grandest ideals into cut and dried dogmas, that Kama became the power that gratifies desire on the animal plane. This is shown by what every *Veda* and some *Brahmanas* say. In the *Atharva Veda*, Kama is represented as the Supreme Deity and Creator. In the Taitarîya Brahmana, he is the child of Dharma, the god of Law and Justice, of Sraddha and faith. In another account he springs from the heart of Brahmâ. Others show him born from water, i.e., from primordial chaos, or the "Deep". Hence one of his many names, *Irâ-ja*, "the water-born"; and *Aja*, "unborn" ; and *Atmabhu* or "Self-existent". Because of the sign of *Makara* (Capricornus) on his banner, he is also called " Makara Ketu". The allegory about Siva, the "Great Yogin ", reducing Kama to ashes by the fire from his *central* (or third) *Eye*, for inspiring the Mahadeva with thoughts of his wife, while he was at his devotions – is very suggestive, as it is said that he thereby reduced Kama to his primeval spiritual form.

Kamaloka (*Sk.*). The *semi*-material plane, to us subjective and invisible, where the disembodied "personalities", the astral forms, called *Kamarupa* remain, until they fade out from it by the complete exhaustion of the effects of the mental impulses that created these eidolons of human and animal passions and desires; (See "Kamarupa".). It is the Hades of the ancient Greeks and the Amenti of the Egyptians, the land of Silent Shadows; a division of the first group of the *Trailôkya*. (See "Kamadhâtu".)

Kamarupa (*Sk.*). Metaphysically, and in our esoteric philosophy, it is the subjective form created through the mental and physical desires and thoughts in connection with things of matter, by all sentient beings, a form which survives the death of their bodies. After that death three of the seven "principles" – or let us say planes of senses and consciousness on which the human instincts and ideation act in turn – viz., the body, its astral prototype and physical vitality, – being of no further use, remain on earth; the three higher principles, grouped into one, merge into the state of Devachan (*q.v.*), in which state the Higher Ego will remain until the hour for a new reincarnation arrives; and the *eidolon* of the ex-Personality is left alone in its new abode. Here, the pale copy of the man that was, vegetates for a period of time, the duration of which is variable and according to the element of materiality which is left in it, and which is determined by the past life of the defunct. Bereft as it is of its higher mind, spirit and physical senses, if left alone to its own senseless devices, it will gradually fade out and disintegrate. But, if forcibly drawn back into the terrestrial sphere whether by the passionate desires and appeals of the surviving friends or by regular necromantic practices – one of the most pernicious of which is mediumship – the "spook" may prevail for a period greatly exceeding the span of the natural life of its body. Once the Kamarupa has learnt the way back to living human bodies, it becomes a vampire, feeding on the vitality of those who are so anxious for its company. In India these *eidolons* are called *Pisâchas,* and are much dreaded, as already explained elsewhere.

Kapila Rishi (*Sk.*). A great sage, a great adept of antiquity; the author of the Sankhya philosophy.

Karabtanos (*Gr.*). The spirit of blind or animal desire; the symbol of Kamarupa. The Spirit "without sense or judgment" in the Codex of the Nazarenes. He is the symbol of matter and stands for the father of the seven spirits of concupiscence begotten by him on his mother, the "Spiritus" or the Astral Light.

Kârana (*Sk.*). Cause (metaphysically).

Kârana Sarîra (*Sk.*). The "Causal body". It is dual in its meaning. Exoterically, it is Avidya, ignorance, or that which is the cause of the evolution of a human ego and its reincarnation ; hence the lower Manas esoterically – the causal body or Kâranopadhi stands in the Taraka Raja yoga as corresponding to Buddhi and the Higher " Manas," or Spiritual Soul.

Kâranopadhi (*Sk.*). The basis or *upadhi* of Karana, the "causal soul". In Taraka Rajayoga, it corresponds with both *Manas* and *Buddhi.* See Table in the *Secret Doctrine,* Vol. I, p. 157.

Karma (*Sk.*). Physically, action: metaphysically, the LAW OF RETRIBUTION, the Law of cause and effect or Ethical Causation. Nemesis, only in one sense, that of bad Karma. It is the eleventh *Nidana* in the concatenation of causes and effects in orthodox Buddhism ; yet it is the power that controls all things, the resultant of moral action, the meta physical *Samskâra,* or the moral effect of an act committed for the attainment of something which gratifies a personal desire. There is the Karma of merit and the Karma of demerit. Karma neither punishes nor rewards, it is simply *the one* Universal LAW which guides unerringly, and, so to say, blindly, all other laws productive of certain effects along the grooves of their respective causations. When Buddhism teaches that "Karma is that moral kernel (of any being) which alone survives death and continues in transmigration ' or reincarnation, it simply means that there remains nought after each Personality but the causes produced by it ; causes which are undying, i.e., which cannot be eliminated from the Universe until replaced by their legitimate effects, and wiped out by them, so to speak, and such causes – unless compensated during the life of the person who produced them with adequate effects, will follow the reincarnated Ego, and reach it in its subsequent reincarnation until a harmony between effects and causes is fully reestablished. No "personality" – a mere bundle of material atoms and of instinctual and mental characteristics – can of course continue, as such, in the world of pure Spirit. Only that which is immortal in its very nature and divine in its essence, namely, the Ego, can exist for ever. And as it is that Ego which chooses the personality it will inform, after each Devachan, and which receives through these personalities the effects of the Karmic causes produced, it is therefore the Ego, that *self* which is the "moral kernel" referred to and embodied karma, "which alone survives death."

Kartikeya (*Sk.*), or *Kartika.* The Indian God of War, son of Siva, born of his seed fallen into the Ganges. He is also the personification of the power of the Logos. The planet Mars. Kartika is a very occult personage, a nursling of the Pleiades, and a Kumâra. (See *Secret Doctrine.*)

Kasyapa (*Sk.*). A Vedic Sage; in the words of *Atharva Veda*, "The self-born who sprang from Time". Besides being the father of the Adityas headed by Indra, Kasyapa is also the progenitor of serpents, reptiles, birds and other walking, flying and creeping beings.

Kosmos (*Gr.*). The Universe, as distinguished from the world, which may mean our globe or earth.

Krishna (*Sk.*).. The most celebrated avatar of Vishnu, the "Saviour" of the Hindus and their most popular god. He is the-eighth Avatar, the son of Devaki, and the nephew of Kansa, the Indian King Herod, who while seeking for him among the shepherds and cow-herds who concealed him, slew thousands of their newly-born babes. The story of Krishna's conception, birth, and childhood are the exact prototype of the New Testament story. The missionaries, of course, try to show that the Hindus stole the story of the Nativity from the early Christians who came to India.

Krita-Yuga (*Sk.*). The first of the four Yugas or Ages of the Brahmans; also called *Satya-Yuga*, a period lasting 1,728,000 years.

Kriyasakti (Gk.). The power of thought; one of the seven forces of Nature. Creative potency of the *Siddhis* (powers) of the full Yogis.

Kronos (*Gr.*). Saturn. The God of Boundless Time and of the Cycles.

Kshanti (*Sk.*). Patience, one of the *Paramîtas* of perfection.

Kshetrajna or *Kshetrajneswara* (*Sk.*). Embodied spirit, the Conscious Ego in its highest manifestations; the reincarnating Principle; the "Lord" in us.

Kumâra (*Sk.*). A virgin boy, or young celibate. The first Kumâras are the seven sons of Brahmâ born out of the limbs of the god, in the so-called ninth creation. It is stated that the name was given to them owing to their formal refusal to "procreate their species", and so they "remained Yogis", as the legend says.

Kundalini Sakti (*Sk.*). The power of life; one of the Forces of Nature; that power that generates a certain light in those who sit for spiritual and clairvoyant development. It is a power known only to those who practise concentration and Yoga.

L

Lanoo (*Sk.*). A disciple, the same as "chela".

Laya or *Layam* (*Sk.*). From the root *Li*, "to dissolve, to disintegrate"; a point of equilibrium (*zero-point*) in physics and chemistry. In occultism, that point where substance becomes homogeneous and is unable to act or differentiate.

Lha (*Tib.*). Spirits of the highest spheres, whence the name of Lhassa, the residence of the Dalaï-Lama. The title of Lha is often given in Tibet to some *Narjols* (Saints and Yogi adepts) who have attained great occult powers.

Lhamayin (*Tib.*). Elemental sprites of the lower terrestrial plane. Popular fancy makes of them demons and devils.

Linga or *Lingam* (*Sk.*). A sign or a symbol of abstract creation. Force becomes the organ of procreation only on this earth. In India there are 12 great Lingams of Siva, some of which are on mountains and rocks, and also in temples. Such is the *Kedâresa* in the Himalaya, a huge and shapeless mass of rock. In its origin the Lingam had never the gross meaning connected with the phallus, an idea which is altogether of a later date. The symbol in India has the same meaning which it had in Egypt, which is simply that the creative or procreative Force is divine. It also denotes who was the dual Creator – male and female, Siva and his Sakti. The gross and immodest idea connected with the phallus is not Indian but Greek and pre-eminently Jewish. The Biblical *Bethels* were real priapic stones, the " Beth-el" (phallus) wherein God dwells. The same symbol was concealed within the ark of the Covenant, the "Holy of Holies". Therefore the "Lingam" even as a phallus is not "a symbol of Siva" only, but that of every "Creator" or creative god in every nation, including the Israelites and their

"God of Abraham and Jacob".

Linga Purâna (*Sk.*). A scripture of the Saivas or worshippers of Siva. Therein *Maheswara*, "the great Lord", concealed in the Agni Linga explains the ethics of life – duty, virtue, self-sacrifice and finally liberation by and through ascetic life at the end of the *Agni Kalpa* (the Seventh Round). As Professor Wilson justly observed "the Spirit of the worship (phallic) is as little influenced by the character of the type as can well be imagined. *There is nothing like the phallic orgies of antiquity; it is all mystical and spiritual.*"

Linga Sharîra (*Sk.*). The "body", i.e., the aerial symbol of the body. This term designates the *döppelganger* or the "astral body" of man or animal. It is the *eidolon* of the Greeks, the vital and *prototypal* body; the reflection of the men of flesh. It is born *before* and dies or fades out, with the disappearance of the last atom of the body.

Lipikas (*Sk.*). The celestial recorders, the "Scribes", those who record every word and deed, said or done by man while on this earth. As Occultism teaches, they are the agents of KARMA – the retributive Law.

Logos (*Gr.*). The manifested deity with every nation and people; the outward expression, or the effect of the cause which is ever concealed. Thus, speech is the Logos of thought; hence it is aptly translated by the "Verbum" and "Word" in its metaphysical sense.

Loka (*Sk.*). A region or circumscribed place. In metaphysics, a world or sphere or plane. The Purânas in India speak incessantly of seven and fourteen Lokas, above, and below our earth; of heavens and hells.

Lotus (*Gr.*). A most occult plant, sacred in Egypt, India and else where; called "the child of the Universe bearing the likeness of its mother in its bosom". There was a time "when the world was a golden lotus" (*padma*) says the allegory. A great variety of these plants, from the majestic Indian lotus, down to the marsh-lotus (bird's foot trefoil) and the Grecian "Dioscoridis", is eaten at Crete and other islands. It is a species of nymphala, first introduced from India to Egypt to which it was-not indigenous. See the text of *Archaic Symbolism* in the Appendix Viii. "The Lotus, as a Universal Symbol".

Lucifer (*Lat.*). The planet Venus, as the bright "Morning Star". Before Milton, Lucifer had never been a name of the Devil. Quite the reverse, since the Christian Saviour is made to say of himself in *Revelations* (xvi. 22.) "I am . . . the bright morning star" or Lucifer. One of the early Popes of Rome bore that name; and there was even a Christian sect in the fourth century which was called the *Luciferians.*

Lunar Pitris (Gods). Called in India the Fathers, "Pitris" or the lunar ancestors. They are subdivided, like the rest, into seven classes or Hierarchies, In Egypt although the moon received less worship than in Chaldea or India, still Isis stands as the representative of Luna-Lunus, "the celestial Hermaphrodite". Strange enough while the modern connect the moon only with lunacy and generation, the ancient nations, who knew better, have, individually and collectively, connected their "wisdom gods" with it. Thus in Egypt the lunar gods are Thoth-Hermes and Chons; in India it is Budha, the Son of *Soma*, the moon; in Chaldea Nebo is the lunar god of Secret Wisdom, etc., etc. The wife of Thoth, *Sifix*, the lunar goddess, holds a pole with five rays or the five-pointed star, symbol of man, the Microcosm, in distinction from the Septenary Macrocosm. As in all theogonies a goddess precedes a god, on the principle most likely that the chick can hardly precede its egg, in Chaldea the moon was held as older and more venerable than the Sun, because, as they said, darkness precedes light at every periodical rebirth (or "creation") of the universe. Osiris although connected with the Sun and a Solar god is, nevertheless, born on Mount *Sinai*, because *Sin* is the Chaldeo-Assyrian word for the moon; so was Dio-Nysos, god of Nyssi or *Nisi*, which latter appellation was that of Sinai in Egypt, where it was called Mount Nissa. The *crescent* is not – as proven by many writers – an ensign of the Turks, but was adopted by Christians for their symbol before the Mahommedans. For ages the crescent was the emblem of the Chaldean Astarte, the Egyptian Isis, and the Greek Diana, all of them Queens of Heaven, and finally became the emblem of Mary the Virgin. "The Greek Christian Empire of Constantinople held it as their palladium. Upon the conquest by the Turks, the Sultan adopted it . . . and since that, the crescent has been made to oppose the idea of the *cross*". (*Eg. Belief.*)

M

Macrocosm (*Gr.*). The "Great Universe" literally, or Kosmos.

Macroprosopus (*Gr.*). A Kabalistic term, made of a compound Greek word: meaning the Vast or Great Countenance (See "Kabalistic Faces"); a title of Kether, the Crown, the highest Sephira. It is the name of the Universe, called *Arikh-Anpin*, the totality of that of which Microprosopus or *Zauir-Anpin* "the lesser countenance", is the part and antithesis. In its high or abstract metaphysical sense, Microprosopus is Adam Kadmon, the *vehicle of Ain-Suph*, and the crown of the Sephirothal Tree, though since Sephira and Adam Kadmon are in fact one under two aspects, it comes to the same thing. Interpretations are many, and they differ.

Madhyama (*Sk.*). Used of something beginningless and endless. Thus Vâch (Sound, the female Logos, or the female counterpart of Brahmâ is said to exist in several states, one of which is that of *Mâdhyama*, which is equivalent to saying that Vâch is *eternal* in one sense "the Word (Vâch) was with God, and *in*

God", for the two are one.

Mâdhyamikas (*Sk.*). A sect mentioned in the *Vishnu Purâna*. Agreeably to the Orientalists, a "Buddhist sect, which is an anachronism. It was probably at first a sect of Hindu atheists. A later school of that name, teaching a system of sophistic nihilism, that reduces every proposition into a thesis and its antithesis, and then denies both, has been started in Tibet and China. It adopts a few principles of Nâgârjuna, who was one of the founders of the esoteric Mahayâna systems, not their *exoteric* travesties. The allegory that regarded Nâgârjuna's "Paramartha" as a gift from the *Nâgas* (Serpents) shows that he received his teachings from the secret school of adepts, and that the real tenets are therefore kept secret.

Mahâ Buddhi (*Sk.*). *Mahat.* The Intelligent Soul of the World. The seven *Prakritis* or seven "natures" or planes, are counted from Mahâbuddhi downwards.

Mahâ Chohan (*Sk.*). The chief of a spiritual Hierarchy, or of a school of Occultism; the head of the trans-Himalayan mystics.

Mahâ Deva (*Sk.*). Lit., "great god"; a title of Siva.

Mahâ Guru (*Sk.*). Lit., "great teacher". The Initiator.

Mahâ Kâla (*Sk.*). "Great Time". A name of Siva as the "Destroyer", and of Vishnu as the "Preserver".

Mahâ Kalpa (*Sk.*). The "great age".

Mahâ Manvantara (*Sk.*). Lit., the great interludes between the "Manus". The period of universal activity. Manvantara implying here simply a period of activity, as opposed to Pralaya, or rest – without reference to the length of the cycle.

Mahâ Mâyâ (*Sk.*). The great illusion of manifestation. This universe, and all in it in their mutual relation, is called the great Illusion or *Mahâmâyâ* It is also the usual title given to Gautama the Buddha's Immaculate Mother – Mayâdêvi, or the "Great Mystery", as she is called by the Mystics.

Mahâ Pralaya (*Sk.*). The opposite of Mahâmanvantara, literally "the great Dissolution", the "Night" following the "Day of Brahmâ". It is the great rest and sleep of all nature after a period of active manifestation; orthodox Christians would refer to it as the "Destruction of the World".

Mahâ Vidyâ (*Sk.*). The great esoteric science. The highest Initiates alone are in possession of this science, which embraces almost universal knowledge.

Mahâ Yogin (*Sk.*). The "great ascetic". A title of Siva.

Mahâ Yuga (*Sk.*). The aggregate of four *Yugas* or ages, of 4,320,000 solar years; a "Day of Brahmâ", in the Brahmanical system; lit., "the great age".

Mahat (*Sk.*). Lit., "The great one". The first principle of Universal Intelligence and Consciousness. In the Purânic philosophy the first product of root-nature or *Pradhâna* (the same as Mulaprakriti); the producer of *Manas* the thinking principle, and of *Ahankâra*, egotism or the feeling of "I am I" (in the lower Manas).

Mahâtma. Lit., "great soul". An adept of the highest order. Exalted beings who, having attained to the mastery over their lower principles are thus living unimpeded by the "man of flesh", and are in possession of knowledge and power commensurate with the stage they have reached in their spiritual evolution. Called in Pali Rahats and Arhats.

Maitreya Buddha (*Sk.*). The same as the *Kalki Avatar* of Vishnu (the "White Horse" Avatar), and of Sosiosh and other Messiahs. The only difference lies in the dates of their appearances. Thus, while Vishnu is expected to appear on his white horse at the end of the present *Kali Yuga* age "for the final destruction of the wicked, the renovation of creation and the restoration of purity", Maitreya is expected earlier. Exoteric or popular teaching making slight variations on the esoteric doctrine states that Sakyamuni (Gautama Buddha) visited him in Tushita (a celestial abode) and commissioned him to issue thence on earth as his successor at the expiration of five thousand years after his (Buddha's) death. This would be in less than 3,000 years hence. Esoteric philosophy teaches that the next Buddha will appear during the seventh (sub) race of this Round. The fact is that Maitreya was a follower of Buddha, a well-known Arhat, though not his direct disciple, and that he was the founder of an esoteric philosophical school. As shown by Eitel (*Sanskrit-Chinese Dict.*), "statues were erected in his honour as early as B.C. 350".

Manas (*Sk.*). Lit., "the mind", the mental faculty which makes of man an intelligent and moral being, and distinguishes him from the mere animal; a synonym of *Mahat. Esoterically,* however, it means, when unqualified, the Higher EGO, or the sentient reincarnating Principle in man. When qualified it is called by Theosophists *Buddhi-Manas* or the Spiritual Soul in contradistinction to its human reflection – *Kâma-Manas.*

Manas, Kâma (*Sk.*). Lit., "the mind of desire." With the Buddhists it is the *sixth* of the Chadâyatana (*q.v.*), or the six organs of knowledge, hence the highest of these, synthesized by the seventh called *Klichta*, the spiritual perception of that which defiles this (lower) Manas, or the "Human-animal Soul", as the Occultists term it. While the Higher Manas or the Ego is directly related to *Vijnâna* (the 10th of the 12 Nidânas) – which is the perfect knowledge of all forms of knowledge, whether relating to object or subject in the nidânic concatenation of causes and effects; the lower, the Kâma Manas is but one of the *Indriya* or organs (roots) of Sense. Very little can be said of the dual Manas here, as the doctrine that treats of it, is correctly stated only in esoteric works.

Its mention can thus be only very superficial.

Manas Sanyama (*Sk.*). Perfect concentration of the mind, and control over it, during Yoga practices.

Manas Taijasi (*Sk.*). Lit., the "radiant" Manas; a state of the Higher Ego, which only high metaphysicians are able to realize and comprehend.

Mânasa or *Manaswin* (*Sk.*). "The efflux of the *divine* mind," and explained as meaning that this efflux signifies the *manasa* or divine sons of Brahmâ-Virâj. Nilakantha who is the authority for this statement, further explains the term "manasa" by *manomâtrasarira*. These Manasa are the *Arupa* or incorporeal sons of the Prajâpati Virâj, in another version. But as Arjuna Misra identifies Virâj with Brahmâ, and as Brahmâ is Mahat, the universal mind, the exoteric blind becomes plain. The Pitris are identical with the Kumâra, the Vairaja, the Manasa-Putra (mind sons), and are finally identified with the human "Egos".

Mânasa Dhyânis (*Sk.*). The highest Pitris in the *Purânas*; the Agnishwatthas, or Solar Ancestors of Man, those who made of Man a rational being, by incarnating in the senseless forms of semi-ethereal flesh of the men of the third race. (See Vol. II. of *Secret Doctrine*.)

Mânasas (*Sk.*). Those who endowed humanity with *manas* or intelligence, the immortal EGOS in men. (See "Manas".)

Mantrika Sakti (*Sk.*). The power, or the occult potency of mystic words, sounds, numbers or letters in these Mantras.

Manus (*Sk.*). The fourteen Manus are the patrons or guardians of the race cycles in a Manvantara, or Day of Brahmâ. The primeval Manus are seven, they become fourteen in the *Purânas.*

Manushi or *Manushi Buddhas (Sk.).* Human Buddhas, Bodhisattvas, or incarnated Dhyan Chohans.

Manvantara (*Sk.*). A period of manifestation, as opposed to Pralaya (dissolution, or rest), applied to various cycles, especially to a Day of Brahmâ, 4,320,000,000 Solar years – and to the reign of one Manu – 308,448,000. (See Vol. II. of the *Secret Doctrine*, p. 68 *et. seq.*) Lit., *Manuantara* – between Manus.

Mârga (*Sk.*). "The "Path", The *Ashthânga mârga*, the "holy" or sacred path is the one that leads to Nirvâna. The eight-fold path has grown out of the seven-fold path, by the addition of the (now) first of the eight Marga; *i.e.*, "the possession of orthodox views"; with which a *real Yogâcharya* would have nothing to do.

Mârttanda (*Sk.*). The Vedic name of the Sun.

Mâyâ *(Sk.).* Illusion ; the cosmic power which renders phenomenal existence and the perceptions thereof possible. In Hindu philosophy that alone which is changeless and eternal is called *reality* ; all that which is subject to change through decay and differentiation and which has therefore a begining and an end is regarded as *mâyâ* – illusion.

Mîmânsâ (*Sk.*). A school of philosophy; one of the six in India. There are two Mîmânsâ the older and the younger. The first, the "Pârva-Mîmânsâ", was founded by Jamini, and the later or "Uttara Mîmânsâ", by a Vyasa—and is now called the Vedânta school. Sankarâchârya was the most prominent apostle of the latter. The Vedânta school is the oldest of all the six *Darshana* (lit., "demonstrations"), but even to the Pûrva-Mîmânsâ no higher antiquity is allowed than 500 B.C. Orientalists in favour of the absurd idea that all these schools are "due to Greek influence", in order to have them fit their theory would make them of still later date. The *Shad-darshana* (or Six Demonstrations) have all a starting point in common, and maintain that *ex nihilo nihil fit*.

Moksha (*Sk.*). "Liberation." The same as Nirvâna; a post mortem state of rest and bliss of the "Soul-Pilgrim".

Monad (*Gr.*). The Unity, the *one* ; but in Occultism it often means the unified triad, Atma-Buddhi-Manas, or the duad, Atma-Buddhi, that immortal part of man which reincarnates in the lower kingdoms, and gradually progresses through them to Man and then to the final goal – Nirvâna.

Monas (*Gr.*). The same as the term *Monad* ; "Alone", a unit. In the Pythagorean system the duad emanates from the higher and solitary Monas, which is thus the "First Cause".

Moon. The earth's satellite has figured very largely as an emblem in the religions of antiquity; and most commonly has been represented as Female, but this is not universal, for in the myths of the Teutons and Arabs, as well as in the conception of the Rajpoots of India (see Tod, *Hist.*), and in Tartary the moon was male. Latin authors speak of Luna. and also of Lunus, but with extreme rarity. The Greek name is Selene, the Hebrew Lebanah and also Yarach. In Egypt the moon was associated with Isis, in Phenicia with Astarte and in Babylon with Ishtar. From certain points of view the ancients regarded the moon also as Androgyne. The astrologers allot an Influence to the moon over the several parts of a man, according to the several Zodiacal signs she traverses; as well as a special influence produced by the house she occupies in a figure.

The division of the Zodiac into the 28 mansions of the moon appears to be older than that into 12 signs: the Copts, Egyptians, Arabs, Persians and Hindoos used the division into 28 parts centuries ago, and the Chinese use it still.

The Hermetists said the moon gave man an astral form, while Theosophy teaches that the Lunar Pitris were the creators of our human bodies and lower principles. (See *Secret Doctrine* 1. 386.) [w.w.w.]

Mukta and **Mukti** (*Sk.*). Liberation from sentient life; one beatified or liberated; a candidate for *Moksha*, freedom from flesh and matter, or life on this earth.

Mûlaprakriti (*Sk.*). The Parabrahmic root, the abstract deific feminine principle—undifferentiated substance. Akâsa. Literally, "the root of Nature" (*Prakriti*) or Matter.

Munis (*Sk.*). Saints, or Sages.

Mysteries. Greek *teletai*, or finishings, celebrations of initiation or the Mysteries. They were observances, generally kept secret from the profane and uninitiated, in which were taught by dramatic representation and other methods, the origin of things, the nature of the human spirit, its relation to the body, and the method of its purification and restoration to higher life. Physical science, medicine, the laws of music, divination, were all taught in the same manner. The Hippocratic oath was but a mystic obligation. Hippocrates was a priest of Asklepios, some of whose writings chanced to become public. But the Asklepiades were initiates of the Æsculapian serpent-worship, as the Bacchantes were of the Dionysia; and both rites were eventually incorporated with the Eleusinia. The Sacred Mysteries were enacted in the ancient Temples by the initiated Hierophants for the benefit and instruction of the candidates. The most solemn and occult Mysteries were certainly those which were performed in Egypt by "the band of secret-keepers", as Mr. Bonwick calls the Hierophants. Maurice describes their nature very graphically in a few lines. Speaking of the Mysteries performed in Philæ (the Nile-island), he says that "it was in these gloomy caverns that the grand and mystic arcana of the goddess (Isis) were unfolded to the adoring aspirant, while the solemn hymn of initiation resounded through the long extent of these stony recesses". The word "mysteries" is derived from the Greek *muô*, "to close the mouth", and every symbol connected with them had, a hidden meaning. As Plato and many other sages of antiquity affirm, the Mysteries were highly religious, moral and beneficent as a school of ethics. The Grecian mysteries, those of Ceres and Bacchus, were only imitations of the Egyptian; and the author of *Egyptian Belief and Modern Thought*, informs us that our own "word *chapel* or *capella* is said to be the *Caph-El* or college of *El*, the Solar divinity". The well-known *Kabiri* are associated with the Mysteries. In short, the Mysteries were in every country a series of dramatic performances, in which the mysteries of cosmogony and nature, in general, were personified by the priests and neophytes, who enacted the part of various gods and goddesses, repeating supposed scenes (allegories) from their respective lives. These were explained in their hidden meaning to the candidates for initiation, and incorporated into philosophical doctrines.

N

Nâga (*Sk.*). Literally "Serpent". The name in the Indian Pantheon of the Serpent or Dragon Spirits, and of the inhabitants of Pâtâla, hell. But as Pâtâla means the *antipodes*, and was the name given to America by the ancients, who knew and visited that continent before Europe had ever heard of it, the term is probably akin to the Mexican Nagals the (now) sorcerers and medicine men. The Nagas are the Burmese *Nats*, serpent-gods, or "dragon demons". In Esotericism, however, and as already stated, this is a nick-name for the "wise men" or adepts in China and Tibet, the "Dragons." are regarded as the titulary deities of the world, and of various spots on the earth, and the word is explained as meaning adepts, yogis, and narjols. The term has simply reference to their great knowledge and wisdom. This is also proven in the ancient Sûtras and Buddha's biographies. The Nâga is ever a wise man, endowed with extraordinary magic powers, in South and Central America as in India, in Chaldea as also in ancient Egypt. In China the "worship" of the Nâgas was widespread, and it has become still more pronounced since Nâgarjuna (the "great Nâga", the "great adept" literally), the fourteenth Buddhist patriarch, visited China. The "Nâgas" are regarded by the Celestials as "the tutelary Spirits or gods of the five regions or the four points of the compass and the centre, as the guardians of the five lakes and four oceans" (Eitel). This, traced to its origin and translated esoterically, means that the five continents and their five root-races had always been under the guardianship of "terrestrial deities", i.e., Wise Adepts. The tradition that Nâgas washed Gautama Buddha at his birth, protected him and guarded the relics of his body when dead, points again to the Nâgas being only wise men, Arhats, and no monsters or Dragons. This is also corroborated by the innumerable stories of the conversion of Nâgas to Buddhism. The Nâga of a lake in a forest near Râjagriha and many other "Dragons" were thus converted by Buddha to the good Law.

Nârada (*Sk.*). One of the Seven great Rishis, a Son of Brahmâ. This "Progenitor" is one of the most mysterious personages in the Brahmanical sacred symbology. Esoterically Nârada is the Ruler of events during various Karmic cycles, and the personification, in a certain sense, of the great human cycle; a Dhyan Chohan. He plays a great part in Brahmanism, which ascribes to him some of the most occult hymns in the *Rig Veda*, in which sacred work he is described as "of the Kanwa family". He is called Deva-Brahmâ, but as such has a distinct character from the one he assumes on earth – or Pâtâla. Daksha cursed him for his interference with his 5,000 and 10,000 sons, whom he persuaded to remain Yogins and *celibates*, to be reborn time after time on this earth (*Mahâbhârata*). But this is an allegory. He was the inventor of the Vina, a kind of lute, and a great "lawgiver". The story is too long to be given here.

Nârâyana (*Sk.*). The "mover on the Waters" of space: a title of Vishnu, in his aspect of the Holy Spirit, moving on the Waters of Creation. (See *Mânu*, Book II.) In esoteric symbology it stands for the primeval manifestation of the *life-principle*, spreading in infinite Space.

Nâstika (*Sk.*). Atheist, or rather he who does not worship or recognize the gods and idols.

Nephesh (*Heb.*). Breath of life. *Anima, Mens, Vita,* Appetites. This term is used very loosely in the Bible. It generally means *prana* "life"; in the Kabbalah it is the animal passions and the animal Soul. [w.w.w.]. Therefore, as maintained in theosophical teachings, *Nephesh* is the synonym of the Prâna-Kâmic Principle, or the vital animal Soul in man. [H. P. B.]

Nidâna (*Sk.*). The 12 causes of existence, or a chain of causation, "a concatenation of cause and effect in the whole range of existence through 12 links". This is the fundamental dogma of Buddhist thought, "the understanding of which solves the riddle of life, revealing the insanity of existence and preparing the mind for Nirvâna". (Eitel's *Sans. Chin. Dict.*) The 12 links stand thus in their enumeration. (1) Jail, or birth, according to one of the four modes of entering the stream of life and reincarnation – or *Chatur Yoni* (*q.v.*), each mode placing the being born in one of the six *Gâti* (*q.v.*). (2) *Jarârnarana*, or decrepitude and death, following the maturity of the *Skandhas* (*q.v.*). (3) *Bhava*, the Karmic agent which leads every new sentient being to be born in this or another mode of existence in the *Trailokya* and Gâti. (4) *Upâdâna*, the creative cause of *Bhava* which thus becomes the cause of *Jati* which is the effect; and this creative cause is the *clinging to life*. (5) Trishnâ, love, whether pure or impure. (6) *Vêdâna*, or sensation; perception by the senses, it is the 5th Skandha. (7) Sparsa, the sense of touch. (8) *Chadâyatana*, the organs of sensation. (9) *Nâmarûpa*, personality, i.e., a form with a name to it, the symbol of the unreality of material phenomenal appearances. (10) *Vijnâna*, the perfect knowledge of every perceptible thing and of all objects in their concatenation and unity. (11) *Samskâra*, action on the plane of illusion. (12) *Avidyâ*, lack of true perception, or ignorance. The Nidânas belonging to the most subtle and abstruse doctrines of the Eastern metaphysical system, it is impossible to go into the subject at any greater length.

Nimitta (*Sk.*). 1. An interior illumination developed by the practice of meditation. 2. The efficient spiritual cause, as contrasted with Upadana, the material cause, in Vedânta philosophy. See also *Pradhâna* in Sankhya philosophy.

Nirguna (*Sk.*). Negative attribute; unbound, or without *Gunas* (attributes), i.e., that which is devoid of all qualities, the opposite of Saguna, that which has attributes (*Secret Doctrine*, II. 95), e.g., Parabrahmam is Nirguna; Brahmâ, Saguna. Nirguna is a term which shows the impersonality of the thing spoken of.

Nirmânakâya (*Sk.*). Something entirely different in esoteric philosophy from the popular meaning attached to it, and from the fancies of the Orientalists. Some call the *Nirmânakâya* body "Nirvana with remains" (Schlagintweit, etc.) on the supposition, probably, that it is a kind of Nirvânic condition during which consciousness and form are retained. Others say that it is one of the *Trikâya* (three bodies), with the "power of assuming any form of appearance in order to propagate Buddhism" (Eitel's idea); again, that "it is the incarnate avatâra of a deity" (*ibid.*), and so on. Occultism, on the other hand, says:that Nirmânakâya, although meaning literally a transformed "body", is a state. The form is that of the adept or yogi who enters, or chooses, that *post mortem* condition in preference to the Dharmakâya or *absolute* Nirvânic state. He does this because the latter *kâya* separates him for ever from the world of form, conferring upon him a state of *selfish* bliss, in which no other living being can participate, the adept being thus precluded from the possibility of helping humanity, or even *devas*. As a Nirmânakâya, however, the man leaves behind him only his physical body, and retains every other "principle" save the Kamic – for he has crushed this out for ever from his nature, during life, and it can never resurrect in his post mortem state. Thus, instead of going into selfish bliss, he chooses a life of self-sacrifice, an existence which ends only with the life-cycle, in order to be enabled to help mankind in an invisible yet most effective manner. (See *The Voice of the Silence*, third treatise, "The Seven Portals".) Thus a Nirmânakâya is not, as popularly believed, the body "in which a Buddha or a Bodhisattva appears on earth", but verily one, who whether a *Chutuktu* or a *Khubilkhan,* an adept or a yogi during life, has since become a member of that invisible Host which ever protects and watches over Humanity within Karmic limits. Mistaken often for a "Spirit", a Deva, God himself, &c., a Nirmânakâya is ever a protecting, compassionate, verily a *guardian* angel, to him who becomes worthy of his help. Whatever objection may be brought forward against this doctrine; however much it is denied, because, forsooth, it has never been hitherto made public in Europe and therefore since it is unknown to Orientalists, it must needs be "a myth of modern invention" – no one will be bold enough to say that this idea of helping suffering mankind at the price of one's own almost interminable self-sacrifice, is not one of the grandest and noblest that was ever evolved from human brain.

Nirupadhi *(Sk.).* Attributeless; the negation of attributes.

Nirvâna *(Sk.).* According to the Orientalists, the entire "blowing out", like the flame of a candle, the utter extinction of existence. But in the esoteric explanations it is the state of absolute existence and absolute consciousness, into which the Ego of a man who has reached the highest degree of perfection and holiness during life goes, after the body dies, and occasionally, as in the case of Gautama Buddha and others, during life. (See "Nirvânî".)

Nirvânî (ee) *(Sk.).* One who has attained Nirvana – an emancipated soul. That Nirvâna means nothing of the kind asserted by Orientalists every scholar who has visited China, India and Japan is well aware. It is "*escape* from misery" but only from that of matter, freedom from *Klêsha,* or *Kâma,* and the complete extinction of animal desires. If we are told that *Abidharma* defines Nirvâna "as a state of absolute annihilation", we concur, adding to the last word the qualification "of everything connected with matter or the physical world", and this simply because the latter (as also all in it) is illusion, *mâyâ*. Sâkya-mûni Buddha said in the last moments of his life that "the spiritual body is immortal" (See *Sans. Chin. Dict.*). As Mr. Eitel, the scholarly Sinologist, explains it: "The popular exoteric systems agree in defining Nirvâna *negatively* as a state of absolute exemption from the circle of transmigration; as a state of entire freedom from all forms of existence; to begin with, freedom from all passion and exertion; a state of indifference to all sensibility" and he might have added "death of all compassion for the world of suffering". And this is why the Bodhisattvas who prefer the Nirmânakâya to the Dharmakâya vesture, stand higher in the popular estimation than the Nirvânîs. But the same scholar adds that: "Positively (and esoterically) they define Nirvâna as the highest state of spiritual bliss, as absolute immortality through absorption of the soul (spirit rather) into itself, but *preserving individuality* so that, e.g., Buddhas, after entering Nirvâna, may reappear on earth" – i.e., in the future Manvantara.

Nitya Pralaya (*Sk.*). Lit., "perpetual" Pralaya or dissolution. It is the constant and imperceptible changes undergone by the atoms which last as long as a Mahâmanvantara, a whole age of Brahmâ, which takes fifteen figures to sum up. A stage of chronic change and dissolution, the stages of growth and decay. It is the duration of "Seven Eternities". (See *Secret Doctrine* I. 371, II. 69, 310.) There are four kinds of Pralayas, or states of changelessness. The Naimittika, when Brahmâ slumbers; the Prakritika, a partial Pralaya of anything during Manvantara; Atyantika, when man has identified himself with the One Absolute synonym of Nirvâna; and Nitya, for physical things especially, as a state of profound and dreamless sleep.

Nitya Sarga (*Sk.*). The state of constant creation or evolution, as opposed to *Nitya Pralaya*—the state of perpetual incessant dissolution (or change of atoms) disintegration of molecules, hence change of forms.

Nous (*Gr.*). A Platonic term for the Higher Mind or Soul. It means Spirit as distinct from animal Soul – *psyche*; divine consciousness or mind in man: *Nous* was the designation given to the Supreme deity (third *logos*) by Anaxagoras. Taken from Egypt where it was called *Nout*, it was adopted by the Gnostics for their first conscious Æon which, with the Occultists, is the third *logos*, cosmically, and the third "principle" (from above) or *manas,* in man. (See "Nout".)

Nout (*Gr.*). In the Pantheon of the Egyptians it meant the "One-only-One", because they did not proceed in their popular or exoteric religion higher than the third manifestation which radiates from the *Unknown* and the *Unknowable*, the first unmanifested and the second *logoi* in the esoteric philosophy of every nation. The Nous of Anaxagoras was the *Mahat* of the Hindu Brahmâ, *the first manifested* Deity – "the Mind or Spirit self-potent"; this creative Principle being of course the *primum mobile* of everything in the Universe – its Soul and Ideation. (See "Seven Principles" in man.)

Nyâya (*Sk.*). One of the six *Darshanas* or schools of Philosophy in India; a system of Hindu logic founded by the Rishi Gautama.

O

Occult Sciences. The science of the secrets of nature – physical and psychic, mental and spiritual; called Hermetic and Esoteric Sciences. In the West, the Kabbalah may be named; in the East, mysticism, magic, and Yoga philosophy, which latter is often referred to by the Chelas in India as the *seventh* "Darshana" (school of philosophy), there being only *six* Darshanas in India known to the world of the profane. These sciences are, and have been for ages, hidden from the vulgar for the very good reason that they would never be appreciated by the selfish educated classes, nor understood by the uneducated; whilst the former might misuse them for their own profit, and thus turn the divine science into *black magic*. It is often brought forward as an accusation against the Esoteric philosophy and the Kabbalah that their literature is full of "a barbarous and meaningless jargon" unintelligible to the ordinary mind. But do not exact Sciences – medicine, physiology, chemistry, and the rest – do the same? Do not official Scientists equally veil their facts and discoveries with a newly coined and most barbarous Græco-Latin terminology? As justly remarked by our late brother, Kenneth Mackenzie – "To juggle thus with words, when the facts are so simple, is the art of the Scientists of the present time, in striking contrast to those of the XVIIth century, who called spades spades, and not 'agricultural implements'." Moreover, whilst their facts would be as simple and as comprehensible if rendered in ordinary language, the facts of Occult Science are of so abstruse a nature, that in most cases no words exist in European languages to express them; in addition to which our "jargon" is a *double* necessity – (a) for the purpose of describing clearly these *facts* to him who is versed in the Occult terminology; and (b) to conceal them from the profane.

Occultist. One who studies the various branches of occult science. The term is used by the French Kabbalists (See Eliphas Lévi's works). Occultism embraces the whole range of psychological, physiological, cosmical, physical, and spiritual phenomena. From the word occultus hidden or secret. It therefore applies to the study of the **Kabbalah**, astrology, alchemy, and all arcane sciences.

Oeaihu, or *Oeaihwu*. The manner of pronunciation depends on the accent. This is an esoteric term for the six in one or the mystic seven. The occult name for the "seven vowelled" ever-present manifestation of the Universal Principle.

Om or Aum (*Sk.*). A mystic syllable, the most solemn of all words in India.

It is "an invocation, a benediction, an affirmation and a promise and it is so sacred, as to be indeed *the word at low breath* of occult, *primitive* masonry. No one must be near when the syllable is pronounced for a purpose. This word is usually placed at the beginning of sacred Scriptures, and is prefixed to prayers. It is a compound of three letters a,u,m, which, in the popular belief, are typical of the three Vedas, also of three gods—**A** (Agni) **V** (Varuna) and **M** (Maruts) or Fire, Water and Air. In esoteric philosophy these are the three sacred fires, or the "triple fire"in the Universe and Man, besides many other things. Occultly, this "triple fire" represents the highest *Tetraktys* also, as it is typified by the Agni named Abhimânin and his transformation into his three sons, Pâvana, Pavamâna and Suchi, "who drinks up water", i.e., destroys material desires. This monosyllable is called Udgîtta, and is sacred with both Brahmins and Buddhists.

Omkâra (*Sk*.). The same as Aum or Om. It is also the name of one of the twelve *lingams*, that was represented by a secret and most sacred shrine at Ujjain—no longer existing, since the time of Buddhism.

Ophiomorphos (*Gr*.). The same, but in its material aspect, as the Ophis-Christos. With the Gnostics the Serpent represented "Wisdom in Eternity".

Ouranos (*Gr*.). The whole expanse of Heaven called the "Waters of Space", the Celestial Ocean, etc. The name very likely comes from the Vedic Varuna, personified as the water god and regarded as the chief Aditya among the seven planetary deities. In Hesiod's Theogony, Ouranos (or Uranus) is the same as Cœlus (Heaven) the oldest of all the gods and the father of the divine Titans.

P

Padma Âsana (*Sk*.). A posture prescribed to and practised by some Yogis for developing concentration.

Padma Kalpa (*Sk*.). The name of the last Kalpa or the preceding Manvantara, which was a year of Brahmâ.

Pancha Kosha (*Sk*.). The five "sheaths". According to Vedantin philosophy, Vijnânamaya Kosha, the fourth sheath, is composed of Buddhi, or is Buddhi. The five sheaths are said to belong to the two higher principles—*Jivâtma* and *Sâkshi*, which represent the *Upathita* and *An-upahita,* divine spirit respectively. The division in the esoteric teaching differs from this, as it divides man's physical-metaphysical aspect into seven principles.

Para (*Sk*.). "Infinite" and "supreme" in philosophy – the final limit.

Parabrahm (*Sk*.). "Beyond Brahmâ", literally. The Supreme Infinite Brahma, "Absolute" – the attributeless, the secondless reality. The impersonal and nameless universal Principle.

Paracelsus. The symbolical name adopted by the greatest Occultist of the middle ages – Philip Bombastes Aureolus Theophrastus von Hohenheim – born in the canton of Zurich in 1493. He was the cleverest physician of his age, and the most renowned for curing almost any illness by the power of talismans prepared by himself. He never had a friend, but was surrounded by enemies, the most bitter of whom were the Churchmen and their party. That he was accused of being in league with the devil stands to reason, nor is it to be wondered at that finally he was murdered by some unknown foe, at the early age of forty-eight. He died at Salzburg, leaving a number of works behind him, which are to this day greatly valued by the Kabbalists and Occultists. Many of his utterances have proved prophetic. He was a clairvoyant of great powers, one of the most learned and erudite philosophers and mystics, and a distinguished Alchemist. Physics is indebted to him for the discovery of nitrogen gas, or **Azote.**

Paramapadha (*Sk.*). The place where—according to Visishtadwaita Vedantins—bliss is enjoyed by those who reach *Moksha* (Bliss). This "place" is not material but made, says the Catechism of that sect, "of *Suddhasatwa*, the essence of which the body of Iswara", the lord, "is made".

Paramartha (*Sk.*). Absolute existence.

Paramâtman (*Sk.*). The Supreme Soul of the Universe.

Paranirvâna (*Sk.*). Absolute *Non-Being*, which is equivalent to absolute *Being* or "Be-ness", the state reached by the human Monad at the end of the great cycle (See *Secret Doctrine* I, 135). The same as *Paraniskpanna*.

Pâtanjala (*Sk.*). The Yoga philosophy; one of the six *Darshanas* or Schools of India.

Patanjali (*Sk.*). The founder of the Yoga philosophy. The date assigned to him by the Orientalists is 200 B.C.; and by the Occultists nearer to 700 than 600 B.C. At any rate he was a contemporary of Pânini.

Personality. In Occultism – which divides man into seven principles, considering him under the three aspects of the *divine*, the *thinking* or the *rational*, and the *animal* man – the lower *quaternary* or the purely astrophysical being; while by *Individuality* is meant the Higher Triad, considered as a Unity. Thus the *Personality* embraces all the characteristics and memories of one physical life, while the *Individuality* is the imperishable *Ego* which re-incarnates and clothes itself in one personality after another.

Phenomenon (*Gr.*). In reality "an appearance", something previously unseen, and puzzling when the cause of it is unknown. Leaving aside various kinds of phenomena, such as cosmic, electrical, chemical, etc., and holding merely to the phenomena of spiritism, let it be remembered that theosophically and esoterically every "miracle" – from the biblical to the theumaturgic – is simply a phenomenon, but that no phenomenon is ever a miracle, *i.e.,* something supernatural or outside of the laws of nature, as all such are impossibilities in nature.

Pitar Devata (*Sk.*). The "Father-Gods", the lunar ancestors of mankind.

Pitaras (*Sk.*). Fathers, Ancestors. The fathers of the human races.

Pitris (*Sk.*). The ancestors, or creators of mankind. They are of seven classes, three of which are incorporeal, *arupa,* and four corporeal. In popular theology they are said to be created from Brahmâ's side. They are variously genealogized, but in esoteric philosophy they are as given in the *Secret Doctrine.* In *Isis Unveiled* it is said of them "It is generally believed that the Hindu term means the spirits of our ancestors, of disembodied people, hence the argument of some Spiritualists that fakirs (and yogis) and other Eastern wonder-workers, are *mediums.* This is in more than one sense erroneous. The Pitris are not the ancestors of the present living men, but those of the human kind, or Adamic races; the spirits of human races, which on the great scale of descending evolution *preceded our races* of men, and they *were physically, as well as spiritually, far superior* to our modern pigmies. In *Mânava Dharma Shâstra* they are called the *Lunar Ancestors.*" The *Secret Doctrine* has now explained that which was cautiously put forward in the earlier Theosophical volumes.

Planetary Spirits. Primarily the rulers or governors of the planets. As our earth has its hierarchy of terrestrial planetary spirits, from the highest to the lowest plane, so has every other heavenly body. In Occultism, however, the term "Planetary Spirit" is generally applied only to the seven highest hierarchies corresponding to the Christian archangels. These have all passed through a stage of evolution corresponding to the humanity of earth on other worlds, in long past cycles. Our earth, being as yet only in its fourth round, is far too young to have produced high planetary spirits. The highest planetary spirit ruling over any globe is in reality the "Personal God" of that planet and far more truly its "over-ruling providence" than the self-contradictory Infinite Personal Deity of modern Churchianity.

Plato. An Initiate into the Mysteries and the greatest Greek philosopher, whose writings are known the world over. He was the pupil of Socrates and the teacher of Aristotle. He flourished over 400 years before our era.

Pragna (*Sk.*). or *Prajna.* A synonym of *Mahat* the Universal Mind. The capacity for perception. (*S. D.,* I. 139) Consciousness.

Prajâpatis (*Sk.*). Progenitors; the givers of life to all on this Earth. They are seven and then ten – corresponding to the seven and ten Kabbalistic Sephiroth;

to the Mazdean Amesha-Spentas, &c. Brahmâ the creator, is called Prajâpati as the synthesis of the Lords of Being.

Prakriti (*Sk.*). Nature in general, nature as opposed to Purusha – spiritual nature and Spirit, which together are the "two primeval aspects of the One Unknown Deity". (*Secret Doctrine*, I. 51.)

Pralaya (*Sk.*). A period of obscuration or repose – planetary, cosmic or universal – the opposite of Manvantara (*S. D.*, I. 370.).

Pramantha (*Sk.*). An accessory to producing the sacred fire by friction. The sticks used by Brahmins to kindle fire by friction.

Prâna (*Sk.*). Life-Principle ; the breath of Life.

Pranidhâna (*Sk.*). The fifth observance of the Yogis; ceaseless devotion. (See *Yoga Shâstras*, ii. 32.)

Pratyasarga (*Sk.*). In Sankhya philosophy the "intellectual evolution of the Universe"; in the *Purânas* the 8th creation.

Prometheus (*Gr.*). The Greek *logos*; he, who by bringing on earth divine fire (intelligence and consciousness) endowed men with reason and mind. Prometheus is the Hellenic type of our Kumâras or *Egos,* those who, by incarnating in men, made of them latent gods instead of animals. The gods (or Elohim) were averse to men becoming "as one of us (*Genesis* iii., 22), and knowing "good and evil". Hence we see these gods in every religious legend punishing man for his desire to know. As the Greek myth has it, for stealing the fire he brought to men from Heaven, Prometheus was chained by the order of Zeus to a crag of the Caucasian Mountains.

Protogonos (*Gr.*). The "first-born"; used of all the manifested gods and of the Sun in our system.

Psyche (*Gr.*). The animal, terrestrial Soul; the lower *Manas*.

Purânas (*Sk.*). Lit., "ancient". A collection of symbolical and allegorical writings – eighteen in number now – supposed to have been composed by Vyâsa, the author of *Mahâbhârata*.

Purusha (*Sk.*). "Man", *heavenly man*. Spirit, the same as Nârâyana in another aspect. "The Spiritual Self."

Pymander (Gr.). The "Thought divine". The Egyptian Prometheus and the personified Nous or divine light, which appears to and instructs Hermes Trismegistus, in a hermetic work called "Pymander".

Pythagoras (*Gr.*). The most famous of mystic philosophers, born at Samos, about 586 B.C. He seems to have travelled all over the world, and to have culled his philosophy from the various systems to which he had access. Thus, he studied the esoteric sciences with the *Brachmanes* of India, and astronomy and astrology in Chaldea and Egypt. He is known to this day in the former country under the name of Yavanâchârya ("Ionian teacher"). After returning he settled in Crotona, in Magna Grecia, where he established a college to which very soon resorted all the best intellects of the civilised centres. His father was one Mnesarchus of Samos, and was a man of noble birth and learning. It was Pythagoras. who was the first to teach the heliocentric system, and who was the greatest proficient in geometry of his century. It was he also who created the word "philosopher", composed of two words meaning a "lover of wisdom"—*philo-sophos*. As the greatest mathematician, geometer and astronomer of historical antiquity, and also the highest of the metaphysicians and scholars, Pythagoras has won imperishable fame. He taught reincarnation as it is professed in India and much else of the Secret Wisdom.

Q

Qadmon, Adam, or *Adam Kadmon (Heb.)*. The Heavenly or Celestial Man, the Microcosm *(q.v.)*, He is the manifested Logos; the *third* Logos according to Occultism, or the Paradigm of Humanity.

R

Râga *(Sk.)*. One of the five *Kleshas* (afflictions) in Patânjali's Yoga philosophy. In *Sânkhya Kârikâ*, it is the "obstruction" called love and desire in the physical or terrestrial sense. The five *Kleshas* are: *Avidyâ*, or ignorance; *Asmitâ*, selfishness, or "I-am-ness" ; *Râga*, love; *Dwesha*, hatred; and *Abhinivesa,* dread of suffering.

Râjas *(Sk.)*. The "quality of foulness" (*i.e.,* differentiation), and activity in the *Purânas.* One of the three *Gunas* or divisions in the correlations of matter and nature, representing form and change.

Rajasâs *(Sk.)*. The elder *Agnishwattas* – the Fire-Pitris, "fire" standing as a symbol of enlightenment and intellect.

Râkshasas *(Sk.)*. *Lit.,* "raw eaters", and in the popular superstition evil spirits, demons. Esoterically, however, they are the *Gibborim* (giants) of the Bible, the Fourth Race or the Atlanteans. (See *Secret Doctrine*, II., 165.)

Ratnâvabhâsa Kalpa *(Sk.)*. The age in which all sexual difference will have ceased to exist, and birth will take place in the *Anupâdaka* mode, as in the second and third Root-races. Esoteric philosophy teaches that it will take place at the end of the sixth and during the seventh and last Root-race in this Round.

Reincarnation. The doctrine of rebirth, believed in by Jesus and the Apostles, as by all men in those days, but denied now by the Christians. All the Egyptian converts to Christianity, Church Fathers and others, believed in this doctrine, as shown by the writings of several. In the still existing symbols, the human-headed bird flying towards a mummy, a body, or "the soul uniting itself with its *sahou* (glorified body of the Ego, and also the *kâmalokic shell*) proves this belief. "The song of the Resurrection" chanted by Isis to recall her dead husband to life, might be translated "Song of Rebirth", as Osiris is collective Humanity. "Oh! Osiris [here follows the name of the Osirified mummy, or the departed], rise again in holy earth (matter), august mummy in the coffin, under thy corporeal substances", was the funeral prayer of the priest over the deceased. "Resurrection" with the Egyptians never meant the resurrection of the mutilated mummy, but of the *Soul* that informed it, the Ego in a new body. The putting on of flesh periodically by the Soul or the Ego, was a universal belief; nor can anything be more consonant with justice and Karmic law.

Rishi Prajâpati (*Sk.*). *Lit.*, "revealers", holy sages in the religious history of Âryavarta. Esoterically the highest of them are the Hierarchies of "Builders" and Architects of the Universe and of living things on earth; they are generally called Dhyan Chohans, Devas and gods.

Rishis (*Sk.*). Adepts; the inspired ones. In Vedic literature the term is employed to denote those persons through whom the various Mantras were revealed.

Rudras (*Sk.*). The mighty ones; the lords of the three upper worlds. One of the classes of the "fallen" or incarnating spirits; they are all born of Brahmâ.

Rûpa (*Sk.*). Body; any form, applied even to the forms of the gods, which are subjective to us.

S

Sabda Brahmam (*Sk.*). "The Unmanifested Logos." The *Vedas*; "Ethereal Vibrations diffused throughout Space ".

Sacred Science. The name given to the *inner* esoteric philosophy, the secrets taught in days of old to the initiated candidates, and divulged during the last and supreme Initiation by the Hierophants.

Sakti (*Sk.*). The active female energy of the gods; in popular Hinduism, their wives and goddesses; in Occultism, the crown of the astral light. Force and the six forces of nature synthesized. Universal Energy.

Sama (*Sk.*). One of the *bhâva pushpas,* or "flowers of sanctity Sama is the fifth, or "resignation". There are eight such flowers, namely: clemency or charity, self-restraint, affection (or love for others), patience, resignation, devotion, meditation and veracity. Sama is also the repression of any mental perturbation,

Sâma Veda (*Sk.*). Lit., "the Scripture, or *Shâstra*, of peace". One of the four Vedas.

Samâdhâna (*Sk.*). That state in which a Yogi can no longer diverge from the path of spiritual progress; when everything terrestrial, except the visible body, has ceased to exist for him.

Samâdhi (*Sk.*). A state of ecstatic and complete trance. The term comes from the words *Sam-âdha*, "self-possession ". He who possesses this power is able to exercise an absolute control over all his faculties, physical or mental; it is the highest state of Yoga.

Samâdhindriya (*Sk.*). Lit., "the root of concentration"; the fourth of the five roots called Pancha Indriyâni, which are said in esoteric philosophy to be the agents in producing a highly moral life, leading to sanctity and liberation ; when these are reached, the two *spiritual roots* lying latent in the body (Atmâ and Buddhi) will send out shoots and blossom. *Samâdhindriya* is the organ of ecstatic meditation in Râj-yoga practices.

Samâpatti (*Sk.*). Absolute concentration in Râja-Yoga; the process of development by which perfect indifference (*Sams*) is reached (*apatti*). This state is the last stage of development before the possibility of entering into Samâdhi is reached.

Samskâra (*Sk.*). Lit., from *Sam* and *Krî*, to improve, refine, impress. In Hindu philosophy the term is used to denote the impressions left upon the mind by individual actions or external circumstances, and capable of being developed on any future favourable occasion—even in a future birth. The *Samskâra* denotes, therefore, the germs of propensities and impulses from previous births to be developed in this, or the coming *janmâs* or reincarnations. In Tibet, Samskâra is called Doodyed, and in China is defined as, or at least connected with, action or Karma. It is, strictly speaking, a metaphysical term, which in exoteric philosophies is variously defined; *e.g.*, in Nepaul as illusion, in Tibet as notion, and in Ceylon as discrimination. The true meaning is as given above, and as such is connected with Karma and its working.

Samvriti (*Sk.*). False conception—the origin of illusion.

Samvritisatya (*Sk.*). Truth mixed with false conceptions (Samvriti); the reverse of absolute truth – or *Paramârthasatya,* self-consciousness in absolute truth or reality.

Sanat Kumâra (*Sk.*). The most prominent of the seven Kumâras, the Vaidhâtra the first of which are called Sanaka, Sananda, Sanâtana and Sanat Kumâra; which names are all significant qualifications of the degrees of human intellect.

Sânkhya (*Sk.*). The system of philosophy founded by Kapila Rishi, a system of analytical metaphysics, and one of the six *Darshanas* or schools of philosophy. It discourses on numerical categories and the meaning of the twenty-five *tatwas* (the forces of nature in various degrees). This "atomistic school", as some call it, explains nature by the interaction of twenty-four elements with *purusha* (spirit) modified by the three gunas (qualities), teaching the eternity of *pradhâna* (primordial, homogeneous matter), or the self-transformation of nature and the eternity of the human Egos.

Sânkhya Yoga (*Sk.*). The system of Yoga as set forth by the above school.

Sanskrit (*Sk.*). The classical language of the Brahmans, never known *nor spoken in its true systematized form* (given later *approximately* by Pânini), except by the initiated Brahmans, as it was pre-eminently "a mystery language". It has now degenerated into the so-called Prâkrita.

Saptarshi (*Sk.*). The seven Rishis. As stars they are the constellation of 'the Great Bear, and called as such the *Riksha* and *Chitrasikhandinas,* bright-crested.

Satya Yuga (*Sk.*). The golden age, or the age of truth and purity; the first of the four Yugas, also called Krita Yuga.

Sattva (*Sk.*). Understanding; quiescence in divine knowledge. It follows 'generally the word *Bodhi* when used as a compound word, e.g., "Bodhisattva".

Sattva or *Satwa,* (*Sk.*). Goodness; the same as Sattva, or purity, one of the trigunas or three divisions of nature.

Satya (*Sk.*). Supreme truth.

Satya Loka (*Sk.*). The world of infinite purity and wisdom, the celestial abode of Brahmâ and the gods.

Satya Yuga (*Sk.*). The golden age, or the age of truth and purity; the first of the four Yugas, also called Krita Yuga.

Secret Doctrine. The general name given to the esoteric teachings of antiquity.

Sephira (*Heb.*). An emanation of Deity; the parent and synthesis of the ten Sephiroth when she stands at the head of the Sephirothal Tree; in the Kabbalah, Sephira,or the " Sacred Aged ", is the divine Intelligence (the same as Sophia or Metis), the first emanation from the "Endless" or Ain-Suph.

Sephiroth (*Heb.*). The ten emanations of Deity; the highest is formed by the concentration of the Ain Soph Aur, or the Limitless Light, and each: Sephira produces by emanation another Sephira. The names of the Ten Sephiroth are – 1. Kether – The Crown; 2. Chokmah – Wisdom; 3. Binah – Understanding; 4. Chesed – Mercy; Geburah – Power; 6. Tiphereth – Beauty; 7. Netzach – Victory; 8. Hod – Splendour; 9. Jesod – Foundation; and 10. Malkuth – The Kingdom.

The conception of Deity embodied in the Ten Sephiroth is a very sublime one, and each Sephira is a picture to the Kabbalist of a group of exalted ideas, titles and attributes, which the name but faintly represents. Each Sephira is called either active or passive, though this attribution may lead to error; passive does not mean a return to negative existence; and the two words only express the relation between individual Sephiroth, and not any absolute quality. [w.w.w.]

Sharîra (Sarîra) (*Sk.*). Envelope or body.

Siddhas (*Sk.*). Saints and sages who have become almost divine also a hierarchy of Dhyan Chohans.

Siddhâsana (*Sk.*). A posture in Hatha-yoga practices.

Siddha-Sena (*Sk.*). Lit., "the leader of Siddhas"; a title of Kârttikeya, the "mysterious youth" (*kumâra guha*).

Siddhis (*Sk.*). Lit., "attributes of perfection"; phenomenal powers acquired through holiness by Yogis.

Sishta (*Sk.*). The great elect or Sages, left after every minor *Pralaya* (that which is called "obscuration" in Mr. Sinnett's *Esoteric Buddhism*), when the globe goes into its night or rest, to become, on its re-awakening, the seed of the next humanity. Lit. "remnant."

Siva (*Sk.*). The third person of the Hindu Trinity (the Trimûrti). He is a god of the first order, and in his character of Destroyer higher than Vishnu, the Preserver, as he destroys only to regenerate on a higher plane. He is born as Rudra, the Kumâra, and is the patron of all the Yogis, being called, as such, Mahâdeva the great ascetic, His titles are significant *Trilochana*, "the three-eyed", *Mahâdeva*, "the great god ", *Sankara*, etc., etc., etc.

Skandha or *Skhanda* (*Sk.*). Lit., "bundles", or groups of attributes; everything finite, inapplicable to the eternal and the absolute. There are five—esoterically, *seven*—attributes in every human living being, which are known as the *Pancha Shandhas*. These are (1) form, *rûpa*; (2) perception, *vidâna*; (3) consciousness, *sanjnâ*; (4) action, *sanskâra*; (5) knowledge, vidyâna. These unite at the birth of man and constitute his personality. After the maturity of these Skandhas, they begin to separate and weaken, and this is followed by *jarâmarana*, or decrepitude and death.

Son-kha-pa (*Tib.*). Written also *Tsong-kha-pa*. A famous Tibetan reformer of the fourteenth century, who introduced a purified Buddhism into his country. He was a great Adept, who being unable to witness any longer the desecration of Buddhist philosophy by the false priests who made of it a marketable commodity, put a forcible stop thereto by a timely revolution and the exile of 40,000 sham monks and Lamas from the country. He is regarded as an Avatar of Buddha, and is the founder of the *Gelukpa* (" yellow-cap ") Sect, and of the mystic Brotherhood connected with its chiefs. The "tree of the 10,000 images" (*khoom boom*) has, it is said, sprung from the long hair of this ascetic, who leaving it behind him disappeared for ever from the view of the profane.

Soul. The **yuch**, or *nephesh* of the *Bible*; the vital principle, or the breath of life, which every animal, down to the infusoria, shares with man. In the translated Bible it stands indifferently for *life*, blood and soul. "Let us not kill his *nephesh*", says the original text: "let us not kill *him* ", translate the Christians (*Genesis* xxxvii. 21), and so on.

Sparsa (*Sk.*). The sense of touch.

Spirit. The lack of any mutual agreement between writers in the use of this word has resulted in dire confusion. It is commonly made synonymous with *soul*; and the lexicographers countenance the usage. In Theosophical teachings. the term "Spirit" is applied solely to that which *belongs directly to Universal Consciousness*, and which is its homogeneous and unadulterated emanation. Thus, the higher Mind in Man or his Ego (Manas) is, when linked indissolubly with Buddhi, a spirit; while the term "Soul", human or even animal (the lower Manas acting in animals as instinct), is applied only to Kâma-Manas, and qualified as the living soul. This is *nephesh*, in Hebrew, the "breath of life". Spirit is formless and *immaterial*, being, when individualised, of the highest spiritual substance – *Suddasatwa*, the divine essence, of which the body of the manifesting *highest* Dhyanis are formed. Therefore, the Theosophists reject the appellation " Spirits" for those phantoms which appear in the phenomenal manifestations of the Spiritualists, and call them "shells", and various other names. (See "Sukshma Sarîra".) Spirit, in short, is no entity in the sense of having form ; for, as Buddhist philosophy has it, where there is a form, there is a cause for pain and suffering. But each *individual* spirit – this individuality lasting only throughout the manvantaric life-cycle – may be described as a *centre of consciousness*, a self-sentient and self-conscious centre; a state, not a conditioned individual. This is why there is such a wealth of words in Sanskrit to express the different States of Being, Beings and Entities, each appellation showing the philosophical difference, the plane to which such *unit* belongs, and the degree of its spirituality or materiality. Unfortunately these terms are almost untranslatable into our Western tongues.

Sraddha (*Sk.*). Lit., faith, respect, reverence.

Sri Sankarâchârya (*Sk.*). The great religious reformer of India, and teacher of the Vedânta philosophy—the greatest of all such teachers, regarded by the *Adwaitas* (Non-dualists) as an incarnation of Siva and a worker of miracles. He established many *mathams* (monasteries), and founded the most learned sect among Brahmans, called the Smârtava. The legends about him are as numerous as his philosophical writings. At the age of thirty-two he went to Kashmir, and reaching Kedâranâth in the Himalayas, entered a cave alone, whence he never returned. His followers claim that he did not die, but only retired from the world.

Sthûla Sarîram (*Sk.*). In metaphysics, the gross physical body.

Sthûlopadhi (*Sk.*). A "principle" answering to the lower triad in man, i.e., body, astral form, and life, in the Târaka Râja Yoga system, which names only three chief principles in man. *Sthûlopadhi* corresponds to the *jagrata*, or waking conscious *state*.

Sûkshma Sarîra (*Sk.*). The dream-like, illusive body akin to *Mânasarûpa* or "thought-body ". It is the vesture of the gods, or the Dhyânis and the Devas. Written also *Sukshama Sharîra* and called *Sukshmopadhi* by the Târaka Râja Yogis. (*Secret Doctrine*, I.,157)

Sûkshmopadhi (*Sk.*). In Târaka Râja Yoga the "principle" containing both the higher and the lower Manas and Kâma. It corresponds to the *Manomaya Kosha* of the Vedantic classification and to the *Svapna* state. (See "Svapna ".)

Suras (*Sk.*). A general term for gods, the same as devas; the contrary to asuras or "no-gods".

Sûryâvarta (*Sk.*). A degree or stage of Samâdhi.

Sushupti Avasthâ (*Sk.*). Deep sleep; one of the four aspects of Prânava.

Sûtrâtman (*Sk.*). Lit., "the thread of spirit"; the immortal Ego, the Individuality which incarnates in men one life after the other, and upon which are strung, like beads on a string, his countless Personalities. The universal life-supporting air, *Samashti prau*; universal energy.

Svabhâvat (*Sk.*). Explained by the Orientalists as "plastic substance", which is an inadequate definition. Svabhâvat is the world-substance and stuff, or rather that which is behind it – the spirit and essence of substance. The name comes from *Subhâva* and is composed of three words – **su**, good, perfect, fair, handsome; **sva,** self; and **bkâva**, being, or *state of being.* From it all nature proceeds and into it all returns at the end of the life-cycles. In Esotericism it is called "Father-Mother". It is the plastic essence of matter.

Svapna Avasthâ (*Sk.*). A dreaming state; one of the four aspects of *Prânava*; a Yoga practice.

Svasam Vedanâ (*Sk.*). Lit., "the reflection which analyses itself "; a synonym of Paramârtha.

Svastikâsana (*Sk.*). The second of the four principal postures of the eighty-four prescribed in Hatha Yoga practices.

T

Taijasi (*Sk.*). The radiant, flaming—from *Tejas* "fire"; used sometimes to designate the *Mânasa-rûpa*, the "thought-body", and also the stars.

Tamas (*Sk.*). The quality of darkness, "foulness" and inertia; also of ignorance, as matter is blind. A term used in metaphysical philosophy. It is the lowest of the three *gunas* or fundamental qualities.

Tanha (*Pali*). The thirst for life. Desire to live and clinging to life on this earth. This clinging is that which causes rebirth or reincarnation.

Tanmâtras (*Sk.*). The types or rudiments of the five Elements; the subtile essence of these, devoid of all qualities and identical with the properties of the five basic Elements – earth, water, fire, air and ether; i.e., the *tanmâtras* are, in one of their aspects, smell, taste, touch, sight, and hearing.

Tapas (*Sk.*). "Abstraction", "meditation". "To perform *tapas*" is to sit for *contemplation*. Therefore ascetics are often called Tâpasas.

Târakâ Râja Yoga (*Sk.*). One of the Brahminical Yoga systems for the development of purely spiritual powers and knowledge which lead to Nirvâna.

Tattwa (*Sk.*). Eternally existing "That"; also, the different principles in Nature, in their occult meaning. *Tattwa Samâsa* is a work of Sânkhya philosophy attributed to Kapila himself.

Also the abstract principles of existence or categories, physical and metaphysical. The subtle elements – five exoterically, seven in esoteric philosophy – which are correlative to the five and the seven senses on the physical plane ; the last two senses are as yet latent in man, but will be developed in the two last root-races.

Theosophia (*Gr.*). Wisdom-religion, or "Divine Wisdom". The substratum and basis of all the world-religions and philosophies, taught and practised by a few elect ever since man became a thinking being. In its practical bearing, Theosophy is purely divine ethics; the definitions in dictionaries are pure nonsense, based on religious prejudice and ignorance of the true spirit of the early Rosicrucians and mediæval philosophers who called themselves Theosophists.

Theosophists. A name by which many mystics at various periods of history have called themselves. The Neo-Platonists of Alexandria were Theosophists; the Alchemists and Kabbalists during the mediæval ages were likewise so called, also the Martinists, the Quietists, and other kinds of mystics, whether acting independently or incorporated in a brotherhood or society. All real lovers of divine Wisdom and Truth had, and have, a right to the name, rather than those who, appropriating the qualification, live lives or perform actions opposed to the principles of Theosophy. As described by Brother Kenneth R. Mackenzie, the Theosophists of the past centuries – "entirely speculative, and founding no schools, have still exercised a silent influence upon philosophy; and, no doubt, when the time arrives, many ideas thus silently propounded may yet give new directions to human thought. One of the ways in which these doctrines have obtained not only authority, but power, has been among certain enthusiasts in the higher degrees of Masonry. This power has, however, to a great degree died with the founders, and modern Freemasonry contains few traces of theosophic influence. However accurate and beautiful some of the ideas of Swedenborg, Pernetty, Paschalis, Saint Martin, Marconis, Ragon, and Chastanier may have been, they have but little direct influence on society." This is true of the Theosophists of the last three centuries, but not of the later ones. For the Theosophists of the current century have already visibly impressed themselves on modern literature, and introduced the desire and craving for some philosophy in place of the blind dogmatic faith of yore, among the most intelligent portions of human-kind. Such is the difference between past and modern THEOSOPHY.

Thread Soul. The same as *Sutrâtmâ (q.v.)*.

Thumos (*Gr.*). The astral, animal soul; the *Kâmas-Manas; Thumos* means passion, desire and confusion and is so used by Homer. The word is probably derived from the Sanskrit *Tamas*, which has the same meaning.

To On (*Gr.*). The "Being", the "Ineffable All" of Plato. He "whom no person has seen except the Son".

Tretâ Yuga (*Sk.*). The second age of the world, a period of 1,296,000 years.

Triad, or *the Three*. The ten Sephiroth are contemplated as a group of three triads: Kether, Chochmah and Binah form the supernal triad; Chesed, Geburah and Tiphereth, the second; and Netzach, Hod and Yesod, the inferior triad. The tenth Sephira, Malkuth, is beyond the three triads. [w.w.w.]

The above is orthodox Western Kabalah. Eastern Occultists recognise but one triad – the upper one (corresponding to Atmâ-Buddhi and the "Envelope" which reflects their light, the three in one) – and count seven lower Sephiroth, everyone of which stands for a "principle", beginning with the Higher Manas and ending with the Physical Body – of which Malkuth is the representative in the Microcosm and the Earth in the Macrocosm.

Trigunas (*Sk.*). The three divisions of the inherent qualities of differentiated matter—i.e., of pure quiescence (*satva*), of activity and desire (*rajas*), of stagnation and decay (*tamas*) They correspond with Vishnu, Brahmâ, and Shiva. (See "Trimûrti".)

U

Upâdhi (*Sk.*). Basis; the vehicle, carrier or bearer of something less material than itself: as the human body is the *upâdhi* of its spirit, ether the *upâdhi* of light, etc., etc.; a mould; a defining or limiting substance.

Upanishad (*Sk.*). Translated as "esoteric doctrine ", or interpretation of the *Vedas* by the *Vedânta* methods. The third division of the *Vedas* appended to the *Brâhmanas* and regarded as a portion of *Sruti* or "revealed" word. They are, however, as records, far older than the *Brâhmanas* the exception of the two, still extant, attached to the *Rig -Veda* of the Aitareyins. The term *Upanishad* is explained by the Hindu pundits as "that which destroys ignorance, and thus produces liberation" of the spirit, through the knowledge of the supreme though *hidden* truth; the same, therefore, as that which was hinted at by Jesus, when he is made to say, "And ye shall know the truth, and the truth shall make you free" (*John* viii. 32). It is from these treatises of the *Upanishads*—themselves the echo of the primeval Wisdom-Religion—that the Vedânta system of philosophy has been developed. (See "Vedânta".) Yet old as the *Upanishads* may be, the Orientalists will not assign to the oldest of them more than an antiquity of 600 years B.C. The accepted number of these treatises is 150, though now no more than about twenty are left unadulterated. They treat of very abstruse, metaphysical questions, such as the origin of the Universe; the nature and the essence of the Unmanifested Deity and the manifested gods the connection, primal and ultimate, of spirit and matter; the universality of mind and the nature of the human Soul and Ego.

The *Upanishads* must be far more ancient than the days of Buddhism, as they show no preference for, nor do they uphold, the superiority of the Brahmans as a caste. On the contrary, it is the (now) second caste, the Kshatriya, or warrior class, who are exalted in the oldest of them. As stated by Professor Cowell in Elphinstone's *History of India* – "they breathe a freedom of spirit unknown to any earlier work except the *Rig Veda*. . . The great teachers of the higher knowledge and Brahmans are continually represented as *going to Kshatriya Kings to become their pupils.*" The "Kshatriya Kings" were in the olden times, like the King Hierophants of Egypt, the receptacles of the highest divine knowledge and wisdom, the *Elect* and the incarnations of the primordial divine Instructors— the Dhyâni Buddhas or Kumâras. There was a time, æons before the Brahmans became a caste, or even the *Upanishads* were written, when there was on earth but one "lip ", one religion and one science, namely, the speech of the gods, the Wisdom-Religion and Truth. This was before the fair fields of the latter, overrun by nations of many languages, became overgrown with the weeds of intentional deception, and national creeds invented by ambition, cruelty and selfishness, broke the one sacred Truth into thousands of fragments.

Uparati (*Sk.*). Absence of outgoing desires; a Yoga state.

V

Vâch (*Sk.*). To call Vâch "speech" simply, is deficient in clearness. Vâch is the mystic personification of speech, and the female *Logos*, being one with Brahmâ, who created her out of one-half of his body, which he divided into two portions; she is also one with Virâj (called the "female" Virâj) who was created in her by Brahmâ. In one sense Vâch is "speech" by which knowledge was taught to man;

in another she is the "mystic, secret speech" which descends upon and enters into the primeval Rishis, as the "tongues of fire" are said to have "sat upon" the apostles. For, she is called "the female creator ", the "mother of the Vedas ", etc., etc. Esoterically, she is the subjective Creative Force which, emanating from the Creative Deity (the subjective Universe, its "privation ", or *ideation*) becomes the manifested "world of speech ", i.e., the *concrete expression of ideation*, hence the "Word" or Logos. Vâch is "the male and female" Adam of the first chapter of *Genesis*, and thus called "Vâch-Virâj" by the sages. (See *Atharva Veda*.) She is also "the celestial Saraswatî produced from the heavens ", a "voice derived from *speechless* Brahmâ" *(Mahâbhârata)*; the goddess of wisdom and eloquence. She is called *Sata-rûpa*, the goddess of *a hundred forms*.

Vâhan(a) (*Sk.*). A vehicle, the carrier of something immaterial and formless. All the gods and goddesses are, therefore, represented as using vâhanas to manifest themselves, which vehicles are ever symbolical. So, for instance, Vishnu has during Pralayas, *Ânanta* the infinite (Space), symbolized by the serpent Sesha, and during the Manvantaras – *Garuda* the gigantic half-eagle, half-man, the symbol of the great cycle; Brahma appears as Brahmâ, descending into the planes of manifestations on *Kâlahamsa*, the "swan in time or finite eternity"; Siva (phonet, Shiva) appears as the bull *Nandi*; Osiris as the sacred bull *Apis*; Indra travels on an elephant; Kârttikeya, on a peacock; Kâmadeva on *Makâra*, at other times a parrot; Agni, the universal (and also solar) Fire-god, who is, as all of them are, "a consuming Fire", manifests itself as a ram and a lamb, *Ajâ*, "the unborn"; Varuna, as a fish; etc., etc., while the vehicle of MAN is his body.

Vaikhari Vâch (*Sk.*). 'That which is uttered; one of the four forms of speech.

Vaisheshika (*Sk.*). One of the six *Darshanas* or schools of philosophy, founded by Kanâda. It is called the Atomistic School, as it teaches the existence of a universe of atoms of a transient character, an endless number of souls and a fixed number of material principles, by the correlation and interaction of which periodical cosmic evolutions take place without any directing Force, save a kind of mechanical law inherent in the atoms; a very materialistic school.

Vaishnava (*Sk.*). A follower of any sect recognising and worshipping Vishnu as the one supreme God. The worshippers of Siva are called *Saivas*.

Vaivaswata (*Sk.*). The name of the Seventh Manu, the forefather of the post-diluvian race, or our own fifth humankind. A reputed son of Sûrya (the Sun), he became, after having been saved in an ark (built by the order of Vishnu) from the Deluge, the father of Ikshwâku, the founder of the solar race of kings. (See "*Sûryavansa*".)

Vâyu (*Sk.*). Air: the god and sovereign of the air; one of the five states of matter, namely the *gaseous*; one of the five elements, called, as wind, *Vâta*.

The *Vishnu Purâna* makes Vâyu King of the Gandharvas. He is the father of Hanumân, in the *Râmâyana*. The trinity of the mystic gods in Kosmos closely related to each other, are Agni (fire) whose place is on earth; Vâyu (air, or one of the forms of Indra), whose place is in the air; and Sûrya (the sun) whose place is in the air (*Nirukta*.) In esoteric interpretation, these three cosmic principles, correspond with the three human principles, Kâma, Kâma-Manas and Manas, the sun of the intellect.

Vedânta (*Sk.*). A mystic system of philosophy which has developed from the efforts of generations of sages to interpret the secret meaning of the *Upanishads* (*q.v.*). It is called in the *Shad-Darshanas* (six schools or systems of demonstration), *Uttara Mîmânsâ*, attributed to *Vyâsa*, the compiler of the *Vedas*, who is thus referred to as the founder of the Vedânta. The orthodox Hindus call Vedânta – a term meaning literally the "end of all (Vedic) knowledge" – *Brahmâ-jnâna*, or pure and spiritual knowledge of Brahmâ. Even if we accept the late dates assigned to various Sanskrit schools and treatises by our Orientalists, the Vedânta must be 3,300 years old, as Vyâsa is said to have lived 1,400 years B.C. If, as Elphinstone has it in his *History of India*, the *Brahmanas* are the *Talmud* of the Hindus, and the *Vedas* the Mosaic books, then the *Vedânta* may be correctly called the *Kabalah* of India. But how vastly more grand! Sankarâchârya, who was the popularizer of the Vedântic system, and the founder of the *Adwaita* philosophy, is sometimes called the founder of the modern schools of the Vedânta.

Vedas (*Sk.*). The "revelation". the scriptures of the Hindus, from the root *vid*, "to know ", or "divine knowledge". They are the most ancient as well as the most sacred of the Sanskrit works. The *Vedas*, on the date and antiquity of which no two Orientalists can agree, are claimed by the Hindus themselves, whose Brahmans and Pundits ought to know best about their own religious works, to have been first taught orally for thousands of years and then compiled on the shores of Lake Mânasa-Sarovara (phonetically, *Mansarovara*) beyond the Himalayas, in Tibet.

The Vedic writings are all classified in two great divisions, exoteric and esoteric, the former being called *Karma-Kânda*, "division of actions or works ", and the *Jnâna Kânda*, "division of (divine) knowledge", the Upanishads (*q.v.*) coming under this last classification. Both departments are regarded as *Sruti* or revelation. To each hymn of the *Rig-Veda*, the name of the Seer or Rishi to whom it was revealed is prefixed. It, thus, becomes evident on the authority of these very names (such as Vasishta, Viswâmitra, Nârada, etc.), all of which belong to men born in various manvantaras and even ages, that centuries, and perhaps millenniums, must have elapsed between the dates of their composition.

Vidyâ (*Sk.*). Knowledge, Occult Science.

Vijnânam (*Sk.***).** The Vedântic name for the principle which dwells in the

Vijñânamaya Kosha (the sheath of intellect) and corresponds to the faculties of the Higher Manas.

Vishnu (*Sk.*). The second person of the Hindu Trimûrti (trinity), composed of Brahmâ, Vishnu and Siva. From the root **vish**, "to pervade". in the *Rig-Veda*, Vishnu is no high god, but simply a manifestation of the solar energy, described as "striding through the seven regions of the Universe in *three* steps and enveloping all things with the dust" (of his beams). Whatever may be the six other occult significances of the statement, this is related to the same class of types as the seven and ten Sephiroth, as the *seven* and *three* orifices of the perfect Adam Kadmon, as the seven "principles" and the higher triad in man, etc., etc. Later on this mystic type becomes a great god, the preserver and the renovator, he "of a thousand names – Sahasranâma ".

W

Will. In metaphysics and occult philosophy, Will is that which governs the manifested universes in eternity. *Will* is the one and sole principle of abstract eternal MOTION, or its ensouling essence. "The will", says Van Helmont, "is the first of all powers. . . . The will is the property of all spiritual beings and displays itself in them the more actively the more they are freed from matter." And Paracelsus teaches that "determined will is the beginning of all magical operations. It is because men do not perfectly imagine and believe the result, that the (occult) arts are so uncertain, while they might he perfectly certain." Like all the rest, the Will is *septenary* in its degrees of manifestation. Emanating from the one, eternal, abstract and purely quiescent Will (Âtmâ in Layam), it becomes Buddhi in its Alaya state, descends lower as Mahat (Manas), and runs down the ladder of degrees until the divine Eros becomes, in its lower, animal manifestation, erotic desire. Will as an eternal principle is neither spirit nor substance but everlasting ideation. As well expressed by Schopenhauer in his *Parerga*, "in sober reality there is neither *matter* nor *spirit.* The tendency to gravitation in a stone is as unexplainable as thought in the human brain. . . If matter can – no one knows why – fall to the ground, then it can also – no one knows why – think. . . . As soon, even in mechanics, as we trespass beyond the purely mathematical, as soon as we reach the inscrutable adhesion, gravitation, and so on, we are faced by phenomena which are to our senses as mysterious as the WILL."

Wisdom. The "very essence of wisdom is contained in the Non-Being". say the Kabbalists; but they also apply the term to the WORD or Logos, the Demiurge, by which the universe was called into existence. "The one Wisdom is in the Sound", say the Occultists; the Logos again being meant by Sound, which is the substratum of Âkâsa. Says the *Zohar,* the "Book of Splendour": "It is the Principle of all the Principles, the mysterious Wisdom, the crown of all that which there is of the most High". (*Zohar*, iii., fol. 288, Myers *Qabbalah*.) And it is explained, "Above Kether is the Ayin, or Ens, i.e., Ain, the NOTHING". "It is so named because we do not know, and it is impossible to know, *that which there is in that Principle*, because . . . it is above Wisdom itself." (iii., fol. 288.) This shows that the real Kabbalists agree with the Occultists that the essence, or that which is in the principle of Wisdom, is still above that highest Wisdom.

Wisdom Religion. The one religion which underlies all the now-existing creeds. That "faith" which, being primordial, and revealed directly to human kind by their *progenitors* and informing EGOS (though the Church regards them as the "fallen angels"), required no "grace", nor *blind* faith to believe, for it was *knowledge*. (See "Gupta Vidyâ", Hidden Knowledge.) It is on this Wisdom Religion that *Theosophy is based*.

Y

Years of Brahmâ. The whole period of "Brahma's Age" (100 Years) equals 311,040,000,000,000 years. (See "Yuga ".)

Yoga (*Sk.*). (1) One of the six Darshanas or schools of India; a school of philosophy founded by Patanjali, though the real Yoga doctrine, the one that is said to have helped to prepare the world for the preaching of Buddha, is attributed with good reasons to the more ancient sage Yâjnawalkya, the writer of the *Shatapatha Brâhmana*, of *Yajur Veda*, the *Brihad Âranyaka*, and other famous works. (2) The practice of meditation as a means of leading to spiritual liberation. Psycho-spiritual powers are obtained thereby, and induced ecstatic states lead to the clear and correct perception of the eternal truths, in both the visible and invisible universe.

Yogâchârya (*Sk.*). (1) A mystic school. (2) Lit., a teacher (*âchârya*) of Yoga, one who has mastered the doctrines and practices of ecstatic meditation – the culmination of which are the *Mahâsiddhis*. It is incorrect to confuse this school with the Tantra, or Mahâtantra school founded by Samantabhadra, for there are two Yogâchârya Schools, one esoteric, the other popular. The doctrines of the latter were compiled and glossed by Asamgha in the sixth century of our era, and his mystic tantras and mantras, his formularies, litanies, spells and mudrâ would certainly, if attempted without a Guru, serve rather purposes of sorcery and black magic than real Yoga. Those who undertake to write upon the subject are generally learned missionaries and haters of Eastern philosophy in general. From these no unbiassed views can be expected. Thus when we read in the *Sanskrit-Chinese Dictionary* of Eitel, that the reciting of mantras (which he calls "spells"!) "should he accompanied by music and distortions of the fingers (mudrâ), that a state of mental fixity (*Samâdhi*} might he reached – one acquainted, however slightly, with the real practice of Yoga can only shrug his shoulders. These distortions of the fingers, or mudrâ, are necessary, the author thinks, for the reaching of Samâdhi, "characterized by there being neither thought nor annihilation of thought, and consisting of six-fold bodily (*sic*) and mental happiness *(yogi) whence would result endowment with supernatural miracle-working power*". Theosophists cannot be too much warned against such fantastic and prejudiced explanations.

Yogi (*Sk.*). (1) Not "a state of six-fold bodily and mental happiness as the result, of ecstatic meditation" (Eitel) but a state which, when reached, makes the practitioner thereof absolute master of his six principles", *he now being merged in the seventh*. It gives him full control, owing to his knowledge of SELF and Self, over his bodily, intellectual and mental states, which, unable any longer to interfere with, or act upon, his Higher Ego, leave it free to exist in its original, pure, and divine state. (2) Also the name of the devotee who practises Yoga.

Yuga (*Sk.*). A 1,000th part of a Kalpa. An age of the World of which there are four, and the series of which proceed in succession during the manvantaric cycle. Each Yuga is preceded by a period called in the *Purânas* Sandhyâ, twilight, or transition period, and is followed by another period of like duration called Sandhyânsa, "portion of twilight". Each is equal to one-tenth of the Yuga. The group of four Yugas is first computed by the *divine* years, or "years of the gods" – each such year being equal to 360 years of mortal men. Thus we have, in "divine" years :

AGE	YEARS
Krita or Satya Yuga	4,000
Sandhyâ	400
Sandhyansa	400
	4,800

Tretâ Yuga	3,000
Sandhyâ	300
Sandhyânsa	300
	3,600

Dwâpara Yuga	2,000
Sandhya	200
Sandhyânsa	200
	2,400

Kali Yuga	1,000
Sandhyâ	100

Sandhyânsa		100
		1,200
Total	**=**	**12,000**

This rendered in years of mortals equals:

4800	X	360	=	1,728,000
3600	X	360	=	1,296,000
2400	X	360	=	864,000
1200	X	360	=	432,000
		Total	=	4,320,000

The above is called a Mahâyuga or Manvantara. 2,000 such Mahâyugas, or a period of 8,640,000 years, make a Kalpa the latter being only a "day and a night", or twenty-four hours, of Brahmâ. Thus an "age of Brahmâ", or one hundred of his divine years, must equal 311,040,000,000,000 of our mortal years. The old Mazdeans or Magi (the modern Parsis) had the same calculation, though the Orientalists do not seem to perceive it, for even the Parsi Moheds themselves have forgotten it. But their "Sovereign time of the Long Period" (*Zervan Dareghâ Hvadâta*) lasts 12,000 years, and these are the 12,000 *divine* years of a Mahâyuga as shown above, whereas the *Zervan Akarana* (Limitless Time), mentioned by Zarathustra, is the *Kâla*, out of space and time, of Parabrahm.

INDEX

A

B

karma 8, 16, 18, 20, 21, 42, 59, 67, 68, 71, 75, 80, 90, 92, 103, 107, 108, 112
karuna 43
kleshas 48, 50, 59, 66, 67, 68, 70, 75, 102, 103, 111, 112
Krishna 31, 53, 87
Kriyashakti 36
krodha 62
kshanti 52, 67
kundalini 93
Kutastha 130

L

languor 37
laziness 37
life-atoms xvi, xvii
line of life's meditation 128
lobha 62
Logos 5, 93, 124, 125, 126, 127
love xv, 67, 72, 73, 116, 125, 126

M

macrocosm 12, 31
Mahat 24
mahavritam 37
maitri 43, 80, 92
manas xii, xvii , 14, 24, 25, 30, 48, 91
Manasa xvii
man of meditation xii, 69, 117, 121, 124, 131
Manu 98
Manushya 48, 124
Master 96, 121
maya 27, 49, 50, 51, 67, 98, 111
meditation vii, xi-xiv, xviii, 2, 5, 7, 12, 29-33, 38, 42, 44, 45, 51-59, 67, 69-77, 86, 88, 91, 95, 99, 105, 107, 115-131
meditation on a seed 51, 52
meditation without a seed 45, 52, 56
memory 19, 39, 44, 48, 53, 56, 108, 110, 126
men of meditation 116, 125
mental deposits 36, 59, 67, 99, 107
mental modifications 5, 6, 39, 40, 46, 48, 49, 55, 56, 59, 60, 69, 109
metanoia 9, 92
Metaphysics 31
microcosm 12, 31, 92

KRISHNA:

This divine discipline, Arjuna, is not to be attained by the man who eateth more than enough or too little, nor by him who hath a habit of sleeping much, nor by him who is given to overwatching. The meditation which destroyeth pain is produced in him who is moderate in eating and in recreation, of moderate exertion in his actions, and regulated in sleeping and waking. When the man, so living, centers his heart in the true Self and is exempt from attachment to all desires, he is said to have attained to Yoga. Of the sage of self-centered heart, at rest and free from attachment to desires, the simile is recorded, 'as a lamp which is sheltered from the wind flickereth not.' When regulated by the practice of yoga and at rest, seeing the self by the self, he is contented; when he becometh acquainted with that boundless bliss which is not connected with objects of the senses, and being where he is not moved from the reality; *having gained which he considereth no other superior to it, and in which, being fixed, he is not moved even by the greatest grief; know that this disconnection from union with pain is distinguished as yoga, spiritual union or devotion, which is to be striven after by a man with faith and steadfastly.

The Bhagavad-Gita, Ch. VI

www.ingramcontent.com/pod-product-compliance
Lightning Source LLC
LaVergne TN
LVHW011347080426
835511LV00005B/170